STAGE 3

Mentals 6

Alan McSeveny Rachel McSeveny Diane McSeveny-Foster

Pearson Australia
(a division of Pearson Australia Group Pty Ltd)
459–471 Church St, Level 1, Building B, Richmond, Victoria, 3121
PO Box 23360, Melbourne, Victoria 8012
www.pearson.com.au

Copyright © Pearson Australia 2025
(a division of Pearson Australia Group Pty Ltd)
First published 2024 by Pearson Australia
2028 2027 2026 2025
10 9 8 7 6 5 4 3 2 1

Reproduction and communication for educational purposes
The Australian *Copyright Act 1968* (the Act) allows a maximum of one chapter or 10% of the pages of this work, whichever is the greater, to be reproduced and/or communicated by any educational institution for its educational purposes provided that that educational institution (or the body that administers it) has given a remuneration notice to the Copyright Agency under the Act. For details of the copyright licence for educational institutions contact the Copyright Agency (www.copyright.com.au).

Reproduction and communication for other purposes
Except as permitted under the Act (for example any fair dealing for the purposes of study, research, criticism or review), no part of this book may be reproduced, stored in a retrieval system, communicated or transmitted in any form or by any means without prior written permission. All enquiries should be made to the publisher at the address above.

This book is not to be treated as a blackline master; that is, any photocopying beyond fair dealing requires prior written permission.

Publishers: Sophie Matta and Kerry Nagle
Project Manager: Michelle Thomas
Production Editor: Laura Rentsch
Editor: Rachel Elliott
Designer: Anne Donald
Proofreader: Ann M. Philpott
Rights & Permissions Editor: Alice McBroom
Cover art: Michael Barter
Illustrator: Michael Barter
Publishing Services: Jit-Pin Chong
Printed in Australia by Pegasus Media + Logistics

ISBN 978 0 6557 0913 8
Pearson Australia Group Pty Ltd ABN 40 004 245 943

Attributions
We would like to thank the following for permission to reproduce copyright material.

Shutterstock: Ilya Akinshin, p. 17 (TV screen); Vovan, p. 53 (laptop).

Acknowledgement of Country
Pearson respects and honours Aboriginal and Torres Strait Islander Elders past, present and future. We acknowledge the stories, traditions and living cultures of the Traditional Custodians of the lands on which our company is located and where we conduct our business. Pearson is committed to honouring Australian Aboriginal and Torres Strait Islander peoples' unique cultural and spiritual relationships to the land, waters and seas and their rich contribution to society.

Aboriginal and Torres Strait Islander peoples are advised that this text may contain images, voices and names of deceased persons.

Introduction

Using the Mentals Books

This book reviews content from the Signpost Student book. It is used most effectively when it aligns with the suggested program in the Student Book contents. Each unit of the Mentals Book is programmed to review Student Book content for the previous two weeks. (The Suggested program overview can be found in the online Teacher Resource.) For example, Unit 15 of the Mentals Book can be set as homework to review weeks 13 and 14 of the Student Book while week 15 of the Student Book is being taught. Units 1 and 2 review work taught in the previous year.

Mixed-topic questions

The units present questions in a mixed-topic format to encourage thorough understanding and continuous review.

Graded questions

- Column 1: Easier
- Column 2 and 3: Harder
- Column 4: Extension and Challenge

Presentation

- Number facts are reinforced to encourage instant recall.
- Essential skills are explained.
- The Arithmetic card (page 5) is a useful teaching tool for practising basic number skills.
- ID cards (pages 6 to 9) review the mathematical terms students need to learn.
- Examples of measurements and Tables of number and measurement (pages 84 and 85) are provided so that students can learn important facts and estimate measurements effectively.

Motivation

- There are two lizards hidden on each page for students to find.
- The header allows students to record their score.

Extra activities

- Problem-solving **strategies** are introduced in a carefully planned sequence throughout the series.

- Important concepts from **Number and algebra** and **Measurement and geometry** are explored.

- **Measurement** concepts and activities are introduced and investigated.

- **Statistics and probability** concepts (Data and chance) are presented for revision and extension.

- A **tables** program for each of the four operations is included.
- It is important for students to learn addition and multiplication tables by heart.

6 **Contents**

Teaching ideas using headers

Unit	Content	Extra Activity
1:1/2 **1:3/4**	+ 3, + 5 Personal measurements	+ tables Measure
2:1/2 **2:3/4**	− 2, − 4 Language	− tables ID card D
3:1/2 **3:3/4**	× 8, × 5 Rounding money	× tables Concept
4:1/2 **4:3/4**	× 2, × 4 + 4, + 6	× tables + tables
5:1/2 **5:3/4**	Percentages Equivalent fractions	Concept Concept
6:1/2 **6:3/4**	Order of operations Square numbers / Multiples	Concept Concept
7:1/2 **7:3/4**	Problem solving Reflections	Strategy time Concept
8:1/2 **8:3/4**	Square numbers Order of operations	Concept Concept
9:1/2 **9:3/4**	Language ÷ 2, ÷ 4	ID card B ÷ tables
10:1/2 **10:3/4**	Language − 13, − 17	ID card B − tables
11:1/2 **11:3/4**	× 3, × 6 Multiplication	× tables × tables
12:1/2 **12:3/4**	÷ 5, ÷ 10 Scale drawing	÷ tables Concept
13:1/2 **13:3/4**	÷ 3, ÷ 6 × 6, × 9	÷ tables × tables
14:1/2 **14:3/4**	Language Language	ID card C ID card C
15:1/2 **15:3/4**	Averages × 7, × 8	Concept × tables
16:1/2 **16:3/4**	÷ 9 Profit and loss	÷ tables Concept
17:1/2 **17:3/4**	Money Chance	Strategy time Chance
18:1/2 **18:3/4**	÷ 7, ÷ 8 Money	÷ tables Strategy time
19:1/2 **19:3/4**	Problem solving Problem solving	Strategy time Strategy time

Unit	Content	Extra Activity
20:1/2 **20:3/4**	− 9, − 5 + 7, + 9	− tables + tables
21:1/2 **21:3/4**	Language Crossnumber puzzle	ID card D Concept
22:1/2 **22:3/4**	Magic squares Crossnumber puzzle	Concept Concept
23:1/2 **23:3/4**	− 3, − 5, − 9 Converting distances	− tables Measure
24:1/2 **24:3/4**	Problem solving Problem solving	Strategy time Strategy time
25:1/2 **25:3/4**	Estimating measurements Factors	Measure Concept
26:1/2 **26:3/4**	− and + with fractions Subtraction with fractions	Concept Concept
27:1/2 **27:3/4**	Fractions to decimals × 8, × 6	Concept × tables
28:1/2 **28:3/4**	Language Problem solving	ID card A Strategy time
29:1/2 **29:3/4**	Average speed Problem solving	Measure Strategy time
30:1/2 **30:3/4**	Problem solving Codes	Strategy time Concept
31:1/2 **31:3/4**	Order of operations Tally	Concept Chance
32:1/2 **32:3/4**	× 6, × 7, × 8 ÷ 4	× tables ÷ tables
33:1/2 **33:3/4**	− 6, − 8 Roman numerals	− tables Concept
34:1/2 **34:3/4**	Scale drawing Coordinates	Concept Concept
35:1/2 **35:3/4**	Codes Factors	Concept Concept
36:1/2 **36:3/4**	Scale drawing Divisibility	Concept Concept
37:1/2 **37:3/4**	Coordinates Personal measurements	Concept Measure
Answers	These can be found in the middle of this book on pages A1 to A16.	

© PEARSON AUSTRALIA 2024 • *AUSTRALIAN SIGNPOST MATHS NSW 6 MENTALS* • ISBN 978 0 6557 0913 8

Arithmetic card

	A	B	C	D	E	F	G	H	I	J	K	L	M
1	20	9	110	20	6	11	$100	$\frac{67}{100}$	0·52	97%	$\frac{56}{100}$	20	67
2	16	1	170	50	14	21	$32	$\frac{3}{10}$	0·2	52%	$\frac{8}{100}$	50	62
3	12	6	200	10	2	27	$48	$\frac{75}{100}$	0·75	39%	$\frac{27}{100}$	10	50
4	18	2	130	70	18	25	$90	$\frac{46}{100}$	0·39	74%	$\frac{15}{100}$	70	41
5	13	8	160	100	10	13	$117	$\frac{5}{100}$	0·4	63%	$\frac{88}{100}$	100	33
6	15	5	180	30	16	17	$150	$\frac{9}{10}$	0·98	6%	$\frac{42}{100}$	30	26
7	19	3	150	80	4	29	$76	$\frac{14}{100}$	0·67	18%	$\frac{74}{100}$	80	19
8	14	7	190	60	12	15	$28	$\frac{83}{100}$	0·5	45%	$\frac{66}{100}$	60	14
9	11	4	140	90	20	23	$55	$\frac{6}{10}$	0·13	87%	$\frac{39}{100}$	90	7
10	17	10	120	40	8	19	$85	$\frac{1}{100}$	0·8	21%	$\frac{95}{100}$	40	3

How to use this card

If students were told to 'subtract B from C', they would write:

1. 110 – 9 = 101
2. 170 – 1 = 169
3. 200 – 6 = 194
4. 130 – 2 = 128
5. 160 – 8 = 152
6. 180 – 5 = 175
7. 150 – 3 = 147
8. 190 – 7 = 183
9. 140 – 4 = 136
10. 120 – 10 = 110

Other instructions might be:

- **What is left from $200 if I spend the amount in column G?**
- **What multiplied by 10 gives column C?**
- **Subtract column B from L.**
- **Write column J as a decimal.**
- **Multiply column B by 4.**
- **Add columns A and C.**
- **Add columns H and K.**
- **Square column B.**
- **Halve column E.**

The applications of this card are endless.

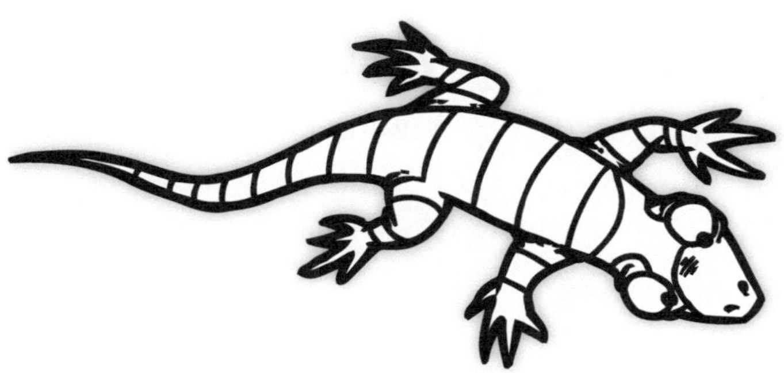

ID card A

Do not write on this card.

1 **mm** stands for m ______.

2 **cm** stands for c ______.

3 **m** stands for m ______.

4 **km** stands for k ______.

5 0 1 2 3 4 — 1 cm = 1 m — s ______

6 **g** stands for g ______.

7 **kg** stands for k ______.

8 **t** stands for t ______.

9 **mL** stands for m ______.

10 **L** stands for l ______.

11 **cm²** stands for s ______ c ______.

12 **m²** stands for s ______ m ______.

13 1m / 1m — 1 square m ______

14 **ha** stands for h ______.

15 100 m | 1 ha | 100 m — 1 hectare = ______ m²

16 **km²** stands for s ______ k ______.

17 **cm³** stands for c ______ c ______.

18 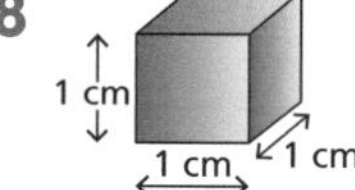

This block has a volume of 1 ______.

19 **1 cm³** has the same volume as ______ mL of liquid.

20 **m³** stands for c ______ m ______.

21 **s** stands for s ______.

22 **min** stands for m ______.

23 **h** stands for h ______.

24 **am** means b ______ n ______.

25 **pm** means a ______ n ______.

26 **05:40** in digital time is ____ : ____ ____.

27 **7:30 pm** in 24-hour time is ____ : ____.

28 **°C** stands for d ______ C ______.

29 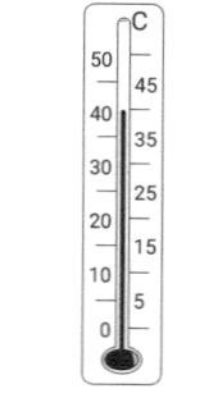

t ______

30 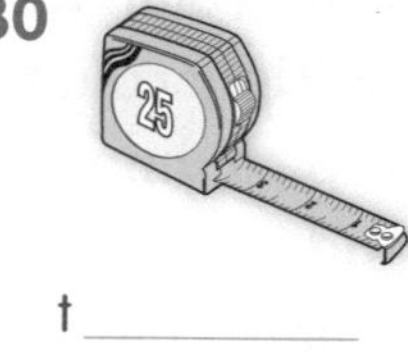

t ______ m ______

See page A1 for answers.

© PEARSON AUSTRALIA 2024 • *AUSTRALIAN SIGNPOST MATHS NSW 6 MENTALS* • ISBN 978 0 6557 0913 8

ID card B

Do not write on this card.

1

..., −3, −2, −1, 0, 1, 2, 3, ...

These are called

i__________.

2

A counting number that has only 2 factors, itself and 1 is a

p __________ number.

3

A counting number that has more than 2 factors is a

c __________ number.

4

7, 14, 21, ...

are multiples of

__________.

5

The factors of 8

are 1, 8,

_____ and _____.

6

35, 40 and 45

are all divisible by

______.

7

$$5\overline{)47}\quad 9 \text{ r } 2$$

'r' means

r__________.

8

1, 4, 9, 16, 25, ...

are the

s __________ numbers.

9

208 650

has 6

d __________.

10

4·395

_____ ones

_____ tenths

_____ hundredths

_____ thousandths

11

19%

means

19 out of __________.

12

v__________ line

13

h__________ line

14

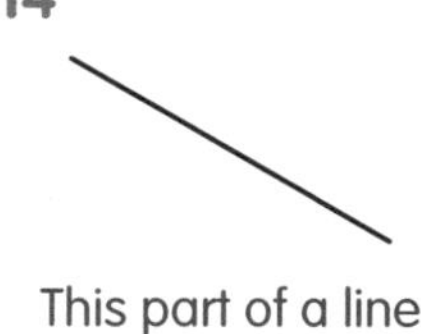

This part of a line is an i__________.

15

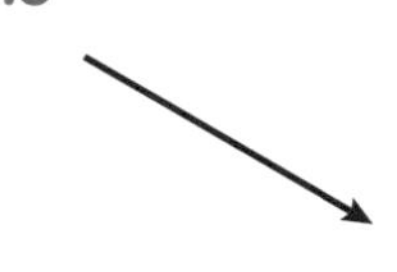

This part of a line is a r __________.

16

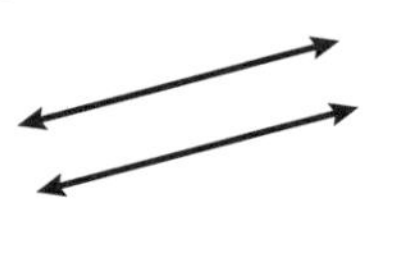

p __________ lines

17

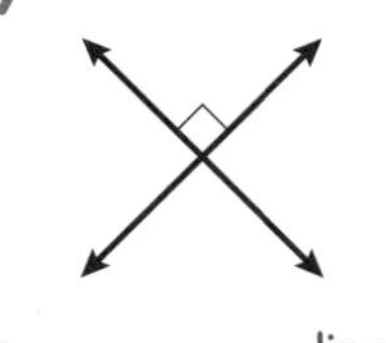

p __________ lines

18

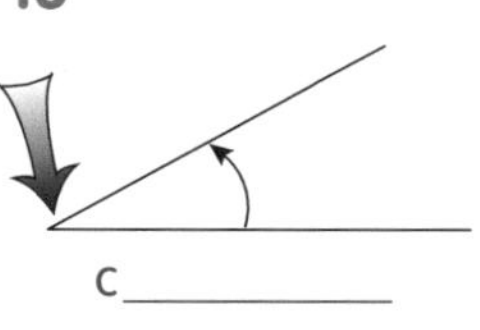

c__________

(or vertex of an angle)

19

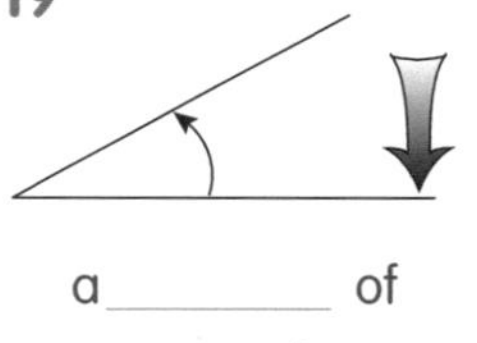

a__________ of an angle

20

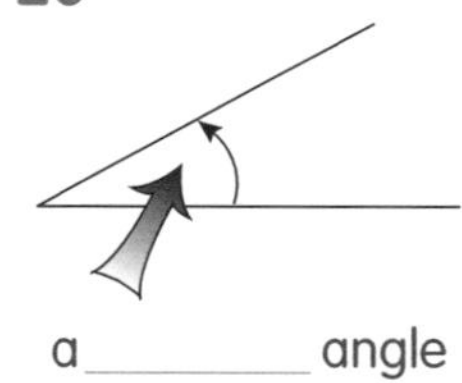

a__________ angle

21

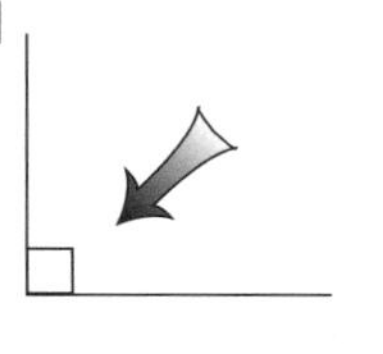

r__________ angle

22

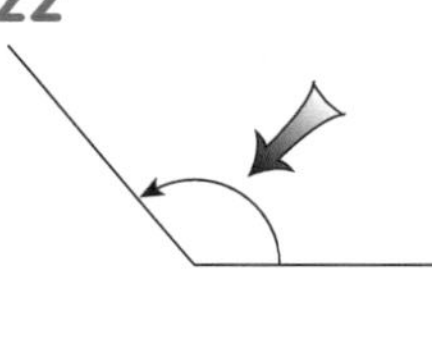

o__________ angle

23

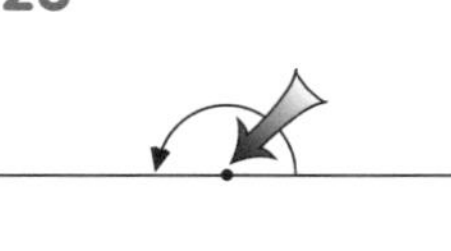

s __________ angle

24

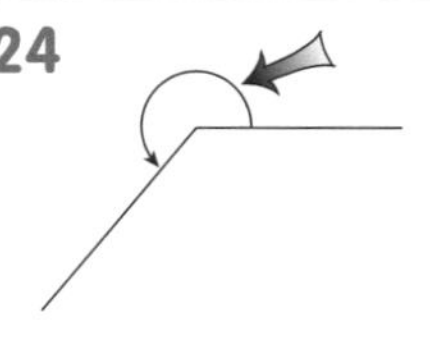

r __________ angle

25

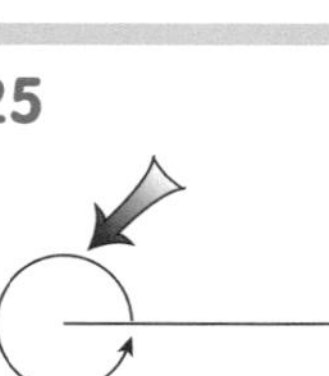

r __________

26

These angles are complementary.

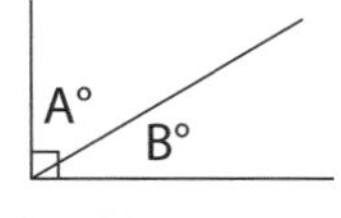

A° + B° = ________

27

These angles are supplementary.

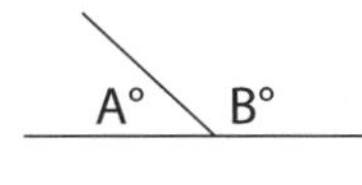

A° + B° = ________

28

Angles at a point

B°
C°
A°
D°

A° + B° + C° + D° = ________

29

Vertically opposite angles

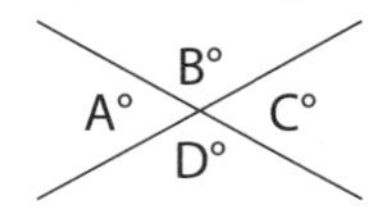

A = _____, B = _____

30

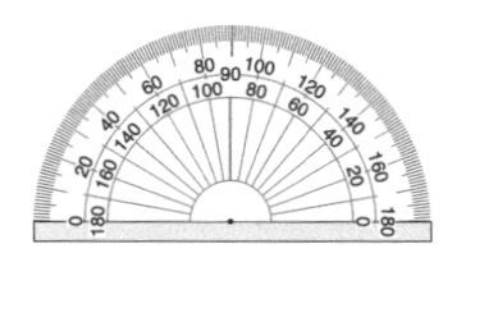

p __________

See page A1 for answers.

ID card C

Do not write on this card.

1

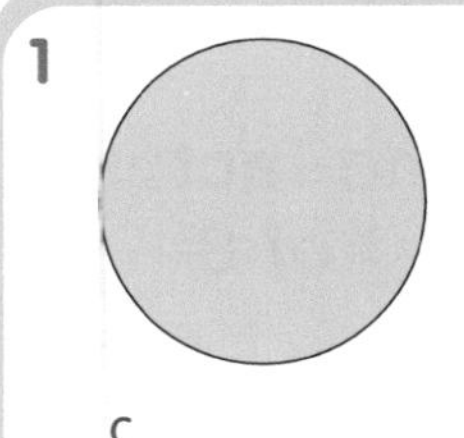

c ______

2

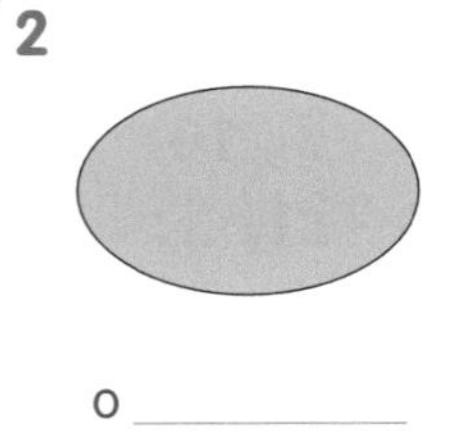

o ______

3

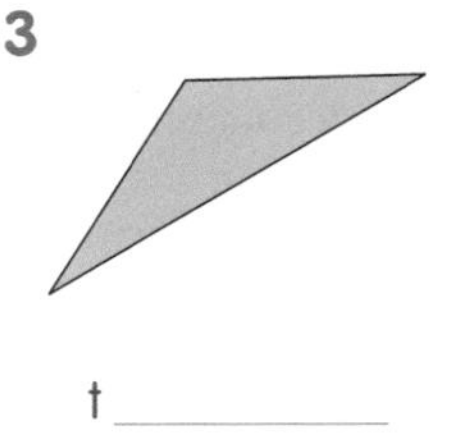

t ______

4

s ______

5

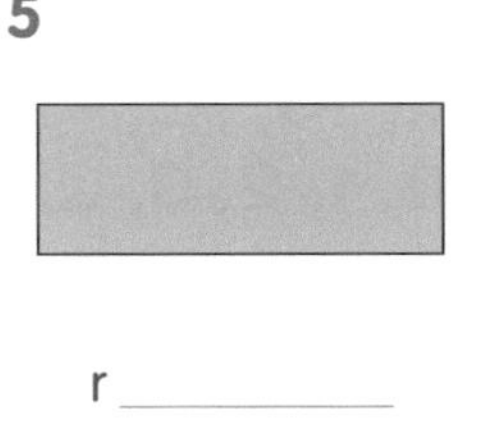

r ______

6

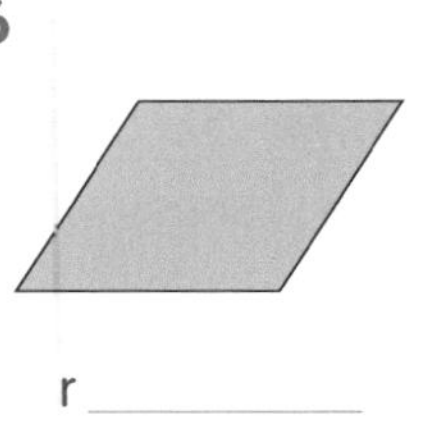

r ______

7

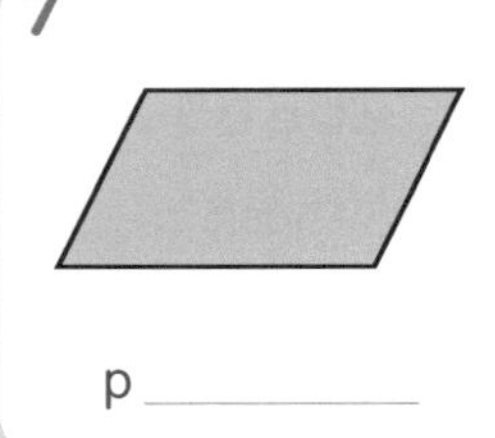

p ______

8

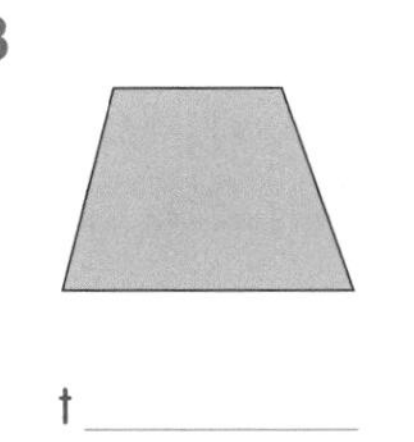

t ______

9

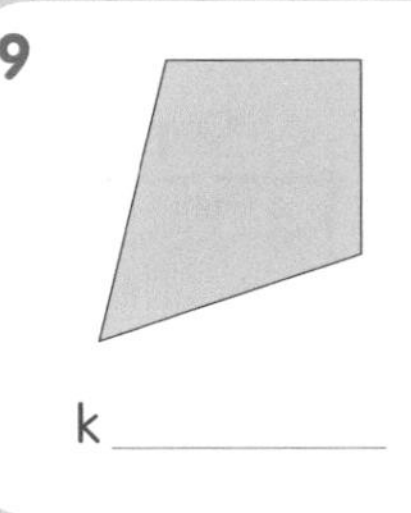

k ______

10

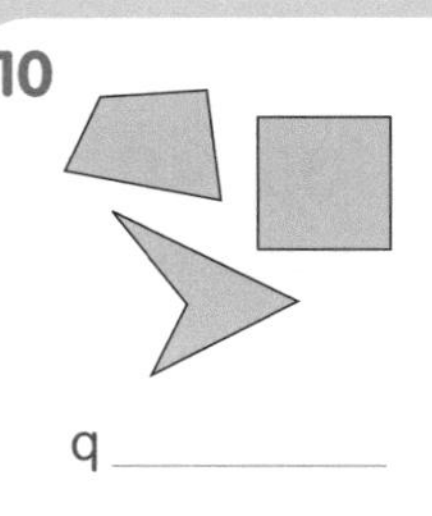

q ______

11

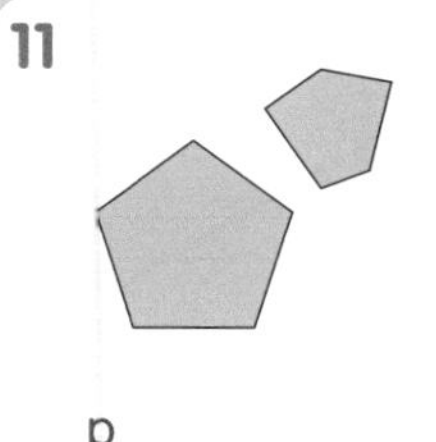

p ______

12

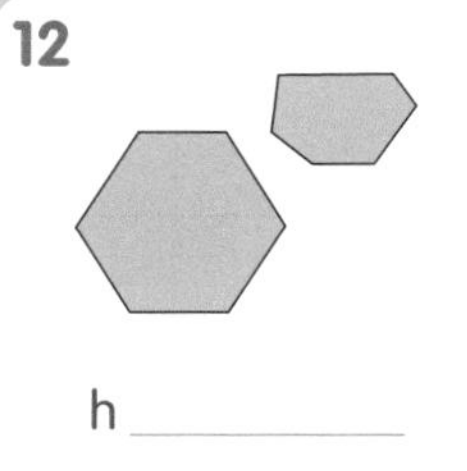

h ______

13

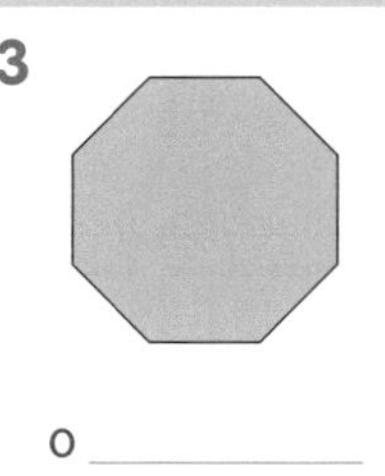

o ______

14

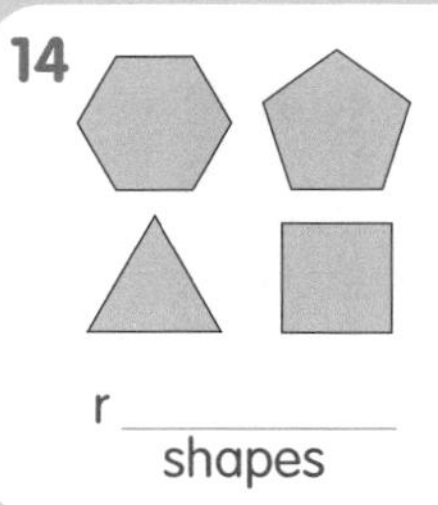

r ______ shapes

15

i ______ shapes

16

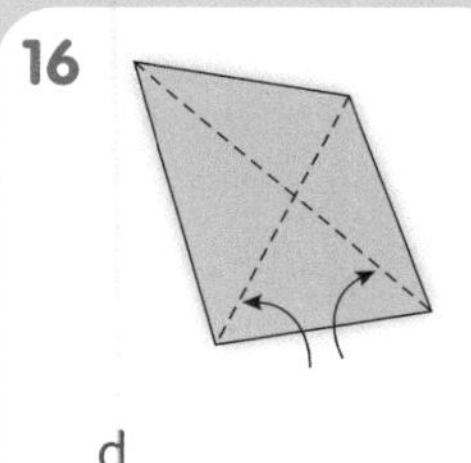

d ______

17

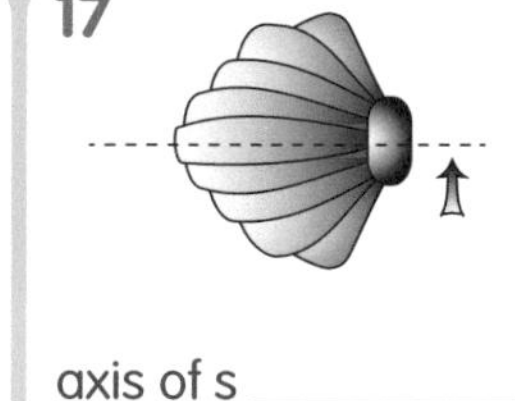

axis of s ______

18

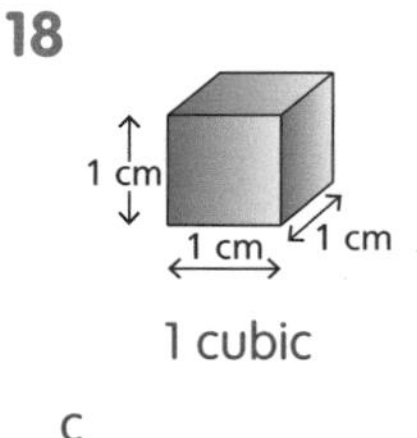

1 cubic

c ______

19

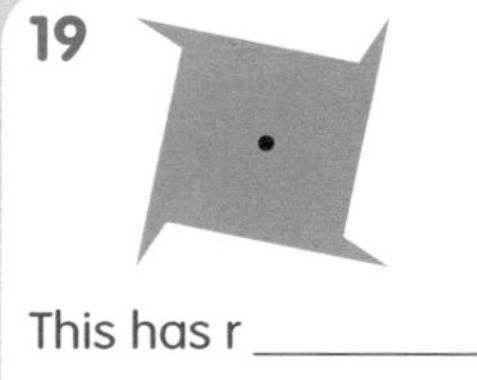

This has r ______

s ______.

20

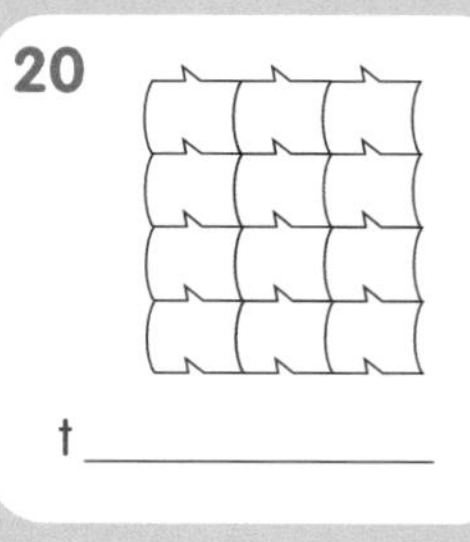

t ______

21

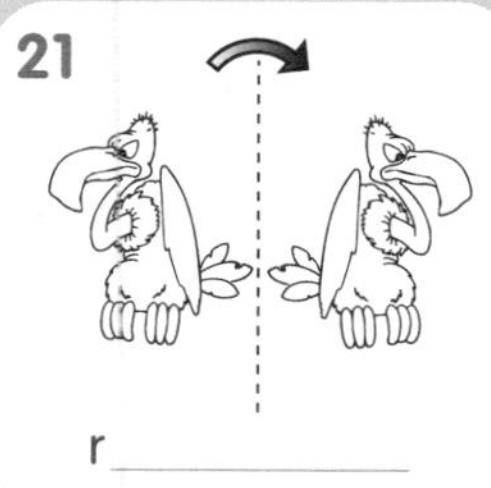

r ______

22

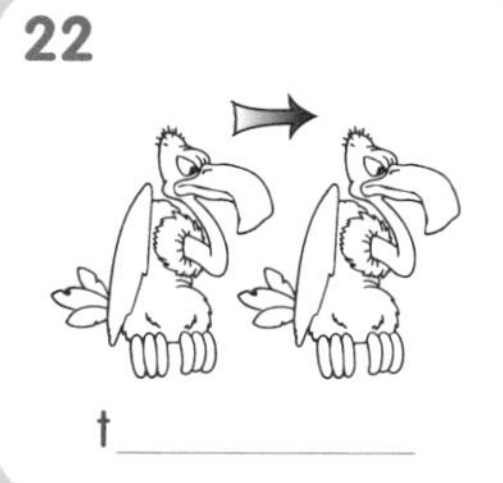

t ______

23

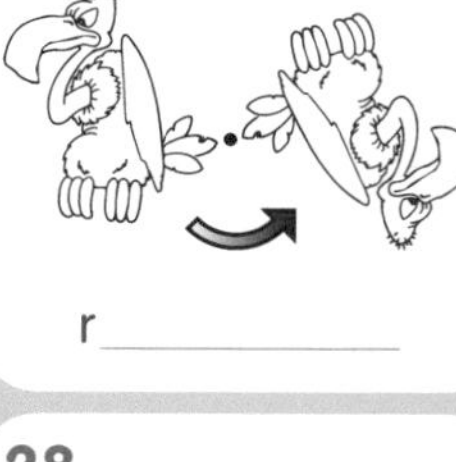

r ______

24

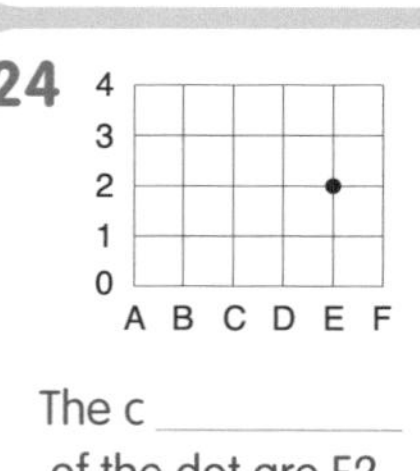

The c ______ of the dot are E2.

25

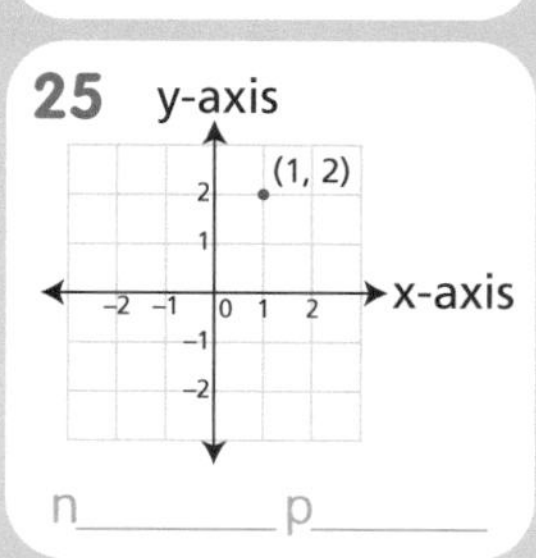

n ______ p ______

26

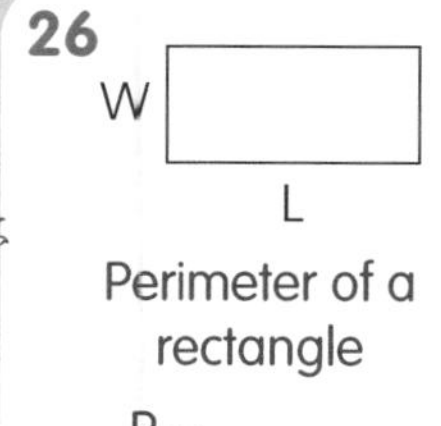

Perimeter of a rectangle

P = ______

27

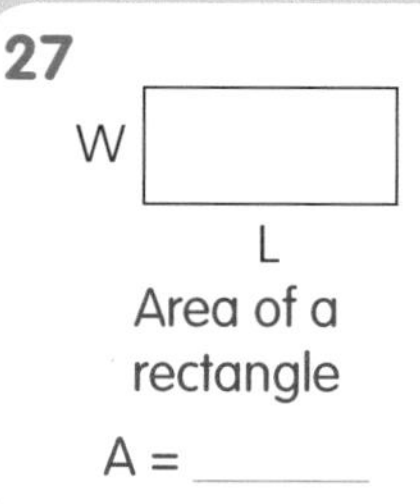

Area of a rectangle

A = ______

28

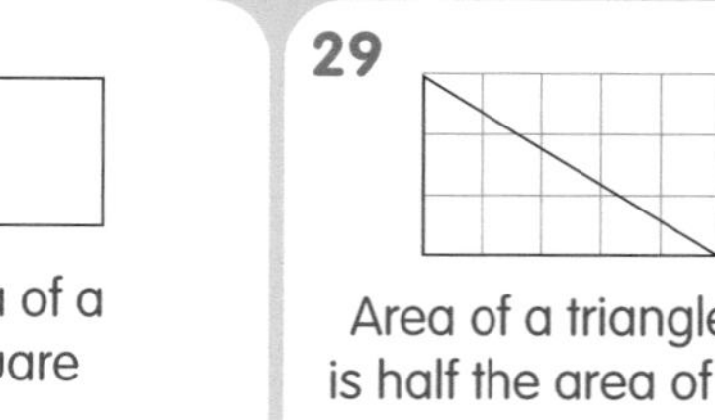

Area of a square

A = ______

29

Area of a triangle is half the area of a

r ______

30

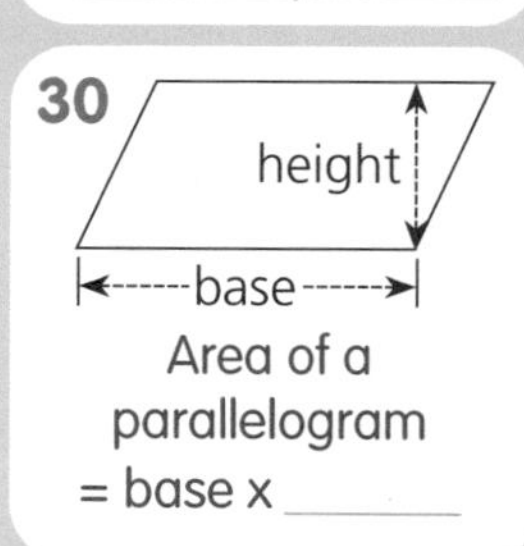

Area of a parallelogram = base x ______

See page A1 for answers.

© PEARSON AUSTRALIA 2024 • *AUSTRALIAN SIGNPOST MATHS NSW 6 MENTALS* • ISBN 978 0 6557 0913 8

ID card D

Do not write on this card.

1

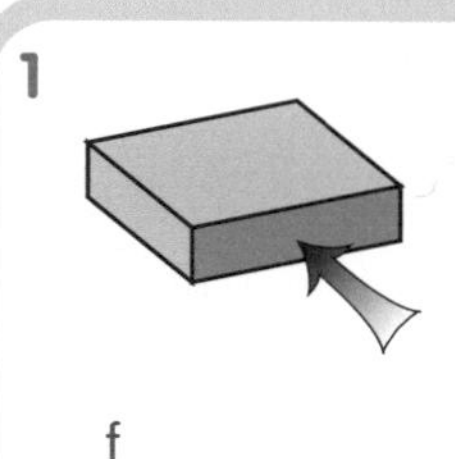

f ____________

2

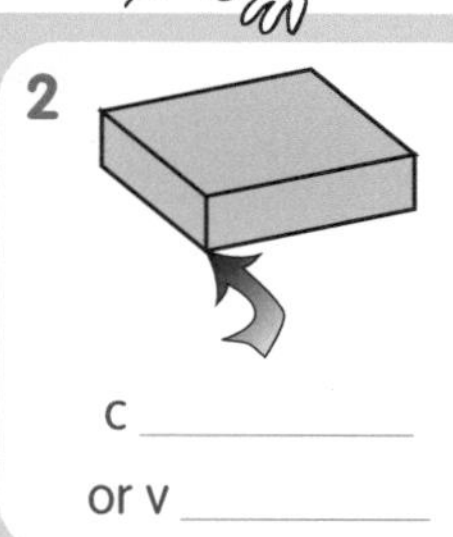

c ____________
or v ____________

3

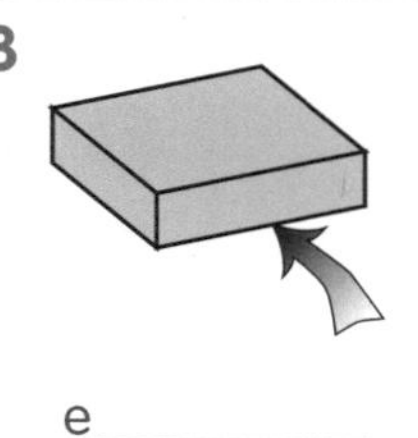

e ____________

4

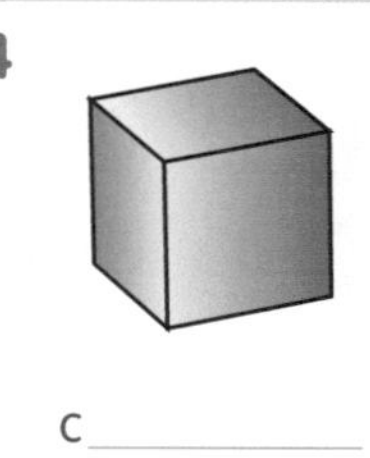

c ____________

5

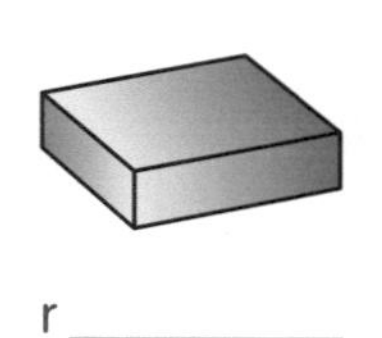

r ____________
p ____________

6

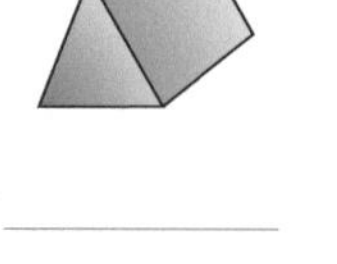

t ____________
p ____________

7

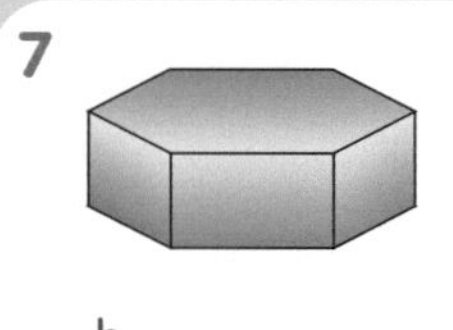

h ____________
p ____________

8

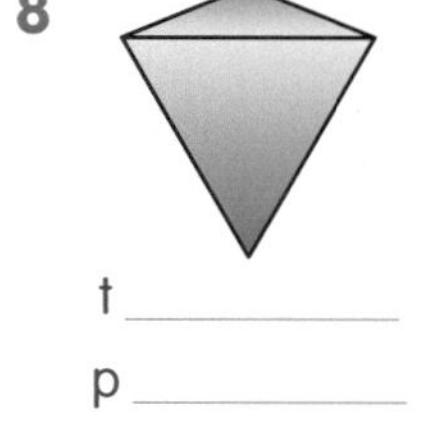

t ____________
p ____________

9

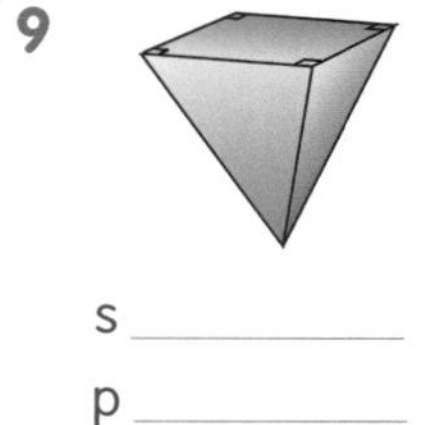

s ____________
p ____________

10

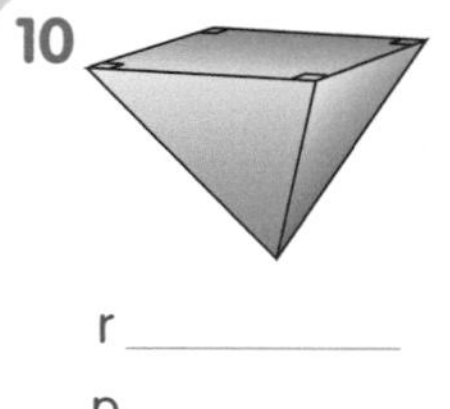

r ____________
p ____________

11

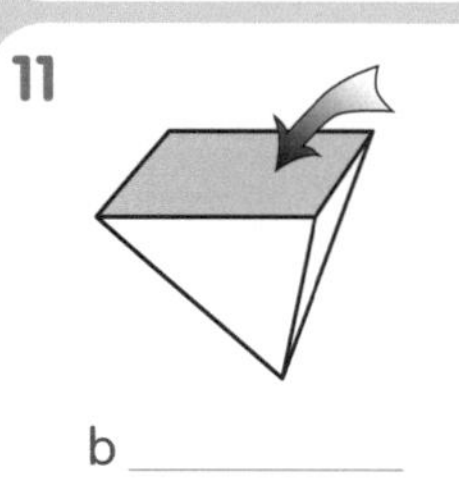

b ____________

12

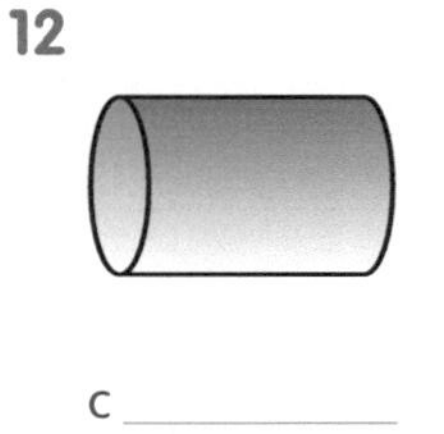

c ____________

13

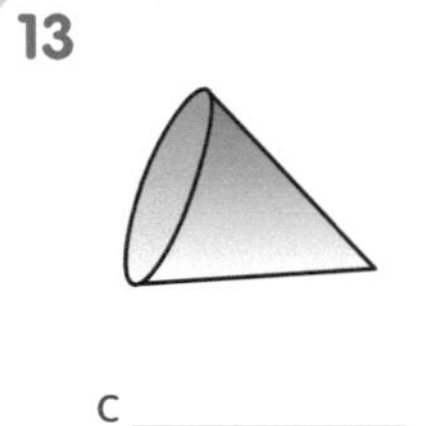

c ____________

14

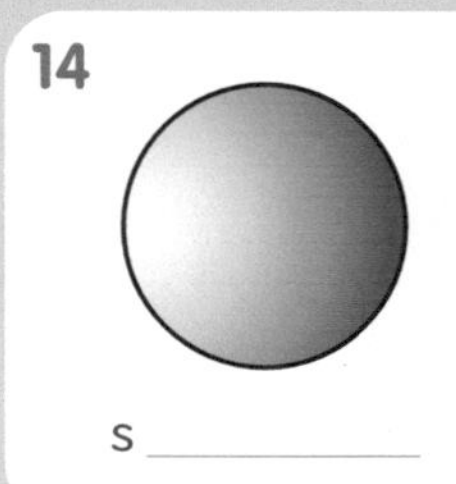

s ____________

15

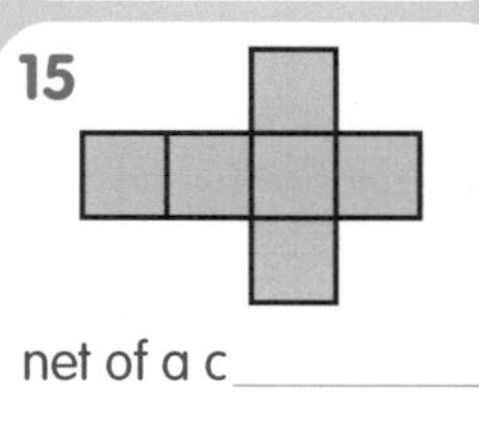

net of a c ____________

16

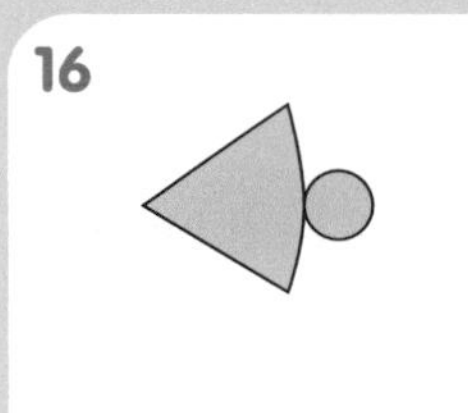

net of a c ____________

17

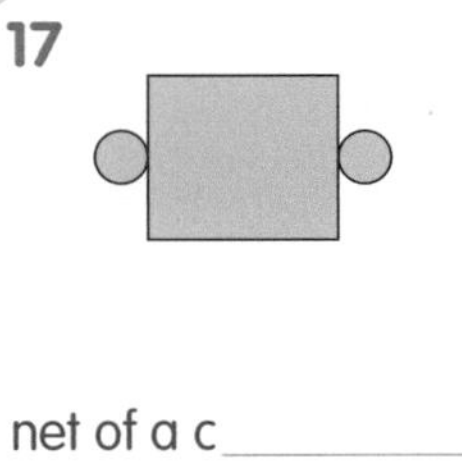

net of a c ____________

18

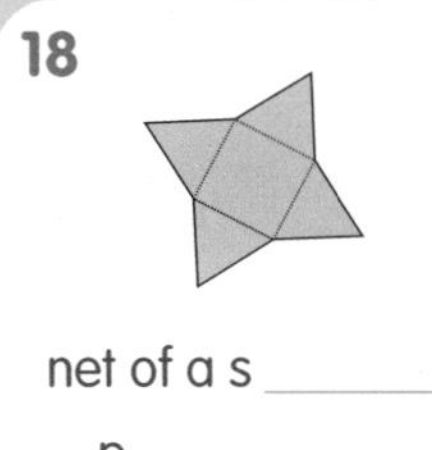

net of a s ____________
p ____________

19

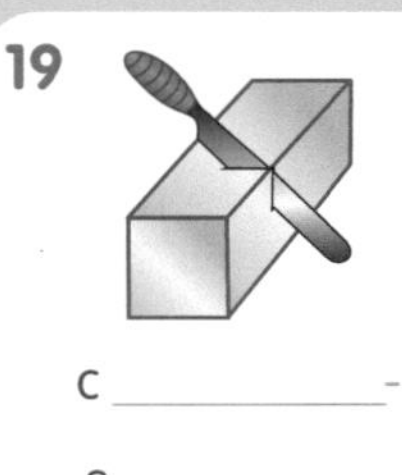

c ____________-
s ____________

20

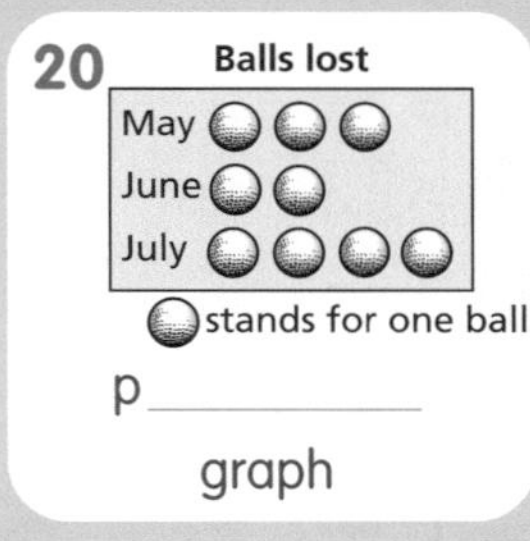

p ____________
graph

21

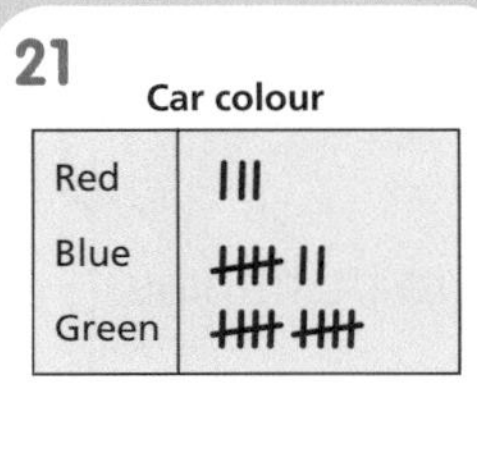

This is a t ____________.

22

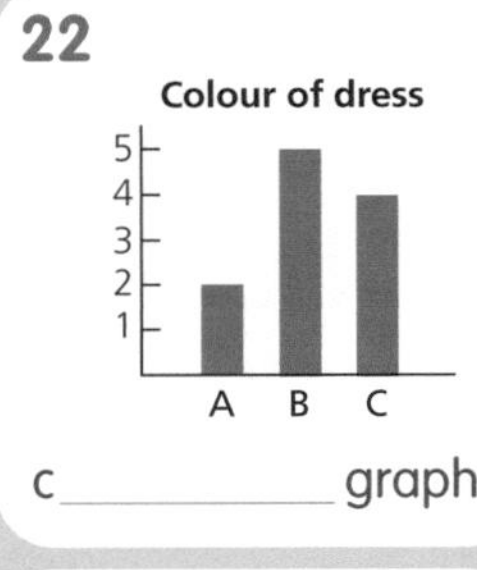

c ____________ graph

23

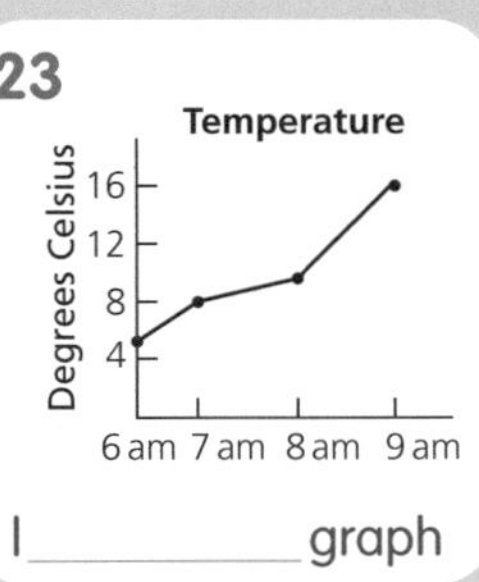

l ____________ graph

24

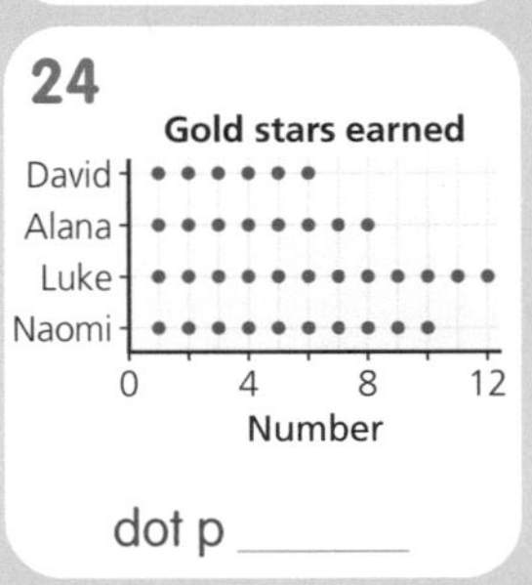

dot p ____________

25

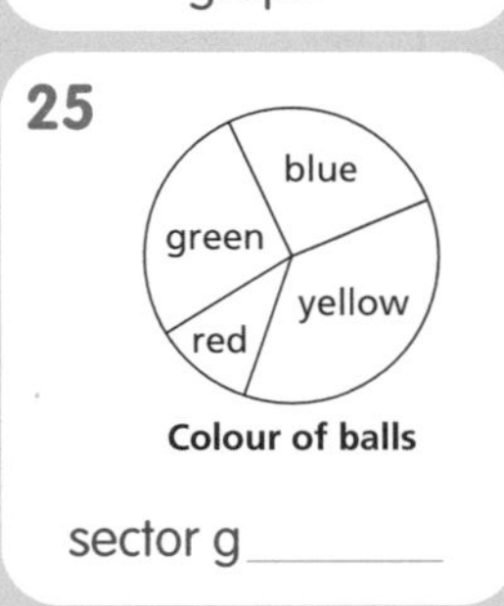

sector g ____________

26

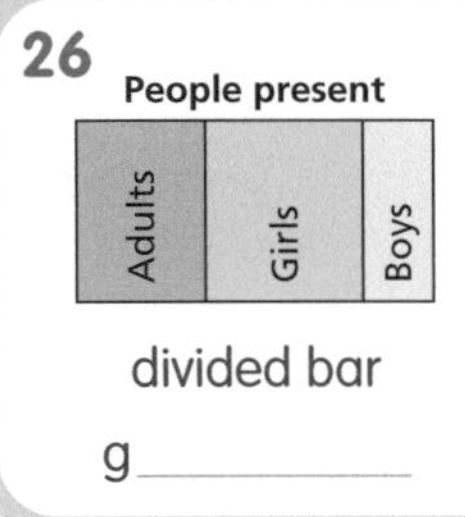

divided bar
g ____________

27

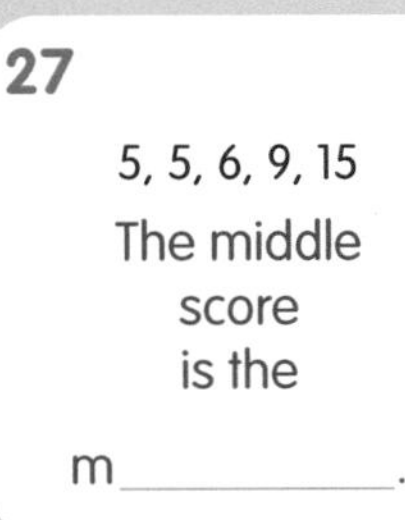

5, 5, 6, 9, 15
The middle score is the
m ____________.

28

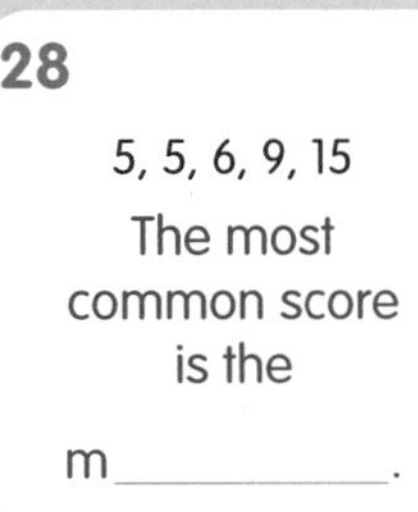

5, 5, 6, 9, 15
The most common score is the
m ____________.

29

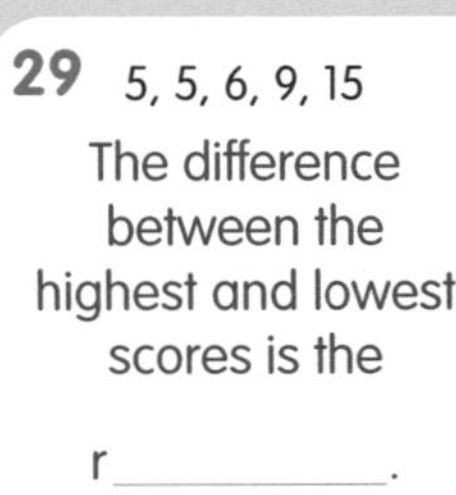

5, 5, 6, 9, 15
The difference between the highest and lowest scores is the
r ____________.

30

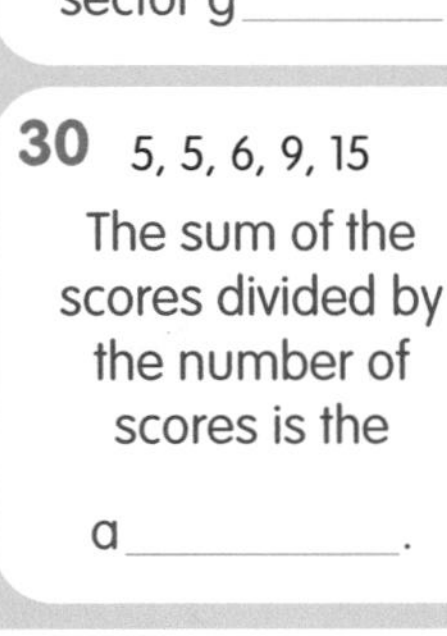

5, 5, 6, 9, 15
The sum of the scores divided by the number of scores is the
a ____________.

See page A1 for answers.

1:1 [ ] out of 18

1. 23 + 31 ____
2. 3 × 3 ____
3. 6 × $3 ____
4. 8 ÷ 2 ____
5. 5475 + 2573 ____
6. Add 235 to 432. ____
7. Multiply 7 by 3. ____
8. 18 divided by 6. ____
9. 0·1 × 10 ____
10. 4253 × 2 ____
11. 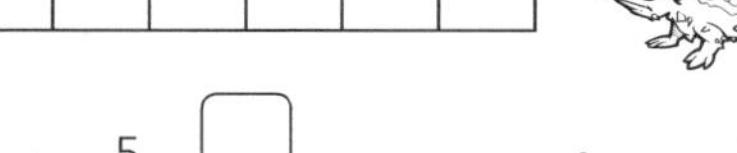

    a $1 - \frac{5}{6}$ [—] b $1 - \frac{2}{6}$ [—]
12. If 19·7 million is 19 700 000, what is:

    49·3 million? ____
13. $\frac{6}{8} - \frac{2}{8} =$ [—] or [—]
14. a 0·48 = ____% b 0·29 = ____%
15. a 20, 24, 28, ____, ____, ____, ____

    b 15, 18, 21, ____, ____, ____, ____

    c 22, 27, 32, ____, ____, ____, ____
16. A cube has ____ edges. See page 85 for help. 
17. a 256 cm = ____ m ____ cm

    b 46 mm = ____ cm

    c 4 kg = ____ g

    d 4750 g = ____ kg
18. The total value of these notes.

____

1:2 [ ] out of 20

1. 64 ÷ 8 ____
2. 7 × $6 ____
3. 648 − 97 ____
4. $\frac{1}{2}$ of 86 ____
5. 8353 − 2647 ____
6. 3 squared. ____
7. Halve $64. ____
8. 684 g − 298 g ____
9. 0·5 mL × 100 ____
10. 5308 × 5 ____
11. Millilitres in $6\frac{1}{2}$ L. ____
12. Make the denominators equal, then subtract.

    $\frac{8}{12} - \frac{1}{3} =$ [—] − [—] = [—]

13. a 0·54, 0·53, 0·52, ____, ____, ____

    b The rule for this pattern is ____.
14. 4 × 164 = (4 × ____) + (4 × ____) + (4 × ____)

    = ____ + ____ + ____

    = ____

    (diagram: 164; 4; 100, 60, 4)
15. If apples cost 90c each, how much would 7 apples cost? ____
16. Find an estimate by rounding each number first.

    a 36 × 29 ____ b 64 × 17 ____

    c 53 × 31 ____ d 69 × 62 ____
17. $5\frac{1}{6}, 5\frac{2}{6}, 5\frac{3}{6},$ [—], [—], [—]
18. 5 hours = ____ minutes
19. Write the fraction equal to zero point nine. [—]
20. I scored 68 out of 100 in a test.

    What percentage did I get correct? ____

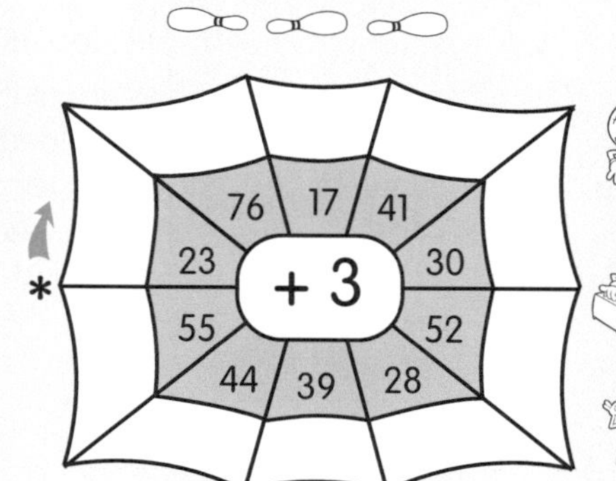

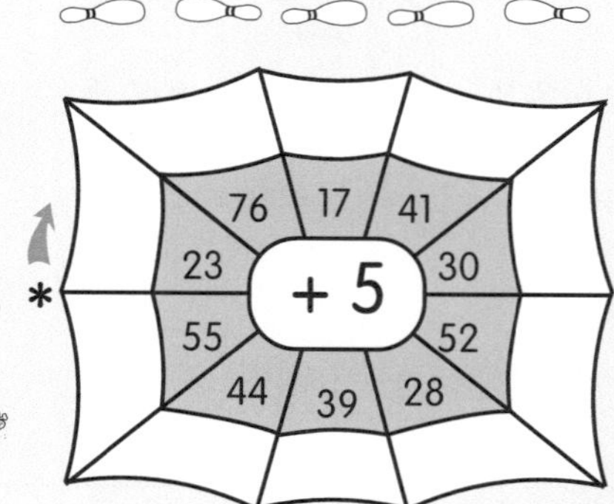

even + odd = ____

odd + odd = ____

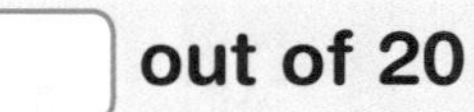

© PEARSON AUSTRALIA 2024 • *AUSTRALIAN SIGNPOST MATHS NSW 6 MENTALS* • ISBN 978 0 6557 0913 8

1:3 out of 18

1 $8\overline{)864}$ 2 $6\overline{)762}$ 3 $5\overline{)835}$

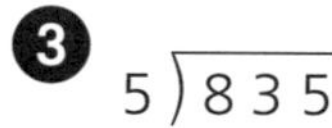

4 700 000 + 45 000 + 300 + 21 = ____

5 List the first 6 multiples of 7.

____, ____, ____, ____, ____, ____

6 Make the largest possible 8-digit number using 4, 2, 7, 4, 7, 9, 1 and 7. ____

7 In every space made by a row of 6 trees, we planted 8 flowers. How many flowers did we plant? ____

8 How many groups of 8 apples in 48? ____

9 Find the area of a rectangle with 4 m and 9 m sides. ____

10 67 − 45 = 62 − ____ = ____

11 500 ha = ____ square kilometres

12 What are the factors of 12?

____, ____, ____, ____, ____, ____

13 Colour 6 tenths red and 3 tenths blue. What fraction have you coloured? ____

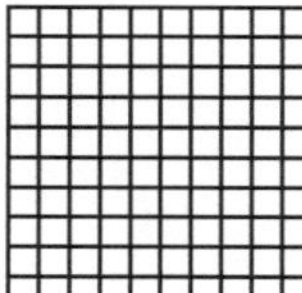

14 **a** 255 more than 121. ____

b 243 more than 456. ____

c 372 more than 627. ____

15 Which of 9, 21, 32 and 36 is both 'even' and 'a multiple of 3'? ____

16 **a** 185, 175, 165, ____, ____, ____

b 16, 24, 32, ____, ____, ____, ____

17 17 + 4 + 8 + 13 + 9 + 6 + 20 ____

18 81 pens shared equally by 9. ____

1:4 out of 8

Extension

1 January 1st is the 1st day of the year.
What day is May 15th, 2023? ____

2 Fill in the boxes.

a □□ × 3 = □92

b $3\overline{)\square\square\square}$ = 1 2 9

3 3 × 3 × 90 ____

4 **a** 108 more than 52. ____

b 108 more than 352. ____

c 108 more than 35 352. ____

5 I must choose an item from each square.
How many groups are possible? ____

6 What fraction of this shape has been shaded? $\frac{\square}{\square}$

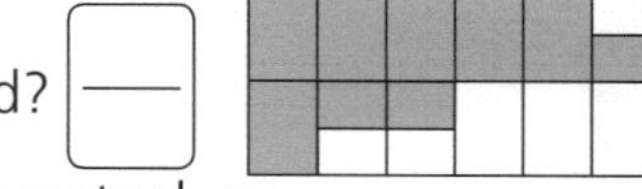

7 How many axes of symmetry has:

a a regular heptagon? (7 sides) ____

b a regular nonagon? (9 sides) ____

8 How many diagonals has a:

a pentagon? ____ **b** hexagon? ____

Challenge

Write facts you know about the number 43·828.

____

____

____

____

____

Measure

Fill out this table about yourself, a relative or a friend.

Name: ____ **Date:** ____

Age: ____	Mass: ____ kg	Shoe size: ____
Height: ____ cm	Waist: ____ cm	Neck size: ____ cm

2:1 ☐ out of 19

1. 2×3 ____
2. 9×2 ____
3. $35 + 45$ ____
4. $38 + 62$ ____
5. $\begin{array}{r} 7456 \\ +\ 1456 \\ \hline \end{array}$
6. 99 more than 123. ____
7. Multiply 0·1 by 100. ____
8. 7 times $4. ____
9. Divide 32 by 8. ____
10. $\begin{array}{r} 1432 \\ \times \quad 5 \\ \hline \end{array}$
11. I scored 76 out of 100 in a test. How many more marks did I need to score 100? ____
12. Use am or pm to write 05:56. ____
13. A mango cost $3.10. Circle the best estimate for the cost of 5 mangos.

    $6 $12 $15 $20 $25
14. Estimate your height. ____
15. Write in order from largest to smallest.

    8 781 344, 8 768 367, 8 780 033

    ____
16. Round 46 354 to the nearest hundred. ____
17. How many tens can be taken from 354 838? ____
18. **a** 5000 mL = ____ L

    b 7·3 L = ____ mL

    c 7365 m = ____ km

    d 5 L 538 mL = ____ mL
19. **a** 18, 24, 30, ____, ____, ____, ____

    b 21, 28, 35, ____, ____, ____, ____

2:2 ☐ out of 19

1. 4×8 ____
2. 6×5 ____
3. $45 \div 9$ ____
4. $35 \div 7$ ____
5. $\begin{array}{r} 6475 \\ -\ 3659 \\ \hline \end{array}$
6. $246 - 137$ ____
7. $673 - 264$ ____
8. Multiply $8 by 9. ____
9. 72 divided by 8. ____
10. $\begin{array}{r} 3751 \\ \times \quad 3 \\ \hline \end{array}$
11. What is the probability, as a fraction, of tossing a 6 on a regular dice? ☐
12. Write 52 million. ____
13. What fraction of a dollar is 65c? ☐
14. Write 9 756 000 in words.

    ____

    ____
15. **a** On this square, shade 49 hundredths.

    b A batsman has scored 49 runs. How many more for a century? ____

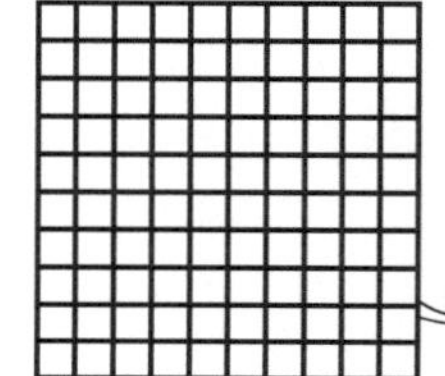

16. Write $2\frac{63}{100}$ as a decimal. ____
17. **a** $\frac{1}{4}$ of 12 ____

    b $\frac{3}{4}$ of 12 ____

18. **a** $2\frac{1}{2}$ m = ____ cm **b** $2\frac{1}{2}$ cm = ____ mm
19. The distance around each square is 16 metres. How far is it around the rectangle?

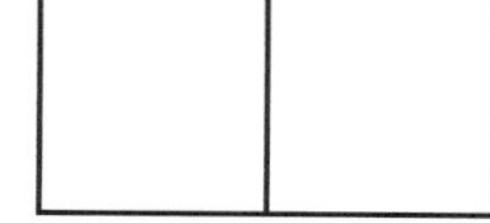

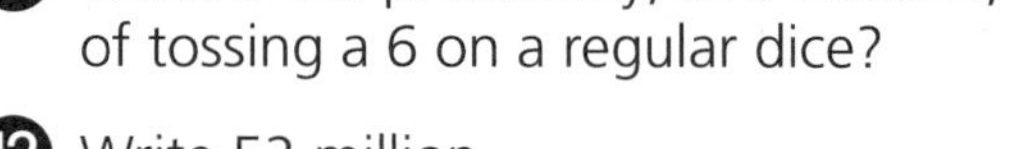

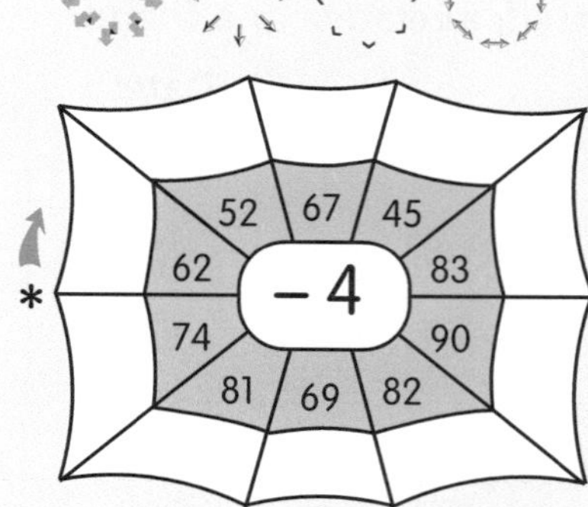

even − even = ____

odd − even = ____

© PEARSON AUSTRALIA 2024 • *AUSTRALIAN SIGNPOST MATHS NSW 6 MENTALS* • ISBN 978 0 6557 0913 8

2:3 ☐ out of 12

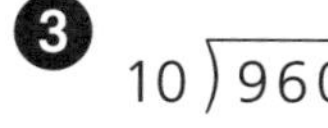

1. $8\overline{)872}$ 2. $4\overline{)812}$ 3. $10\overline{)960}$
4. How many hundreds can be taken from 2 456 064? ________
5. Which is larger:
   a 6·09 or 4·87? ________
   b 17·25 or 19·3? ________
6. Our cricket team needed 260 runs to win the match. We scored only 123. How far short were we? ________

7. 9 o'clock, quarter past 12, half past 9, 3 o'clock. At which of the above times are the hour and minute hands at right angles?
   ____
8. What is the perimeter of the square that has an area of 16 cm^2? ________
9. What is the digital time 36 minutes after 15:27? ________
10. a What is the total capacity of these containers? ________

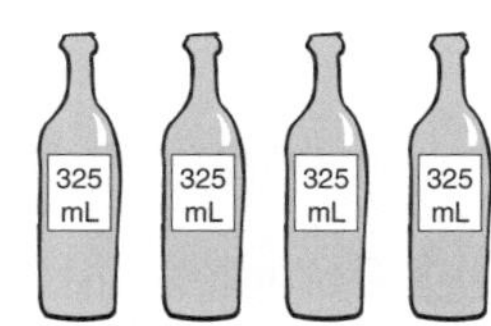

   b How many mL more would be needed to reach 2L? ________
11. 201·79 = ____ hundreds, ____ tens, ____ ones, ____ tenths, ____ hundredths
12. 

   What fraction is:
   a shaded? $\frac{\square}{\square}$ b not shaded? $\frac{\square}{\square}$

2:4 ☐ out of 6

Extension

1. How many axes of symmetry has:
   a a regular decagon? ________
   b a regular dodecagon? (12 sides) ________
2. This figure has hexagons of different size and shape. How many hexagons are there altogether? ________

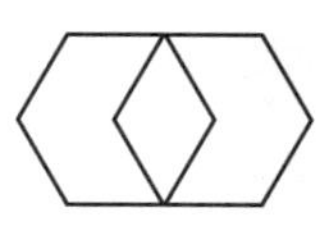

3. In how many different ways can you make 45 cents using only 5c, 10c and 20c coins? ________
4. A plane ticket to Armidale costs $174. What is the cost of:

   a 5 tickets? ________
   b 6 tickets? ________
5. a 435 + 297 = ____ + 300 = ____
   b 824 − 392 = ____ − 390 = ____
   c 725 − 409 = ____ − 410 = ____
6. If the length, breadth and height of this model are all multiplied by 3, how many cubes will be in the new model's:

   a top view? ________
   b total volume? ________

Challenge

Write numbers sentences that are equal to 36.

____
____
____
____
____

Turn to ID card D on page 9.
Give the answers for these numbers.

(1) ________ (2) ________
(3) ________ (12) ________
(13) ________ (14) ________
(15) net of a ________ (16) net of a ________
(17) net of a ________ (18) net of a ________

3:1 ☐ out of 14

1. 4×5 ______
2. 5×3 ______
3. $6 \div 2$ ______
4. $12 \div 3$ ______
5. $\begin{array}{r} 6576 \\ -\ 3657 \\ \hline \end{array}$
6. Halve 282. ______
7. Double 432. ______
8. $0{\cdot}4 \times 100$ ______
9. $\frac{1}{2}$ of \$124. ______
10. $\begin{array}{r} 8063 \\ \times \quad 2 \\ \hline \end{array}$

11. 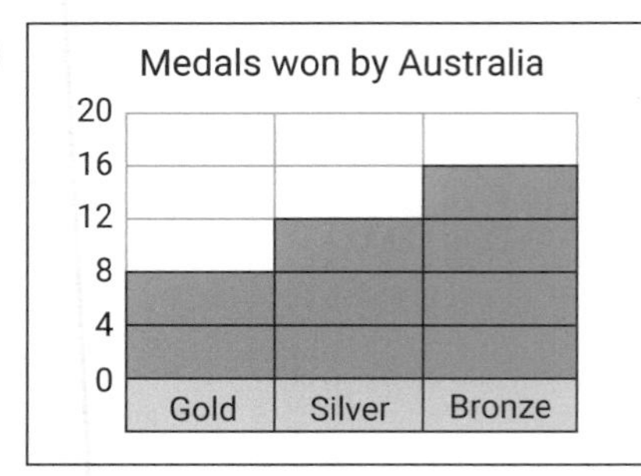

 a How many of each medal were won?
 G = ______ S = ______ B = ______

 b The type of medal won most. ______

 c How many more Bronze than gold were won? ______

12. In a 200 m race, I fell after running 154 m. How far was I from the finish line? ______

13. A  B 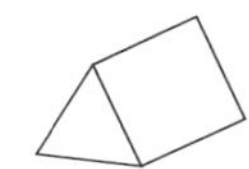 C 

D 

 a Which of the objects has a top view that is a circle? ______

 b Which of the objects has a top view that is a square? ______

14. $7\,000\,000 + 50\,000 + 300 + 21 =$ ______

3:2 ☐ out of 18

1. $7 \times 9 - 38$ ______
2. $8 \times \$62$ ______
3. $21 \div 7$ ______
4. $32 \div 8$ ______
5. $\begin{array}{r} 5735 \\ +\ 2545 \\ \hline \end{array}$
6. Halve 356. ______
7. Multiply \$7 by 8. ______
8. $\square \times 7 = 42, \square =$ ______
9. $\square \times 9 = 63, \square =$ ______
10. $\begin{array}{r} 6347 \\ \times \quad 8 \\ \hline \end{array}$

11. Write a digital label for each time.

 a 
 morning
 ☐ : ☐

 b 
 evening
 ☐ : ☐

12. $2 \times 3 \times 6 =$ ______
13. $87 - 35 = 92 -$ ______ = ______
14. Use am or pm to write the time $1\frac{1}{2}$ hours before:
 a 16:32 ______ b 19:09 ______
 c 09:23 ______ d 05:58 ______
15. Complete this pattern:

Pentagons	1	2	3	4	5
Sides	5				

16. How many \$10 notes have the same value as \$150? ______
17. Alana is 27 years older than Flynn. How old will Alana be when Flynn is 18? ______
18. $167 + 354 =$ ______ $+ 350$

× Tables

$\times 8$: 5, 3, 10, 7, 4, 8, 2, 9, 6, 1 *

$\times 5$: 5, 3, 10, 7, 4, 8, 2, 9, 6, 1 *

6 × 5 is half of 6 × 10.

30 + 30 = 60

© PEARSON AUSTRALIA 2024 • *AUSTRALIAN SIGNPOST MATHS NSW 6 MENTALS* • ISBN 978 0 6557 0913 8

3:3 ☐ out of 13

❶ $5\overline{)830}$ ❷ $7\overline{)825}$ ❸ $9\overline{)846}$

❹ 28 pants, 30 pairs of shoes.
How many more shoes than pants? ________

❺

Vehicles passing home

Buses
Cars
Trucks

2 4 6 8 10

How many vehicles passed my home altogether? ________

❻ Rachel was 43 when Lachlan was 5. How old will Rachel be when Lachlan is 37? ________

❼ What is the average of 14, 12, 16 and 23? ________

❽ Write in order from largest to smallest:
0·67 1·2 0·8 0·99

____

❾ True or false?
700 − 428 = 699 + 1 − 428 ________

❿ 8 + 8 + 8 + 8 + 8 + 8 + 8 ________

⓫ Label each angle with obtuse, acute or reflex.

 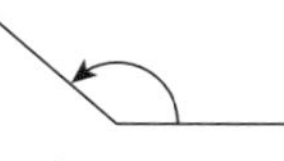 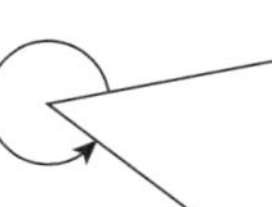

________ ________ ________

⓬ Write the numeral four thousand and two point two one. ________

⓭ Make the smallest possible 7-digit whole number using the digits 3, 6, 0, 4, 3, 2 and 9. ________

3:4 ☐ out of 7

Extension

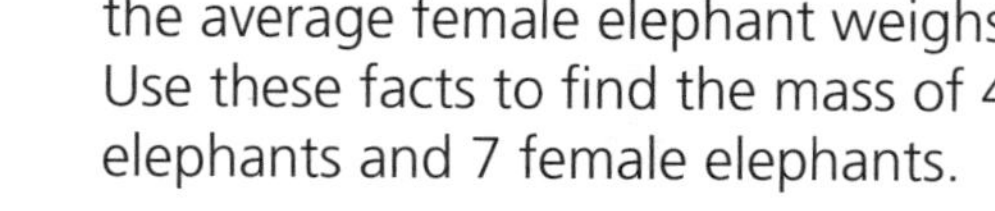

❶ The average male elephant weighs 5465 kg and the average female elephant weighs 3221 kg. Use these facts to find the mass of 4 male elephants and 7 female elephants. ________

❷ What is:

a one third of half an hour? ________

b two thirds of half an hour? ________

❸ For this solid, calculate the number of corners plus the number of faces minus the number of edges. ________

❹ I have 8 boxes. Each box has 4 or 5 books in it. There were 35 books altogether.

How many boxes had 4 books? ________

❺ I bought at least one of each of these items. The cost was $3.85. How many apples did I buy? ________

❻ Use the jump strategy to find 856 + 425.

856 ————————————→

❼ 567 + 286 − 186 + 297 ________

Challenge

Write questions that are equal to:

a 748 + 268 **b** 274 + 377 **c** 2978 + 5382

= ________ = ________ = ________
= ________ = ________ = ________
= ________ = ________ = ________
= ________ = ________ = ________
= ________ = ________ = ________

To round off to the nearest 5 cents, give the closest answer that ends in 5 or 0.

a Is $37.47 closer to $37.45 or $37.50? ________

Round each of these to the nearest 5 cents.

b $43.88 ________ **c** $29.99 ________ **d** $84.63 ________

e $117.12 ________ **f** $265.14 ________ **g** $630.97 ________

h $365.28 ________ **i** $289.09 ________ **j** $836.34 ________

4:1 ☐ out of 22

1. 8×2 ____
2. 8×4 ____
3. $32 \div 8$ ____
4. $16 \div 2$ ____
5. $\begin{array}{r} 2564 \\ +\ 5463 \\ \hline \end{array}$
6. Take 4 from 800. ____
7. Multiply 5 by 6. ____
8. $0{\cdot}5 \times 100$ ____
9. Double 423. ____
10. $\begin{array}{r} 6208 \\ \times\ \ \ 3 \\ \hline \end{array}$
11. Write all the factors of 15. ____
12. The first 10 multiples of 6 are: ____
13. **a** 4 squared ____ **b** 8 squared ____
14. These 21 toys are equally shared between 7 children. One share = ____

15. **a** $3 \times$ ____ $= 27$ **b** $6 \times$ ____ $= 42$
16. 4 baskets with 20 eggs each. ____ eggs
17. How many days in 5 weeks? ____
18. Haley cut 15 cm from a 1 m ruler. How much of the ruler remained? ____
19. Is a population of 2 706 000 closer to 2 000 000 or 3 000 000? ____
20. Complete the labels for the shaded section. ____ tenths or 0· ____

21. Write fifty-one hundredths as a decimal. ____
22. How many thousandths in 0·364? ____

4:2 ☐ out of 20

1. 5 squared. ____
2. $6 \times 8 - 46$ ____
3. $48 \div 8 + 3$ ____
4. $21 \div 7 \times 9$ ____
5. $\begin{array}{r} 8354 \\ -\ 2746 \\ \hline \end{array}$
6. Years in 4 decades. ____
7. Months in 6 years. ____
8. Minutes in 4 hours. ____
9. Years in 3 centuries. ____
10. $\begin{array}{r} 7463 \\ \times\ \ \ 8 \\ \hline \end{array}$
11. 36 cards shared between 4 people. One share = ____
12. **a** $6 \times$ ____ $= 42$ **b** $49 \div 7 =$ ____
13. How many 50c apples can be bought for $3.70? ____
14. I poured 375 mL out of a full 3 L container. How much was left in the container? ____
15. 18 pairs of shoes are in a shop window. How many shoes are there? ____
16. Each hat has 4 corks attached.
    a How many corks are on 6 hats? ____
    b How many hats could be made with 32 corks? ____

17. How many minutes in 8 hours? ____
18. How many are left over if 22 toys are shared by:
    a 3 girls? ____ **b** 4 girls? ____
19. Write 3 out of 10 as a:
    a decimal ____ **b** fraction $\frac{\square}{\square}$
20. Circle the numbers that are *not* multiples of 12. 3 24 4 36 6

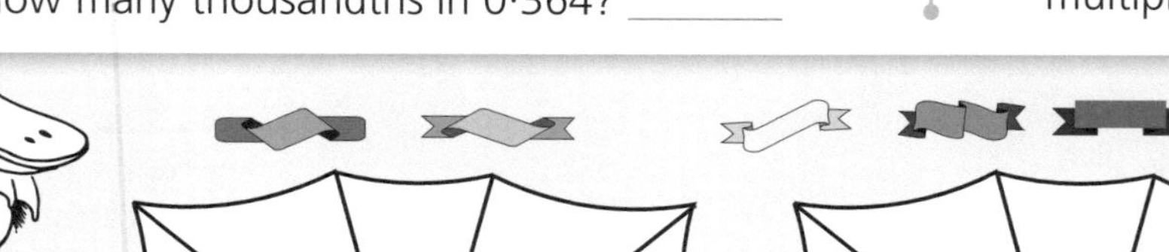

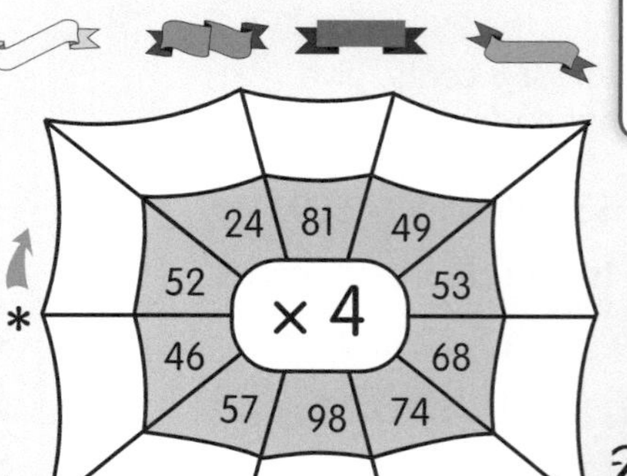

© PEARSON AUSTRALIA 2024 • *AUSTRALIAN SIGNPOST MATHS NSW 6 MENTALS* • ISBN 978 0 6557 0913 8

4:3 out of 13

1. $8\overline{)872}$
2. $3\overline{)813}$
3. $4\overline{)724}$
4. Scott was 44 when Felicity was 7. How old will Scott be when Felicity is 36? ______
5. Write all the factors of 24. ______
6. The first 10 multiples of 8 are:

______

7. **a** 3 squared ______ **b** 9 squared ______
8. I shared 36 bananas in bags of 6. How many bags of 6 bananas do I have? ______

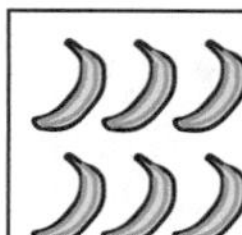

9. What is the smallest even number that is a multiple of 9? ______
10. **a** 8 × ____ = 56 **b** 49 ÷ 7 = ____
11. **a** Two emus were 1·75 m and 1·89 m tall. What was the difference between their heights? ______

b The emus had a mass of 42·89 kg and 53·92 kg. What was their total mass? ______

12. How many different straight lines of 3 circles can be found on this picture? ______

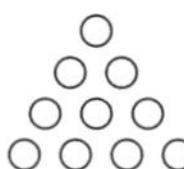

13. Two darts are thrown into this dartboard. Which totals (below 16) are impossible to obtain?

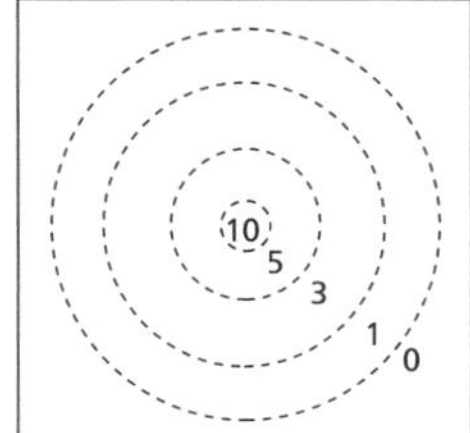

______

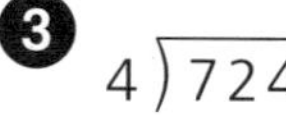

4:4 Extension out of 7

1. After opening a book, the sum of the two page numbers I could see was 145. What were the page numbers? ______
2. Halve the number that is 53 bigger than 177. ______
3. In one week, Chloe watched 14 h 30 min of TV. Jenna watched 10 h 45 min. How much did they watch altogether? ______

4. 12 boxes of pens held either 5 or 6 pens. There was a total of 64 pens. How many boxes held 6 pens? ______
5. Four of these cockatoos have an average mass of 536 g. The other four have an average mass of 723 g. What is their total mass? ______

6. **a** What is the sum of the first four square numbers? ______

   b What is the product of the first three square numbers? ______
7. A book has 194 pages. How many times was the digit 8 used in numbering its pages? ______

Challenge

Write questions that are equal to:

a 894 − 283 **b** 674 − 276 **c** 7685 − 4526

a	b	c
= ______	= ______	= ______
= ______	= ______	= ______
= ______	= ______	= ______
= ______	= ______	= ______
= ______	= ______	= ______

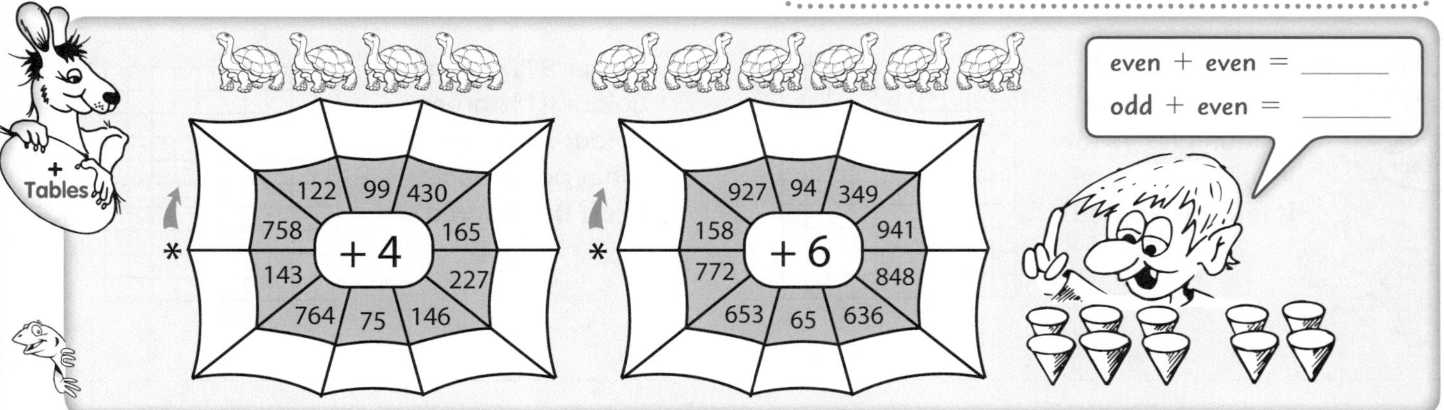

© PEARSON AUSTRALIA 2024

5:1 ☐ out of 21

1. 3 × 7 ______
2. 3 × $4 ______
3. 24 ÷ 8 ______
4. 50 ÷ 10 ______
5. $\begin{array}{r} 2967 \\ -\ 1974 \\ \hline \end{array}$
6. 2 squared. ______
7. 24 divided by 6. ______
8. Multiply 7 by 5. ______
9. 0·7 × 100 ______
10. $\begin{array}{r} 2648 \\ \times\ \ \ 3 \\ \hline \end{array}$
11. Write all the factors of 12. ______
12. How many groups of 4 in 12 apples? ______
13. Equal numbers of birds are put in four cages. If there are 24 birds, how many are in each cage? ______

14. **a** 5 × ____ = 60 **b** 32 ÷ 8 = ____
15. Write in ascending order.

    37 631 713 33 761 301 31 763 116

    ______

16. Name the solid for each net below.

a

b

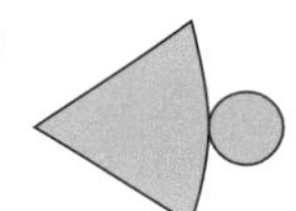

______ ______

17. Thomas constructed 4 triangular prisms. Each had 5 faces. How many faces altogether? ______
18. The numeral for 10^2? ______
19. Count on from 76 to find 85 − 76. ______
20. What is 0·98 as a percentage? ______
21. $(7 \times 10^3) + (2 \times 10^2) + (7 \times 10^1) + 7$ ______

5:2 ☐ out of 18

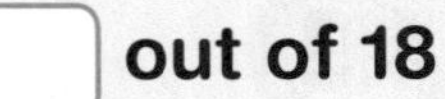

1. 6 × 9 ______
2. $\frac{4}{6} - \frac{1}{3}$ ______
3. $40 ÷ 8 ______
4. 36 ÷ 4 ______
5. $\begin{array}{r} 3967 \\ +\ 4786 \\ \hline \end{array}$
6. 5 squared. ______
7. Multiply 9 by 5. ______
8. Divide $36 by 4. ______
9. 0·9 × 1000 ______
10. $\begin{array}{r} 2945 \\ \times\ \ \ 6 \\ \hline \end{array}$
11. The first 10 multiples of 7 are:

    ______.

12. 

    For these trees, how many groups of:

    a 6 trees? ______ groups ______ left

    b 5 trees? ______ groups ______ left

13. **a** 9 × ____ = 63 **b** 81 ÷ 9 = ______
14. **a** How many vertices has a cube? ______

    b How many faces has a cube? ______

15. Round off each number to the nearest hundred, then use these to estimate:

    a 873 − 204 ______ **b** 1907 − 743 ______

16. A man's step is 60 cm long.

    How far does he walk in 7 steps? ______

17. Count on from 157 to find 165 − 157. ______
18. Draw lines to join equivalent numbers.

0·61	80%
0·49	61%
0·80	25%
0·10	49%
0·25	10%

a Colour 34% red.
Colour 27% blue.
Colour 19% yellow.
What percentage is left uncoloured?

______

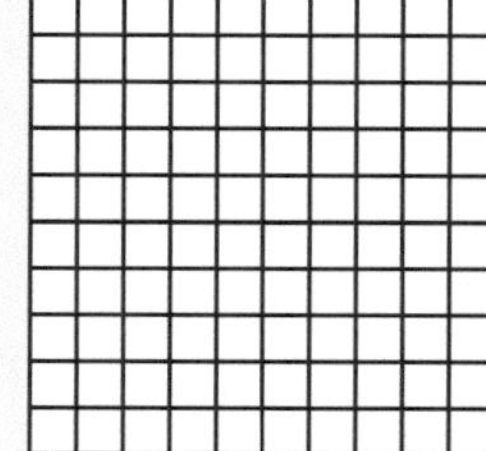

b Colour 9% orange.
Colour 41% green.
Colour 38% purple.
What percentage is left uncoloured?

______

© PEARSON AUSTRALIA 2024 • *AUSTRALIAN SIGNPOST MATHS NSW 6 MENTALS* • ISBN 978 0 6557 0913 8

5:3 □ out of 15

1. 5)720
2. 3)927
3. 7)719

4.
```
  7465
+ 1598
```

5.
```
  4657
×    7
```

6. 27 exercise books shared between 5 students.

   Books each = ______

   Remainder = ______

7. Write all the factors of 36.

   ____

8. **a** 6 × ____ = 42 **b** 49 ÷ 7 = ____

9. Which of 1, 15, 23, 49, 60 are:

   a multiples of 5? ________

   b square numbers? ________

10. If one cake will serve 7 people, how many are needed to serve 100? ______

11. Carlos has a part-time job. He is paid $148 per week. From this amount $16 is deducted as tax. How much does he receive for 3 weeks work? ______

12. Elizabeth has 526 stamps. Max has 8 times as many.

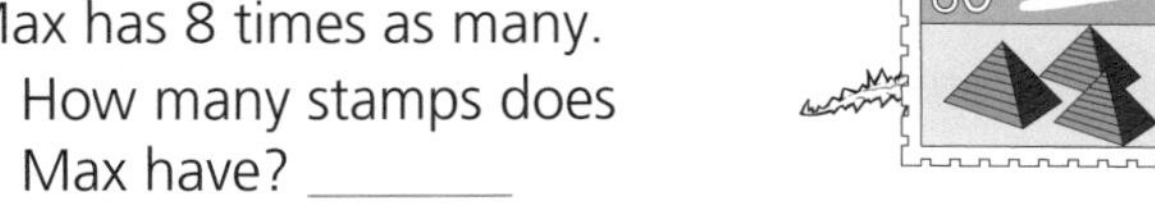

   a How many stamps does Max have? ______

   b How many do they have altogether? ______

13. Write a number sentence for 114 more than a certain number gives 539.

    ____

14. What percentage of a metre is 1cm? ______

15. How many axes of symmetry has a:

    a kite? ______ **b** rhombus? ______

5:4 □ out of 9 **Extension**

1. What is the smallest square number that is also a multiple of 8? ______

2. Which is larger, $2^2 + 3^2 + 4^2$ or $1^2 + 5^2$? ______

3. A corner has been cut off this block.

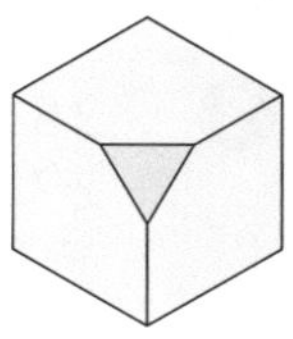

   a How many faces would the block have if each of the corners were cut off? ______

   b How many edges would it have? ______

4. □ ÷ 2 = 55, □ = ____

5. The shaded part has a value of 30. What is the value of the whole? ______

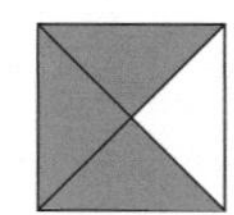

6. If 4 small squares make a quado and 2 quados make an octo, could 68 small squares make:

   a 7 quados and 5 octos? ______

   b 4 quados and 7 octos? ______

7. I am paid between $12 to $14 an hour. Which could be my pay for 6 hours of work: $70.50, $71.80, $83.10 or $84.10? ______

8. How many days in 42 weeks? ______

9. (5 × 37) + (5 × 37) ______

Challenge

List as many square numbers as you can using number sentences, e.g. 2 × 2 = 4, 2 squared = 4 or $2^2 = 4$.

____

____

____

____

Complete this table for the shaded part.

	‾/10	‾/100	0·__	__%
	‾/10	‾/100	0·__	__%

© PEARSON AUSTRALIA 2024 • *AUSTRALIAN SIGNPOST MATHS NSW 6 MENTALS* • ISBN 978 0 6557 0913 8

6:1 out of 19

1. $5 \times 7 + 12$ ____
2. $6 \times 2 - 8$ ____
3. $20 \div 4 + 1$ ____
4. $36 \div (6 + 3)$ ____
5. $\begin{array}{r} 3574 \\ +\ 2768 \\ \hline \end{array}$
6. $36 - (6 \times 4)$ ____
7. $41 - 16 + 8$ ____
8. $46 +$ ____ $= 100$
9. $35 +$ ____ $= 82$
10. $\begin{array}{r} 1423 \\ \times \quad 3 \\ \hline \end{array}$

11. Complete the labels for the shaded part.

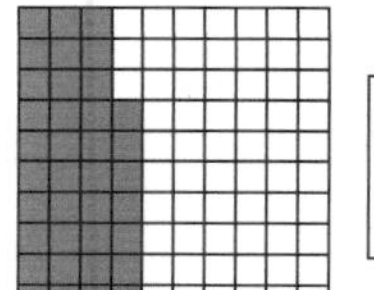

·	$\overline{100}$	%

12. Arrange in descending order:
67 541 234 67 647 324 67 747 324

____

13. Use numerals to write ninety-five million seven hundred and forty-seven thousand and thirteen. ____
14. Is 35 465 798 closer to 35 000 000 or 36 000 000? ____
15. **a** $3 \times 4 \times 2$ ____ **b** $60 - 40 + 23$ ____
16. What 2D shape has 4 right angles and has its opposite sides equal? ____
17. An angle of size 120° is an ____ angle.

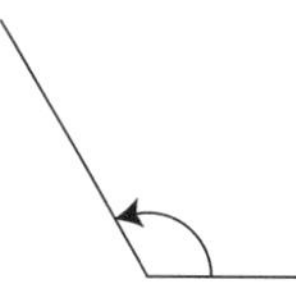

18. How many faces on three cubes? ____
19. Order 4·5, 4·25, 4·8 from largest to smallest.

____

6:2 out of 19

1. $9 \times 8 - 35$ ____
2. 6 squared. ____
3. $7 \times$ ____ $= 56$
4. $4 \times$ ____ $= 24$
5. $\begin{array}{r} 4675 \\ -\ 2798 \\ \hline \end{array}$
6. $\frac{9}{12} - \frac{2}{6}$ ____
7. Increase 465 by 67. ____
8. $167 + 45 =$ ____ $+ 50$
9. $534 +$ ____ $= 536 + 160$
10. $\begin{array}{r} 3647 \\ \times \quad 4 \\ \hline \end{array}$
11. Write the value of the 6 in 35 674 725.

____

12. 76 out of 100 $= \frac{76}{100} =$ ____·____
$=$ ____ %
13. $(5 \times 10^4) + (3 \times 10^3) + (8 \times 10^2) + 3$ ____
14. Is this a reflection, translation or rotation? ____

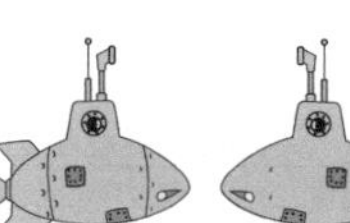

15. Write all the factors of 42.

____

16. Is 72 576 098 closer to 72 000 000 or 73 000 000? ____
17. **a** $8 + (4 \times 3) - 8$ ____ **b** $5 \times 4 + 9$ ____
18. Which of these nets could not fold to make a solid shape like this?

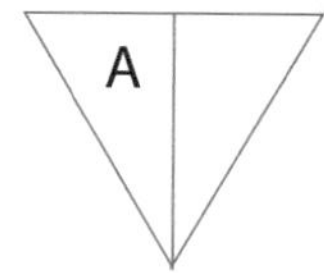

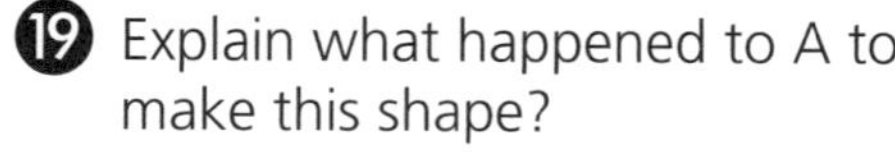

____

19. Explain what happened to A to make this shape?

____

Order of operations

❶ ( ) ❷ × and ÷ ❸ + and −

Example

$4 \times (11 - 9) + 20 \div 2$
Remove the ( ).
$= 4 \times 2 + 20 \div 2$
Do × and ÷, (left to right).
$= 8 + 10$
$= 18$

a $11 - (8 - 3)$ ____ **b** $14 - (20 - 10)$ ____
c $8 + 2 \times 4$ ____ **d** $16 - 2 \times 6$ ____
e $20 - 12 \div 4$ ____ **f** $15 + 6 \div 3$ ____
g $6 \div 3 \times 2$ ____ **h** $20 \div 5 \times 4$ ____
i $11 - 4 + 5$ ____ **j** $21 - 11 + 6$ ____
k $63 + 12 \div 6 - (8 + 12) \div (9 - 4 + 5)$ ____

© PEARSON AUSTRALIA 2024 • *AUSTRALIAN SIGNPOST MATHS NSW 6 MENTALS* • ISBN 978 0 6557 0913 8

6:3 ☐ out of 14

1. $8\overline{)368}$
2. $6\overline{)936}$
3. $4\overline{)275}$

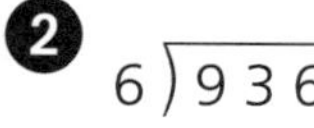

4.
```
  6846
- 4709
```
5.
```
  3809
×    5
```

6. If one pizza is needed to serve 3 people, how many pizzas are needed to serve 23 people? ______

7. Draw lines to connect equal numbers.

0·6	$\frac{1}{2}$	0·06	$\frac{5}{100}$

50%	6%	60%	5%

8. Which of these angles is:
   a acute? ______
   b obtuse? ______

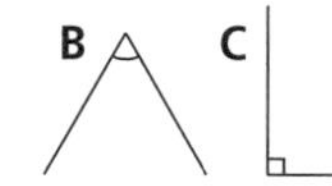

9. $(5 \times 10^4) + (6 \times 10^3) + (4 \times 10^2) + (9 \times 10^1) + 9$
   = ______

10. Is 89 465 736 closer to 89 000 000 or 90 000 000? ______

11. a $24 \div 6 \times 5 \div 4$ ______ b $6 \times 5 - 17$ ______

12. 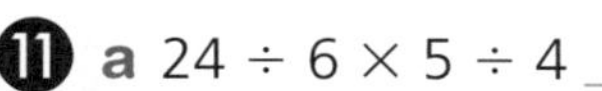

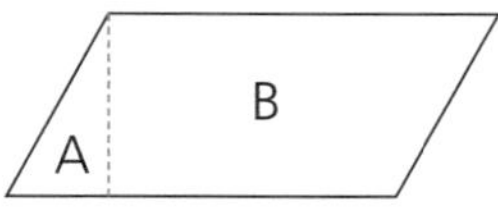

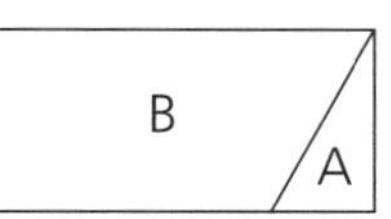

The left shape above is changed to make the right shape. What happened to A to change the shape?

______

13. The value of 4 in 35·46 is ______.

14. What is 2 more than 54·35? ______

6:4 Extension ☐ out of 5

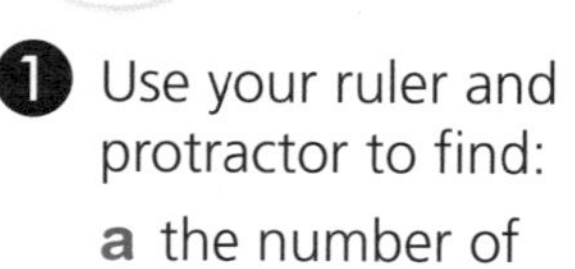

1. Use your ruler and protractor to find:
   a the number of equal sides ______
   b the number of equal angles ______

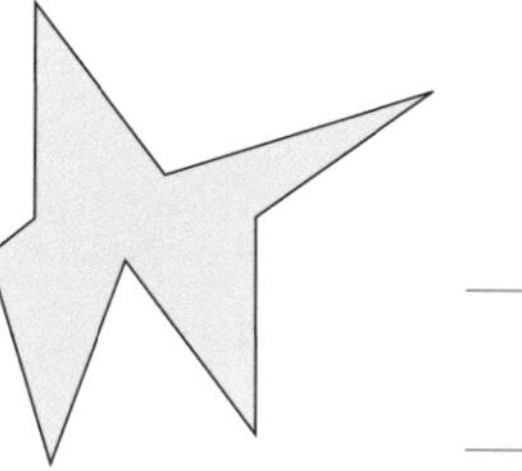

2. If 3 small squares make a *trio* and 3 *trios* make a *nino*, could 57 small squares make:

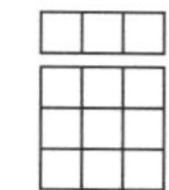

   a one *trio* and 6 *ninos*? ______
   b 7 *trios* and 4 *ninos*? ______

3. Which number below is a multiple of 5, 6 and 7?
   1764 1470 1120 1560 ______

4. $756 + 546 + 293 - 93$ ______

5. 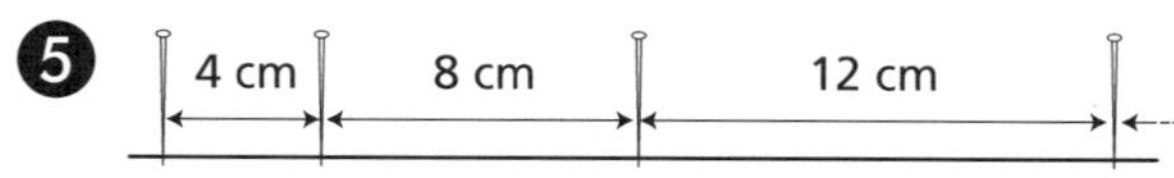

Pins were stuck onto a board using the pattern shown above.
What was the distance between:
   a the 5th and 6th pins? ______
   b the 1st and 6th pins? ______

Challenge

Write number sentences that are equal to 14, using 2 or more operations (+, −, × and ÷) and brackets, e.g. $4 + 5 \times 2 - (4 \times 0) = 14$.

______

______

______

______

Concept

4, 45, 16, 21, 23, 100, 35, 36, 81, 49, 14

1 Which of the numbers above are square numbers? ______

2 Which are multiples of:
   a 2? ______
   b 5? ______
   c 7? ______

© PEARSON AUSTRALIA 2024 • • ISBN 978 0 6557 0913 8

7:1 ☐ out of 17

1. $3 \times 6 + 9$ ____
2. $4 \times 3 + 16$ ____
3. $5 + 2 \times 10$ ____
4. $2 \times 4 + 34$ ____
5. $\begin{array}{r} 7463 \\ +\ 2589 \\ \hline \end{array}$
6. $24 \div 3 + 20$ ____
7. $15 \div (20 - 15)$ ____
8. $60 \div 6 \times 5$ ____
9. $80 \div 10 - 7$ ____
10. $\begin{array}{r} 5163 \\ \times \quad 4 \\ \hline \end{array}$
11. Write the decimal for:
    a 59 hundredths ____
    b 857 thousandths ____
12. a 4 squared = ____ b 3^2 = ____
13. Write $1\frac{1}{2}$ as an improper fraction. $\frac{\square}{\square}$
14. Write as a percentage:
    a 0·72 ____ b 0·09 ____
15. Complete this picture so that it is symmetrical about the dotted line.

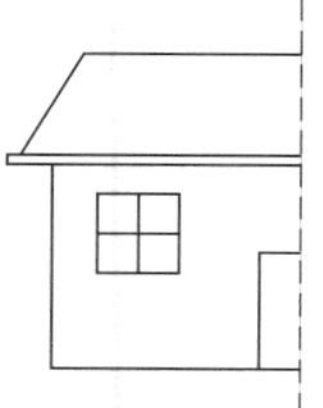

16.

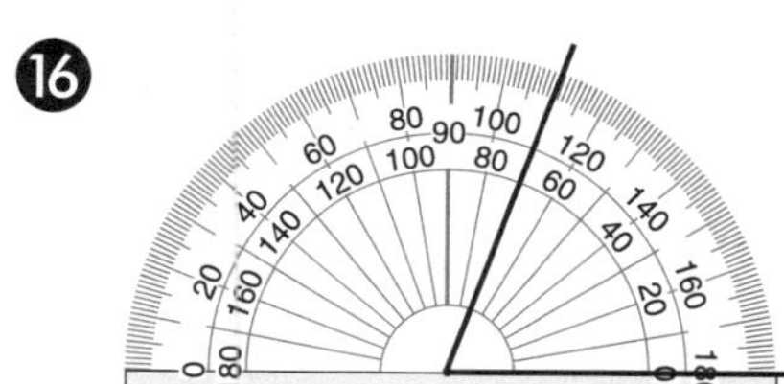

a The size of the angle shown? ____
b Is this angle acute or obtuse? ____

17. Write 4:53 am using 24-hour time. ____

7:2 ☐ out of 19

1. $9 \times 8 - 65$ ____
2. $57 + 6 \times 7$ ____
3. $45 \div (18 - 9)$ ____
4. $0{\cdot}4 \times 100$ ____
5. $\begin{array}{r} 9054 \\ -\ 3646 \\ \hline \end{array}$
6. $4 \times 7 + 134$ ____
7. $100 \div 10 + 465$ ____
8. $\$37 + 6 \times \$7$ ____
9. $6 \times 4 + (35 \div 7)$ ____
10. $\begin{array}{r} 2074 \\ \times \quad 4 \\ \hline \end{array}$
11. Write the percentage equivalent for:
    a $\frac{60}{100}$ ____ b 0·3 ____
12. $(9 \times 10^4) + (6 \times 10^3) + (4 \times 10^2) + 8$ ____
13. For a sphere, how many:
    a surfaces? ____ b edges? ____
14. Order from smallest to largest.
    4·4142 4·142 4·11 4·444
    ____
15. a Write 892 thousandths as a decimal. ____
    b Write 46 hundredths as a decimal. ____
16. a 8 squared = ____ b 6^2 = ____
17. Write an improper fraction and mixed number for the shaded part. $\frac{\square}{\square}$ $\square\frac{\square}{\square}$

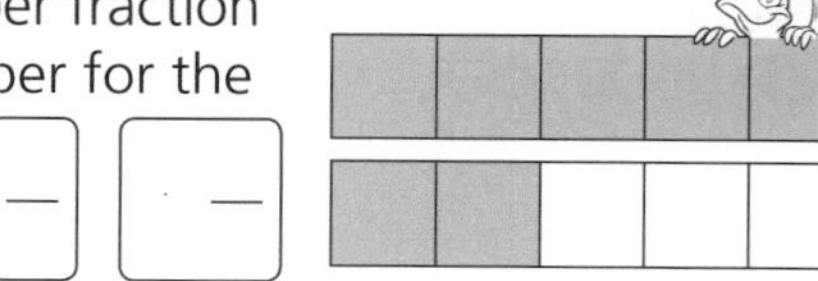

18. What shape can be made from this net?

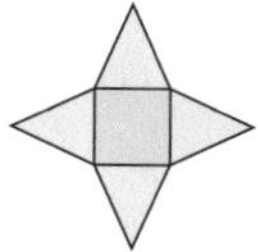

____

19. Write as a percentage:
    a 0·35 ____ b $\frac{1}{4}$ ____

a How many stakes are needed for a fence 30 m long if the stakes are 5 m apart? ____
b The sum of two numbers is 11 and their product is 24. What are the numbers? ____
c The average of two numbers is 9. If one number is 4, what is the other? ____

© PEARSON AUSTRALIA 2024 • *AUSTRALIAN SIGNPOST MATHS NSW 6 MENTALS* • ISBN 978 0 6557 0913 8

7:3 out of 11

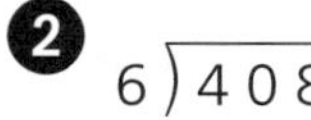

1. $3\overline{)936}$
2. $6\overline{)408}$
3. $9\overline{)585}$
4. True or false?
   $0{\cdot}25 = 25\% = \frac{1}{4}$ ______
5. $(9 \times 10^4) + (2 \times 10^3) + (4 \times 10^2) + (8 \times 10^1) + 5$
   = ______
6. a $9^2 =$ ______ b 7 squared = ______
7. Circle the car that is correctly parked.

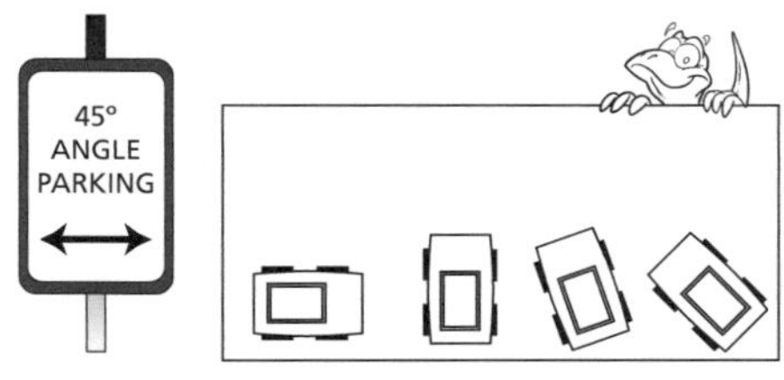

8. Complete:

Number of years	1	2	3	4	5
Number of months	12				

   a Write a rule to describe the pattern.
   ______
   b How many months in 30 years? ______
9. a Colour $1\frac{4}{10}$.

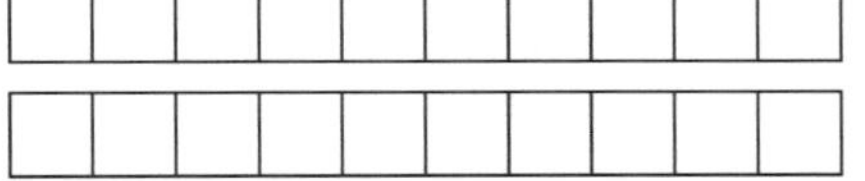

   b Write this as an improper fraction. $\frac{\square}{\square}$
10. The improper fraction modelled here.  $\frac{\square}{\square}$
11. Write 0·56 as a:
   a percentage ______ b fraction $\frac{\square}{\square}$

7:4 out of 5

Extension

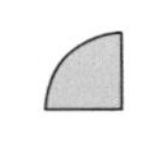

1. Circle the options that are equal to square numbers.
   49, $2^2 + 3^2$, 16, 9 + 13, 49 − 13
2. a Fraction shaded ______
   b Decimal shaded ______
   c Percentage shaded ______
   d Percentage not shaded ______
3. Which of the shapes below can be joined to shape **S** to make a square? ______

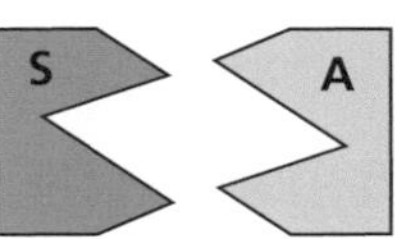

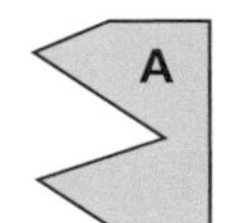

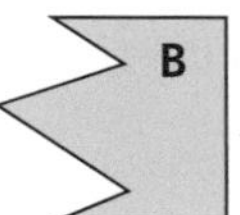

4. Which angle is:
   a obtuse? ______
   b acute? ______
   c straight? ______
   d reflex? ______

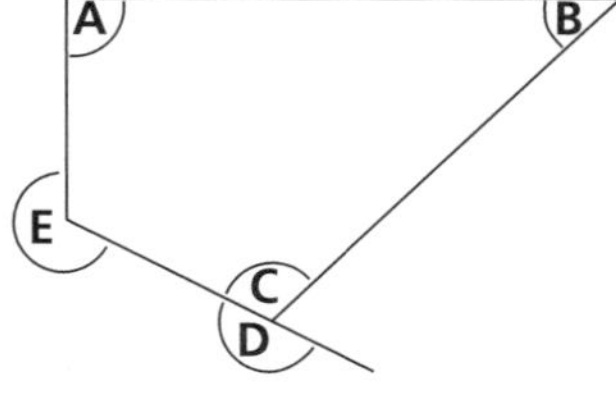

5. If this net is folded to make a cube, which side would be opposite **A**? ______

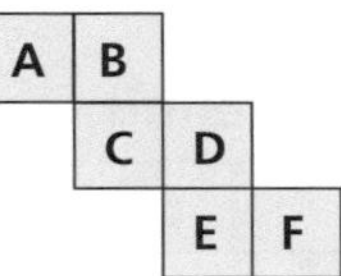

Challenge

Write numerals then record them as powers of ten, e.g.
$8724 = (8 \times 10^3) + (7 \times 10^2) + (2 \times 10^1) + 4$

______
______
______
______

Reflections

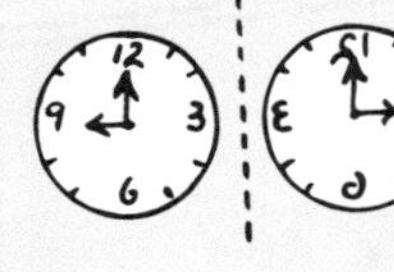

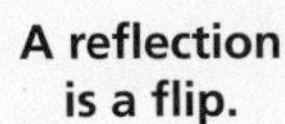

A reflection is a flip.

a I saw the clock in the mirror. It looked like 2 o'clock but it was really ______.

Refer to the flip on the left.

b Do the lengths of the arms change? ______
c Does the angle between arms change? ______
d Does the size of the clock change? ______

8:1

out of 17

1. $4 \times 2 + 14$ ______
2. $7 \times 2 + 34$ ______
3. $9 + 6 \times 5$ ______
4. $67 - 5 + 9$ ______
5. $\begin{array}{r} 8603 \\ -\ 2649 \\ \hline \end{array}$
6. $80 \div (45 - 35)$ ______
7. $100 - 9 \times 7$ ______
8. $\$56 + 8 \times \$4$ ______
9. $90 \div (67 - 57)$ ______
10. $\begin{array}{r} 1856 \\ \times \quad 5 \\ \hline \end{array}$
11. Write 0·45 as a percentage. ______
12. **a** $5^2 =$ ______ **b** 6 squared = ______
13. Name this 3D solid. ______

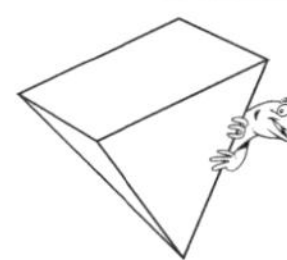

14. Write 78% as a decimal. ______
15. Write $\frac{19}{3}$ as a mixed numeral. $\square\,\frac{\square}{\square}$
16. Which is lower, −5°C or −17°C? ______
17. **Tennis matches won**

Name	
Naomi	● ● ● ● ●
Alana	● ● ◖
Luke	● ● ● ● ●
Rachel	● ● ● ◖
Heather	● ● ● ● ● ●

● = 4 matches

a How many matches were won by Alana? ______

b Which player won 14 matches? ______

c Which player won more than 20 matches? ______

8:2

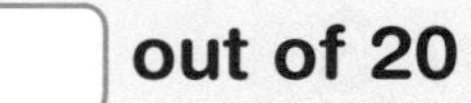

out of 20

1. $0{\cdot}8 \times 100$ ______
2. $9 \times (10 - 7)$ ______
3. $20 + 56 \div 8$ ______
4. $\frac{9}{10} + \frac{4}{5}$ ______
5. $\begin{array}{r} 3647 \\ +\ 6809 \\ \hline \end{array}$
6. −10, −9, −8, ______, ______
7. Increase 45 by 89. ______
8. 78 − ______ = 34
9. \$45 + ______ = \$135
10. $\begin{array}{r} 2704 \\ \times \quad 8 \\ \hline \end{array}$
11. $(7 \times 10^4) + (8 \times 10^3) + (3 \times 10^2) + (1 \times 10^1) + 8$ = ______
12. List all the square numbers up to 100. ______
13. Write $\frac{83}{100}$ as:
    a a percentage ______ **b** a decimal ______
14. How many edges are on a cube? ______
15. Write $1\frac{3}{4}$ as an improper fraction. $\frac{\square}{\square}$
16. What is 5°C lower than −14 degrees Celsius? ______
17. Write the factors of 56? ______
18. How many dots would be in the 6th row? ______

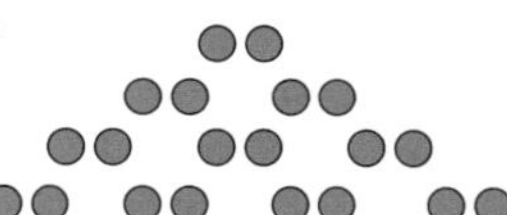

19. Complete this pattern:

Squares	1	2	3	4	5
Sides	4	8			

20. Complete the missing numbers.

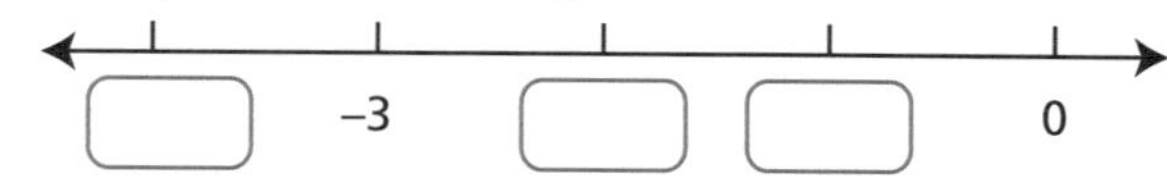

The Square of a number

To square a number multiply it by itself.

6 × 6 = 6 squared

$6 \times 6 = 6^2$

Find the value of:

a 5 squared ______ **b** 3 squared ______ **c** 10^2 ______

d 4 squared ______ **e** 8^2 ______ **f** 1^2 ______

g 9 squared ______ **h** 2 squared ______ **i** 6^2 ______

© PEARSON AUSTRALIA 2024 • *AUSTRALIAN SIGNPOST MATHS NSW 6 MENTALS* • ISBN 978 0 6557 0913 8

8:3

 out of 16

❶ $4\overline{)596}$ ❷ $3\overline{)527}$ ❸ $8\overline{)944}$

❹ Write $\frac{19}{5}$ as a mixed numeral. $\square\frac{\square}{\square}$

❺ $(2 \times 10^4) + (7 \times 10^3) + (6 \times 10^2) + (7 \times 10^1) + 1$

= ____________

❻ Complete this pattern.

1st number	50	51	52	53
2nd number	65	66	67	

Write a rule for the pattern above. ____________

❼ Order from smallest to largest:
2, −2, −8, 4, 0 ____________

❽ 1, 4, 9, 16, ______, ______, ______, ______

❾ **a** 0·7 = ______ % **b** 0·1 = ______ %
c 0·07 = ______ % **d** 0·01 = ______ %

❿ 807, ______, 819, 825, ______, 837

⓫ Which of the numbers 9, 14 and 17 have exactly 2 factors?
This is called a 'prime number'. ____________

⓬ Complete the number line.

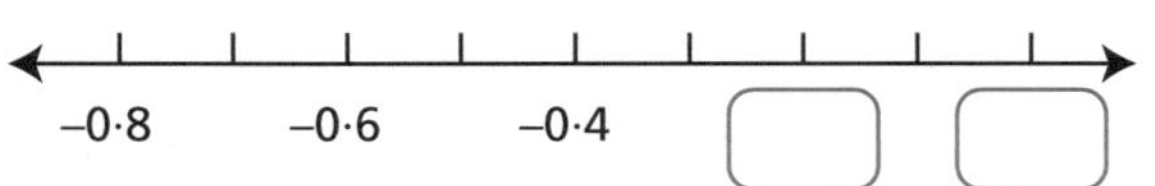

⓭ Which is lower, −23°C or −7°C? ____________

⓮ Write the factors of 81. ____________

⓯ Write 38 hundredths as:
a a decimal ____________ **b** percentage ____________

⓰ 56 ÷ 7 + (287 − 53) ____________

8:4

Extension

out of 5

❶ What is the smallest two-digit square number that is also odd? ____________

❷ Common means 'belongs to all'.
What is the lowest common multiple of:
a 4 and 6? ______ **b** 3 and 5? ______

❸ 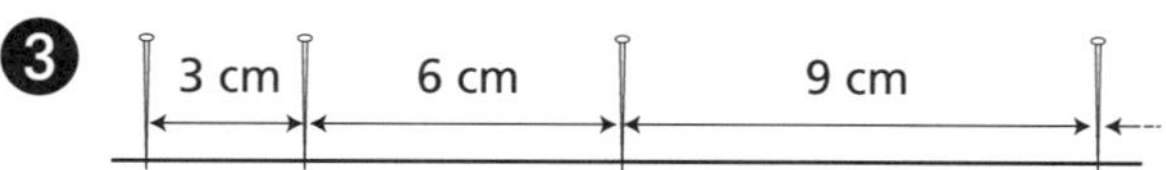

Pins were stuck onto a board using the pattern shown above. What was the distance between:
a the 7th and 8th pins? ____________
b the 1st and 8th pins? ____________

❹ Complete this table if △ = □ + 39.

□	15	25	35	44	54
△					

❺ **a** What two numbers have a difference of 3 and a product of 208? ____________
b 5 squared plus 8 squared. ____________

Challenge

Draw and label 3D objects, showing their features.

Order of operations
Example
28 − (7 − 3) ÷ 2
Remove the ( ).
= 28 − 4 ÷ 2
Do × and ÷.
= 28 − 2
= 26

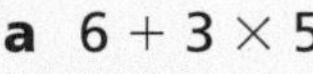

a 6 + 3 × 5 ______ **b** 10 − 2 × 4 ______
c 7 − (10 − 3) ______ **d** 28 − (20 − 10) ______
e 10 − 3 + 4 ______ **f** 10 − (3 + 4) ______
g 20 − 4 + 9 ______ **h** 25 − 19 + 1 ______
i 20 ÷ 5 × 12 ______ **j** 20 ÷ (5 × 2) ______
k 10 + (6 ÷ 2) × 3 + 15 ÷ 3 ______

© PEARSON AUSTRALIA 2024

9:1 ☐ out of 16

1. $3 \times 8 + 53$ ______
2. Halve 264. ______
3. $100 - 4 \times 10$ ______
4. $15 +$ ______ $= 58$
5. $\begin{array}{r} 5473 \\ -\ 2547 \\ \hline \end{array}$
6. $100 \div (2 \times 5)$ ______
7. $89 - 5 \times 4$ ______
8. $\$72 \div 8$ ______
9. $9 \times$ ______ $= 45$
10. $\begin{array}{r} \$5368 \\ \times\quad 5 \\ \hline \end{array}$
11. Complete the number line.

    ☐ ☐ −10% −5% 0

12. Which is lower, −2°C or −12°C? ______
13. 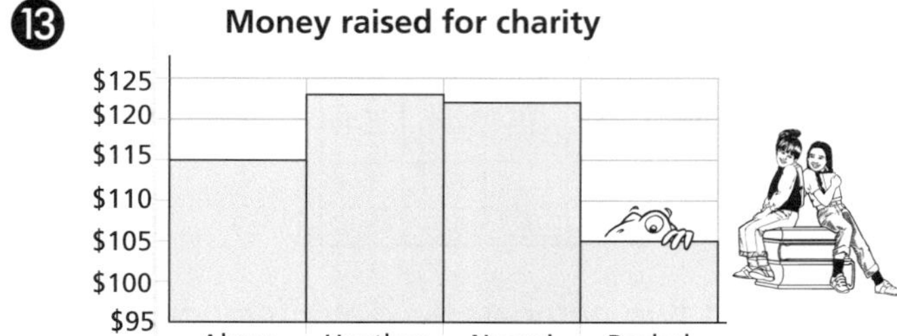

    a How much did Rachel raise? ______

    b How much did these girls raise together? ______

14. In this design, trace over two perpendicular lines using red. Trace over 2 parallel lines using blue.

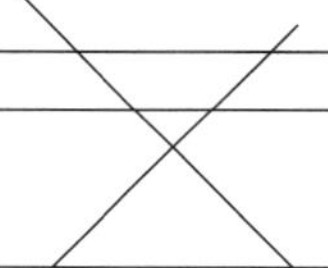

15. Which is lower, −7 or −2? ______
16. C −9 −8 A −6 −5 B −3

    What number would be at:

    a A? ______ b B? ______ c C? ______

9:2 ☐ out of 18

1. $54 \div 6$ ______
2. $\$90 \div 10$ ______
3. 4×19 ______
4. $9 \times \$27$ ______
5. $\begin{array}{r} \$3576 \\ +\$4797 \\ \hline \end{array}$
6. Increase 76 by 89. ______
7. $56 + 46 =$ ______ $+ 50$
8. $354 - 78 =$ ______ $- 80$
9. 6 less than 4. ______
10. $\begin{array}{r} \$6476 \\ \times\quad 3 \\ \hline \end{array}$
11. $(6 \times 10^4) + (3 \times 10^3) + (9 \times 10^2) + (2 \times 10^1) + 9$ = ______
12. Which is lower, −15°C or −49°C? ______
13. 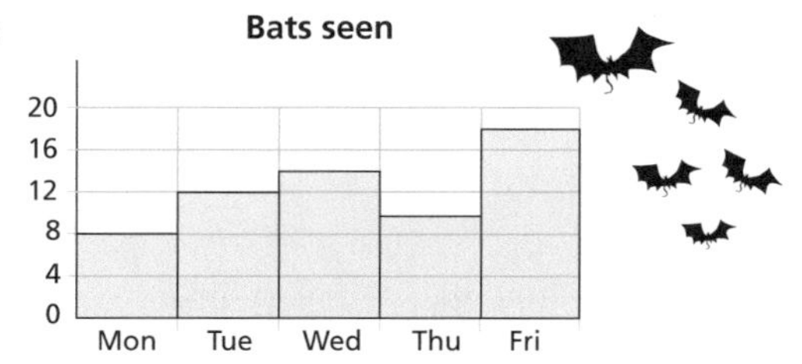

    a How many more bats were seen on Friday than Monday? ______

    b On which two days were the least number of bats seen? ______

14. Write which two angles together make a:

    a right angle? ______

    b straight angle? ______

    B A C E D

15. Arrange in order of size from lowest to highest.

    −7, 8, −2, −9, 4

    ______

16. Write $\frac{24}{5}$ as a mixed number. ☐
17. $0{\cdot}29 =$ ______ $\% = \frac{\square}{\square}$
18. The difference between 87 and 34 is ______.

Turn to ID card B on page 7.

Give the answers for these numbers.

(16)	______ lines	(17)	______ lines
(18)	______	(19)	______ of an angle
(20)	______ angle	(21)	______ angle
(22)	______ angle	(23)	______ angle
(24)	______ angle	(25)	______

© PEARSON AUSTRALIA 2024 • *AUSTRALIAN SIGNPOST MATHS NSW 6 MENTALS* • ISBN 978 0 6557 0913 8

9:3 ☐ out of 9

1 $6\overline{)726}$ 2 $3\overline{)973}$ 3 $10\overline{)460}$

4 How many 30° angles make a right angle? ______

5 Write < (less than) or > (greater than) to make these number sentences true.

a 4 ______ −5 **b** −8 ______ 3

c −3 ______ −21 **d** −7 ______ −1

6 Shade seven tenths and complete the labels.

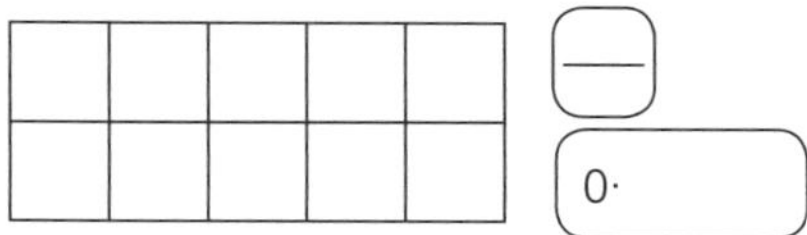

7

	Miss breakfast			Arrive late		
	Primary (%)	High (%)	Total (%)	Primary (%)	High (%)	Total (%)
Always	16	24	20	9	3	6
Often	37	31	34	24	18	21
Occasionally	27	25	26	23	21	22
Rarely	14	2	8	35	39	37
Never	6	18	12	9	19	14

a What fraction of students always miss breakfast? ______

b What percentage said they always or often arrive late? ______

c If 1000 students were surveyed, how many *never* miss breakfast? ______

8 Write fifty-one hundredths:

a as a decimal ______

b as a percentage ______

9 **a** Colour $\frac{1}{4}$ of this shape red.

b Colour $\frac{1}{3}$ of this shape blue.

c Is $\frac{1}{3}$ smaller than $\frac{1}{4}$? ______

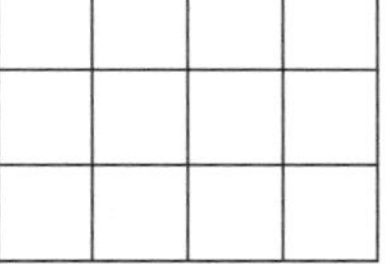

9:4 ☐ out of 9 Extension

1 How many minutes in 2 days and 19 hours? ______

2 How many triangles can be found on this figure? ______

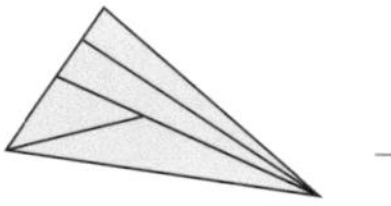

3 Name the angles in this diagram that together make up a:

a right angle ______

b revolution ______

4 $15 \times (87 - 79) - 46 =$ ______

5 What is the smaller angle size between the hands of a clock at 20 past 6? ______

6 How many $1 coins (2·5 cm wide) are needed side by side to make a length of 27 cm? ______

7 How many octagons of any shape are present? ______

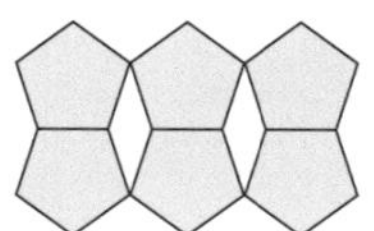

8 Does $2{\cdot}5^2 = 1{\cdot}5^2 + 2^2$? ______

9 I am able to save $9 each week. How many weeks will it take me to save $684? ______

Challenge

Write number sentences that are equal to 56.

______

______

______

______

______

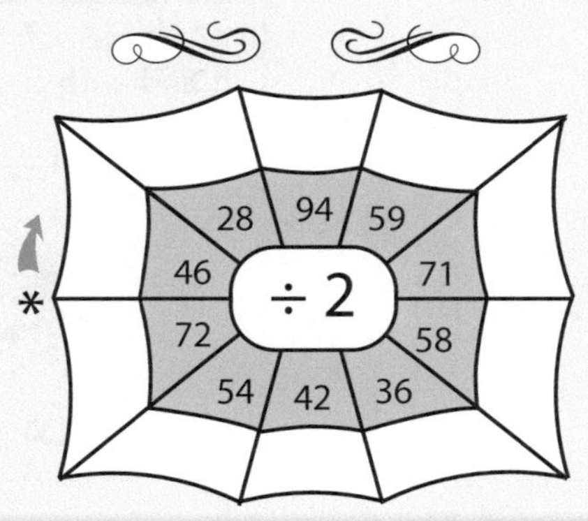

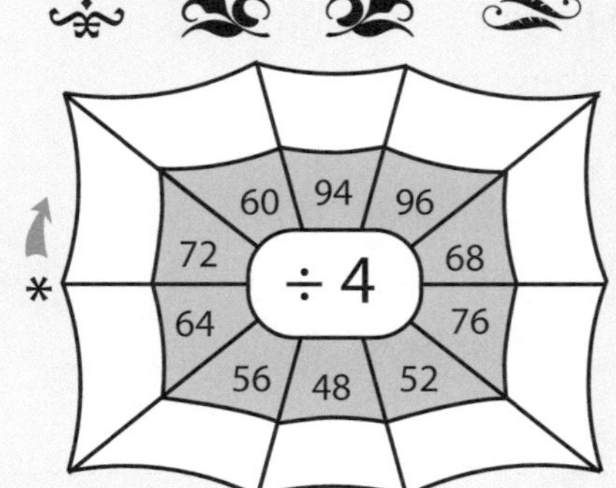

10:1 ☐ out of 17

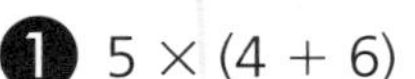

1. $5 \times (4 + 6)$ ____
2. $78 - 67$ ____
3. $14 - 14 \div 2$ ____
4. $37 - 2 \times 6$ ____
5. $\begin{array}{r} 6476 \\ +\ 1463 \\ \hline \end{array}$
6. $0{\cdot}6 \times 1000$ ____
7. $245 - 35 =$ ____ $- 40$
8. $154 + 34 =$ ____ $+ 30$
9. $7 \times$ ____ $= 56$
10. $\begin{array}{r} 6047 \\ \times\ \ \ \ 4 \\ \hline \end{array}$

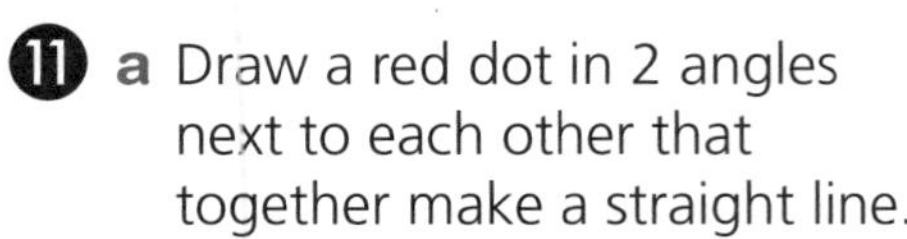

11. **a** Draw a red dot in 2 angles next to each other that together make a straight line.
    b Draw a black dot in 2 angles next to each other that together make a right angle.

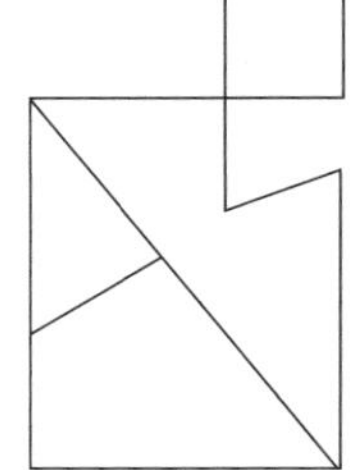

12. Order these numbers from smallest to largest.
    56 798 453   56 480 093   56 350 356
    ____

13. Write $3 \div 5$ as a fraction, then colour 3 fifths of each row. $\frac{\square}{\square}$

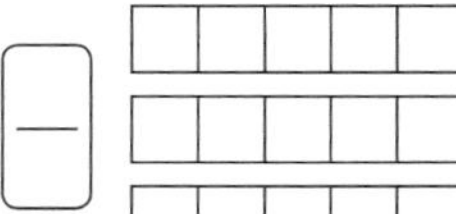

14. **a** $\frac{1}{5}$ of 15 ____
    b $\frac{1}{3}$ of 15 ____

15. 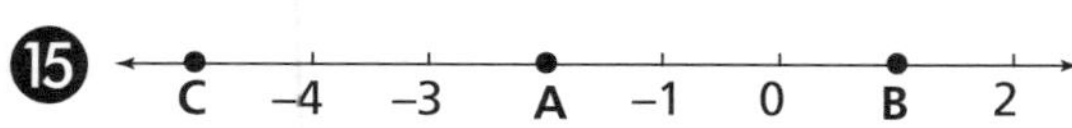

    What number would be at:
    a A? ____ **b** B? ____ **c** C? ____

16. Write the numeral five hundred and three thousand and fifty-four. ____
17. How many tenths in 78·37? ____

10:2 ☐ out of 15

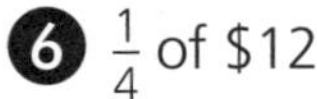

1. $56 + 846$ ____
2. $759 - 79$ ____
3. $2 \times (12 - 6)$ ____
4. $4 \times$ ____ $= 24$
5. $\begin{array}{r} 86757 \\ -\ 36579 \\ \hline \end{array}$
6. $\frac{1}{4}$ of \$12 ____
7. $278 - 57 =$ ____ $- 60$
8. $9 \times (100 - 97)$ ____
9. $64 - 14 - 28$ ____
10. $\begin{array}{r} \$6057 \\ \times\ \ \ \ \ 7 \\ \hline \end{array}$

11. How many degrees are in a straight angle? ____
12. What is the size of the missing angle?
    a 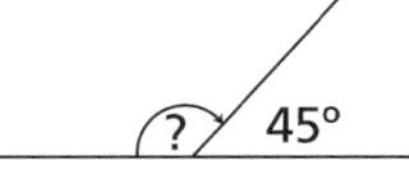

    ____
    b 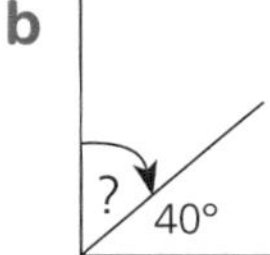

    ____

13. Convert to yen:
    a 25c ____
    b 60c ____

    Convert to cents:
    c 40 yen ____
    d 60 yen ____

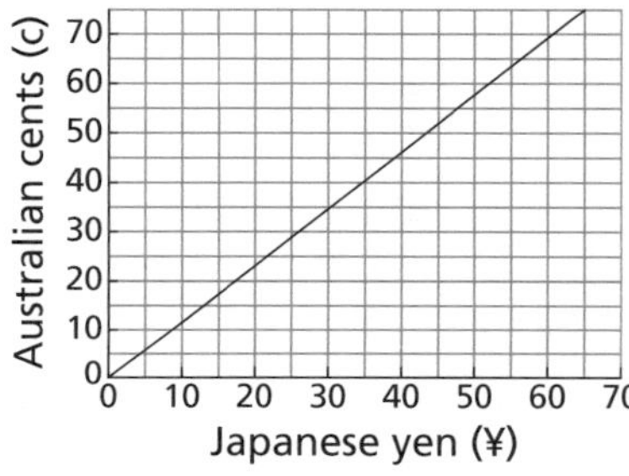

14. **a** Label what fraction of the hexagon's area is covered by each shape within the hexagon.

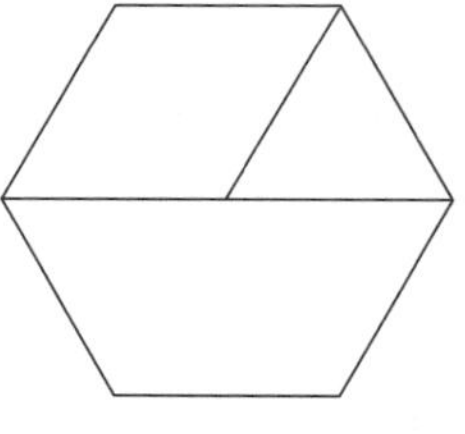

    b Is $\frac{1}{3}$ less than $\frac{1}{2}$? ____
    c Is $\frac{1}{6}$ more than $\frac{1}{3}$? ____

15. **a** $\frac{1}{4}$ of 12 ____
    b $\frac{1}{3}$ of 12 ____

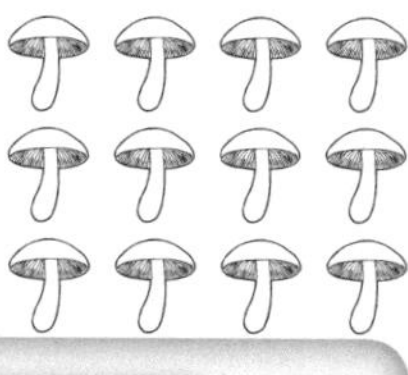

ID Card B

Turn to ID Card B on page 7.
Give the answers for these numbers.

(1) ____________ (2) ____________ number
(3) ____________ number (4) ____________
(5) ______ and ______ (7) ____________
(8) ____________ numbers (9) ____________
(10) ______ ones, ______ tenths, ______ hundredths, ______ thousandths

Multiples of 5 end with 5 or 0.

© PEARSON AUSTRALIA 2024 • *AUSTRALIAN SIGNPOST MATHS NSW 6 MENTALS* • ISBN 978 0 6557 0913 8

 ☐ out of 12

1. $6\overline{)744}$ 2. $7\overline{)847}$ 3. $4\overline{)376}$

4. $(3 \times 10^4) + (4 \times 10^3) + (6 \times 10^1) + 7$

= ____________

5. Write $\frac{7}{2}$ as a mixed number.

6. Write < (less than) or > (greater than) to make these number sentences true.

a −3 ______ −7 **b** 6 ______ −5

c 0 ______ − 1 **d** −10 ______ −8

7. C   −1 $-\frac{1}{2}$ A $\frac{1}{2}$ B $1\frac{1}{2}$

What number would be at:

a **A**? ____ **b** **B**? ____ **c** **C**? ____

8. **a** $\frac{1}{2}$ of 24 ____

b $\frac{5}{6}$ of 24 ____

c $\frac{3}{4}$ of 24 ____

d $\frac{2}{3}$ of 24 ____

9. What is the size of angle:

a A? __________

b B? __________

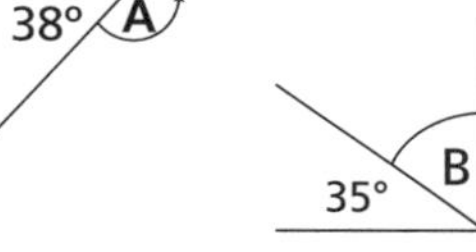

10. C   −80%   −60%   A   −20%   B   20%

What number would be at:

a **A**? ____ **b** **B**? ____ **c** **C**? ____

11. How many hundreds could be taken from 6 786 453? ________

12. Write 3:27 pm using 24-hour time. ________

 Extension ☐ out of 6

1. I keep rabbits and birds. There are 12 heads and 32 feet. How many birds do I have? ________

2. A man, born in 210 BCE, died 35 years later. His grandson was born 19 years after he died. His grandson was born in ________.

3. In how many ways can we draw 3 crosses in a row, on this grid? ________

×			×	×	×
	×				
		×			

4. **a** $(13 \times 16) + (13 \times 4)$ ____

b $(245 - 15 \times 15) \div 2$ ____

5. We had 68 more red scrunchies than green scrunchies. After giving away 56, we had 356 left. How many red scrunchies did we start with altogether? ____

6. One sixth of a whole is 3. Write the value of each shaded part.

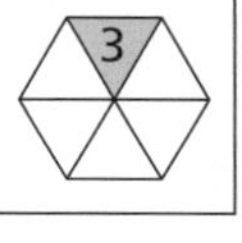

a

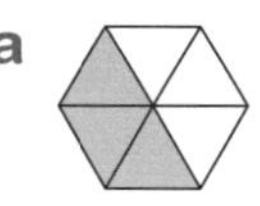

____

b

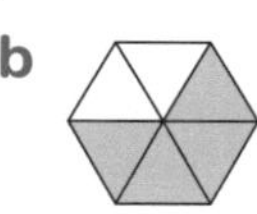

____

c Find the value of $8\frac{1}{3}$ hexagons. ____

Challenge

Describe this angle. List places you might see an angle this size.

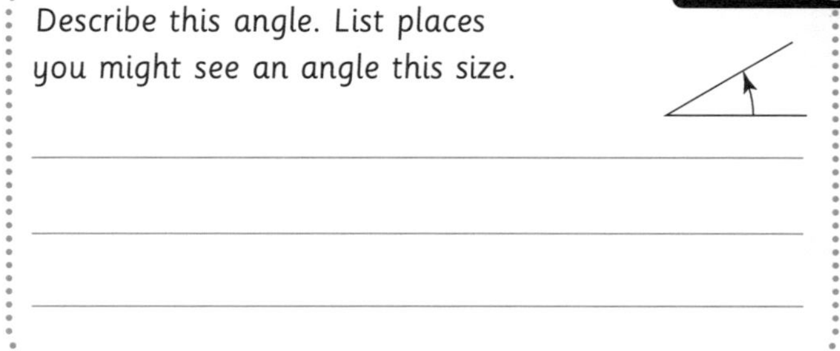

____

____

____

© PEARSON AUSTRALIA 2024 • *AUSTRALIAN SIGNPOST MATHS NSW 6 MENTALS* • ISBN 978 0 6557 0913 8

11:1

[ ] out of 17

1. 60 × 4 ______
2. 3 × 90 ______
3. 156 − 24 ______
4. 0·6 × 10 ______
5. $\begin{array}{r} 8568 \\ -\,3647 \\ \hline \end{array}$
6. 800 × 3 ______
7. 3 × 500 ______
8. 8 × (56 − 47) ______
9. $\frac{4}{9} + \frac{3}{9}$ ______
10. $\begin{array}{r} 1404 \\ \times \quad 3 \\ \hline \end{array}$
11. Write 6 ÷ 10 as a fraction, then write the division as a decimal. $\frac{\square}{\square}$ ______
12. Our family pays $200 for groceries each week. How much do we pay over 9 weeks? ______
13. a $\frac{1}{3}$ of 18 ______
    b $\frac{2}{3}$ of 18 ______
    c $\frac{1}{6}$ of 18 ______
    d $\frac{5}{6}$ of 18 ______
14. What is the size of angle:
    a A? ______
    b B? ______

    120° B

    45° A
15. $10^3 + 10^2 + 10 + 1$ ______
16. Order these numbers from smallest to largest.
    48 576 386 48 376 098 48 265 980
    ______
17. Write 05:23 using am or pm time. ______

 11:2

[ ] out of 17

1. 2 × 700 ______
2. 700 ÷ 10 ______
3. 0·9 × 100 ______
4. 978 − 59 ______
5. $\begin{array}{r} 3645 \\ +\,3698 \\ \hline \end{array}$
6. 8 × (97 − 89) ______
7. $\frac{8}{10} - \frac{3}{5}$ ______
8. 18 + 7 × 10 ______
9. Increase 97 by 18. ______
10. $\begin{array}{r} 3869 \\ \times \quad 8 \\ \hline \end{array}$
11. a $\frac{1}{3}$ of 18 ______
    b $\frac{1}{6}$ of 18 ______
    c $\frac{5}{6}$ of 18 ______
    d Is $\frac{1}{6}$ less than $\frac{1}{3}$? ______
12. I bought 6 packets of pasta for $2.95 each. What is the total cost? ______
13. What is the size of angle:

    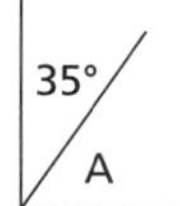

    55° B

    a A? ______ b B? ______
14. Order these decimals from largest to smallest.
    57·352 57·239 57·521
    ______
15. What is the value of the 7 in 14·987? ______
16. Write $\frac{15}{4}$ as a mixed numeral. $\square\frac{\square}{\square}$
17. What fraction is equal to 75%? $\frac{\square}{\square}$

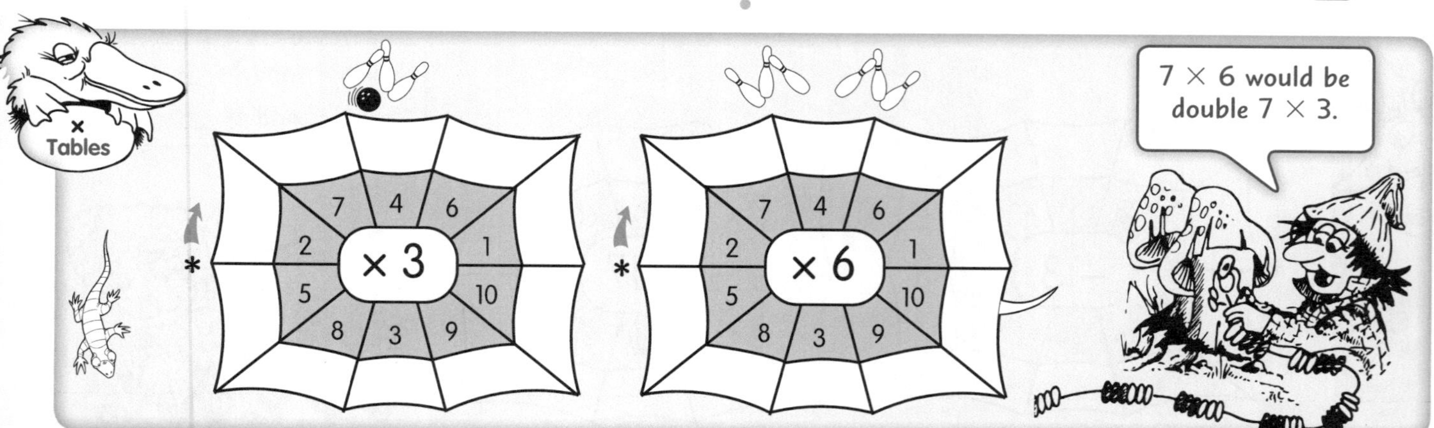

© PEARSON AUSTRALIA 2024 • *AUSTRALIAN SIGNPOST MATHS NSW 6 MENTALS* • ISBN 978 0 6557 0913 8

11:3

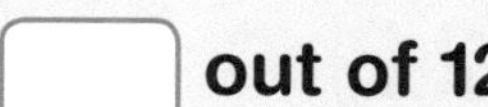

out of 12

1. $5\overline{)970}$ 2. $6\overline{)468}$ 3. $7\overline{)238}$

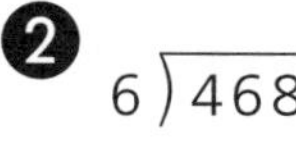

4. Each day this week, I read an average of 236 pages of my book. How many pages did I read this week? ______
5. What is the size of angle:

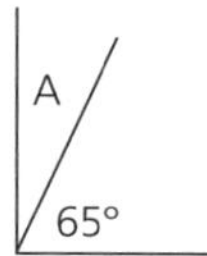

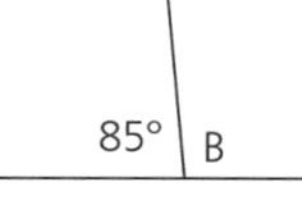

   a A? ______ b B? ______
6. Order these decimals from largest to smallest.

   91·709 91·699 91·711

   ______
7. a $\frac{1}{4}$ of 16 ____ b $\frac{3}{4}$ of 16 ____

   c $\frac{1}{8}$ of 16 ____ d $\frac{7}{8}$ of 16 ____
8. A temperature of 2°C dropped 4 degrees. What was it now? ______
9. The value of the 6 in 23 640 878 is ______.
10. A bag of marbles was dropped and 70 marbles were lost. If 297 remained, how many marbles were in the bag before it was dropped? ______

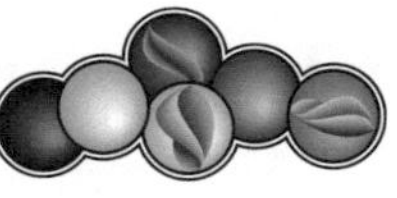

11. Write the decimal for:

    a 7 and 686 thousandths ______

    b 465 and 78 hundredths ______
12. How many teams of six can be made using 59 children? ______

11:4 Extension

out of 6

1. Two tins of beans are sold for $5.50. Find:

   a the cost of 1 tin ______

   b the cost of 17 tins ______
2. How long would it take me to pay for a stove that costs $490 if I pay $99 each week?

   ______
3. I can run around the large square once or around the small square four times. What is the difference in distance? ______

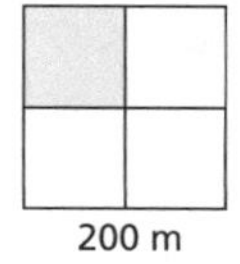

4. a $6\frac{1}{2} + 13\frac{1}{2}$ ______

   b $20 - 3\frac{1}{2}$ ______
5. Circle the square below that completes the pattern.

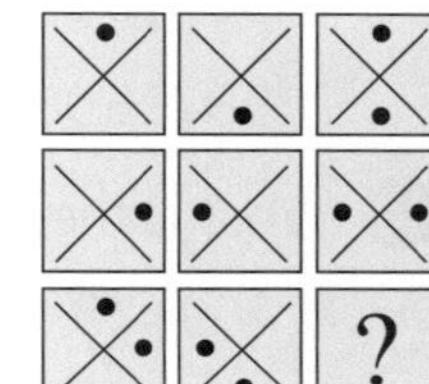

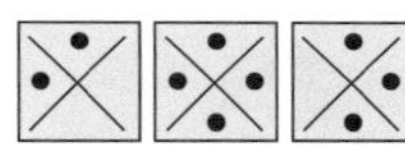

6. One pizza is enough for 4 people. How many do I need to satisfy 33 people? ______

Challenge

Write number sentences that are equal to 100.

______

______

______

Multiplying numbers ending in zeros

Write down the end zeros, and multiply the other numbers.

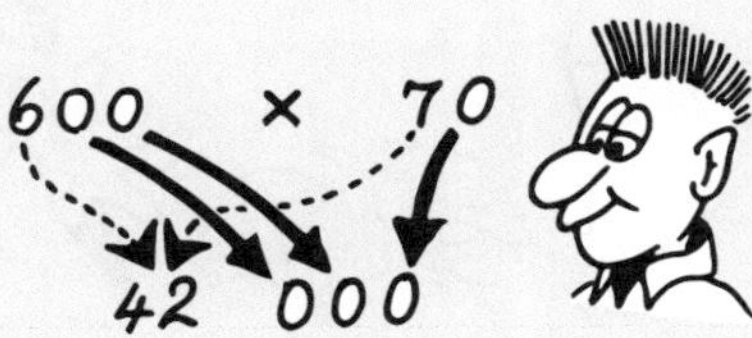

a 50 × 30	______	**b** 70 × 80	______
c 40 × 60	______	**d** 50 × 50	______
e 90 × 50	______	**f** 100 × 50	______
g 80 × 50	______	**h** 300 × 40	______
i 50^2	______	**j** 800^2	______

© PEARSON AUSTRALIA 2024

12:1 ☐ out of 16

1. 36 + 57 ____
2. $\frac{1}{2} + \frac{1}{2}$ ____
3. 93 − 45 ____
4. 103 − 47 ____
5. $\begin{array}{r} 4657 \\ +\ 3987 \\ \hline \end{array}$
6. Multiply 3 by 20. ____
7. Divide 90 by 9. ____
8. 45 + 9 × 4 ____
9. 56 + 87 = ____ + 90
10. $\begin{array}{r} 1024 \\ \times \quad 5 \\ \hline \end{array}$
11. Con carries 6 loads of milk, each with a capacity of 128 L. How much milk did he carry? ____

12. Round 675 756 038 to the nearest million. ____
13. Use < (less than) or > (greater than) in:
    - **a** 82 576 354 ____ 82 586 739
    - **b** 98 735 089 ____ 98 735 900
14. What is the size of:
    - **a** angle ● ? ____
    - **b** angle ▲ ? ____

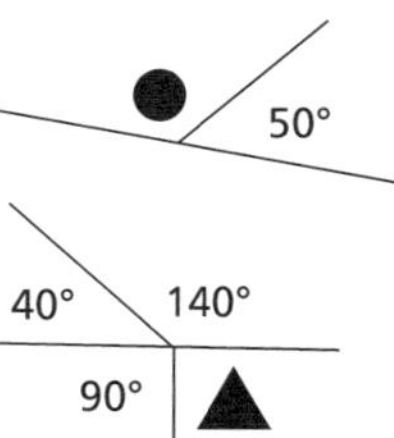

15. How many:
    - **a** months in 9 years? ____
    - **b** days in 11 weeks? ____
    - **c** months in 5 centuries? ____
16. **a** 6 kilograms = ____ grams
    - **b** 14 litres = ____ millilitres
    - **c** 97 centimetres = ____ millimetres
    - **d** 18 kilometres = ____ metres
    - **e** 6·7 metres = ____ centimetres
    - **f** 6 tonnes = ____ kilograms

12:2 ☐ out of 16

1. 560 − 24 ____
2. 489 − 49 ____
3. 457 + 79 ____
4. $\frac{5}{6} + \frac{1}{3}$ ____
5. $\begin{array}{r} 8576 \\ -\ 2954 \\ \hline \end{array}$
6. 0·7 × 1000 ____
7. Days in 9 weeks. ____
8. Double 567. ____
9. Halve 878. ____
10. $\begin{array}{r} 2098 \\ \times \quad 7 \\ \hline \end{array}$
11. What is the size of angle:
    - **a** ____
    - **b** ____

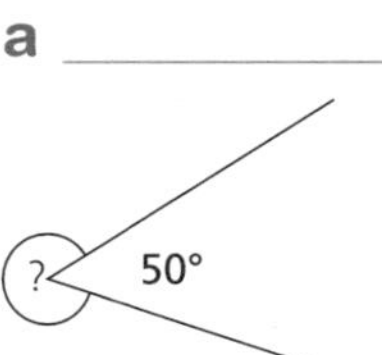

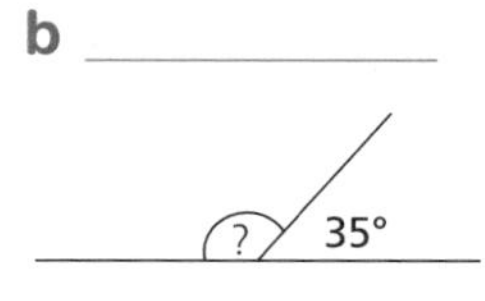

12. Complete the labels.
    - **a** ____ after ____
    - **b** ____ to ____

13. Write this fraction:
    - **a** as a mixed number
    - **b** as an improper fraction
14. **a** ● = ____ **b** ▲ = ____

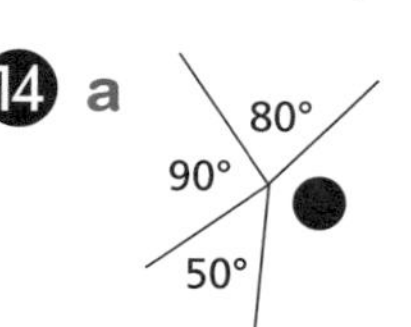

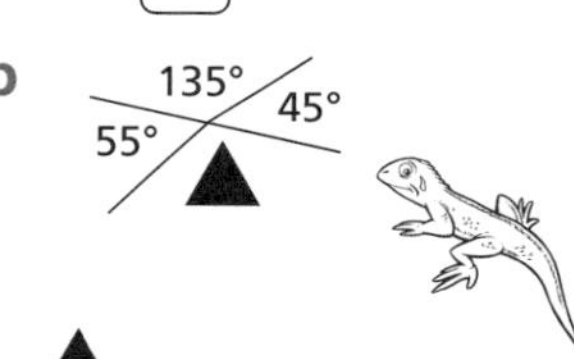

15. 100 – 9 – 9 – 9 – 9 – 9 – 9 ____
16. The opposite direction to south is ____.

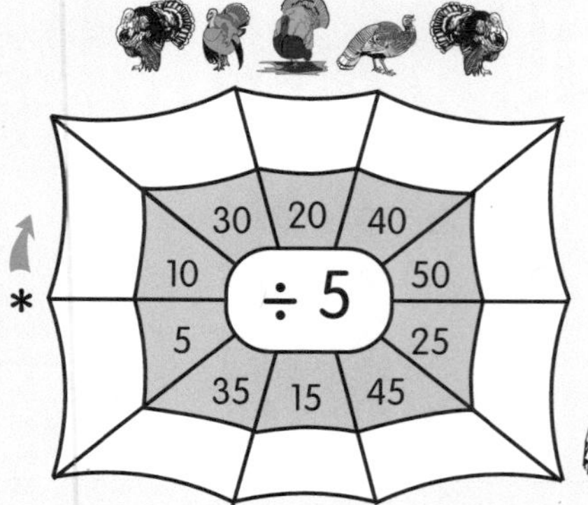

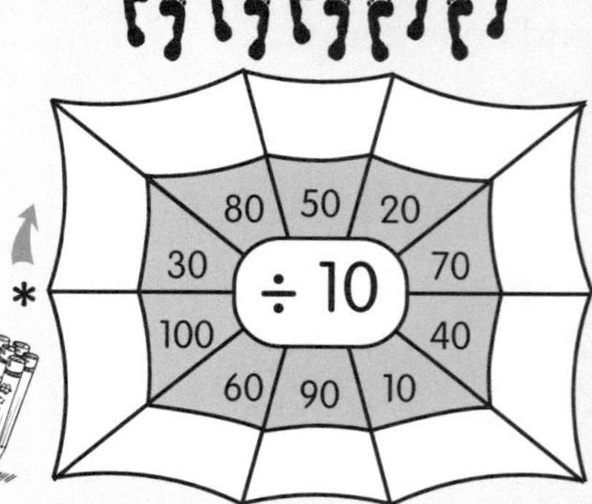

© PEARSON AUSTRALIA 2024 • *AUSTRALIAN SIGNPOST MATHS NSW 6 MENTALS* • ISBN 978 0 6557 0913 8

❶ $4\overline{)396}$ ❷ $8\overline{)256}$ 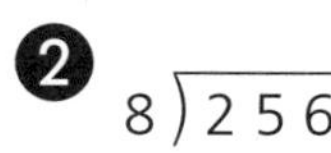 ❸ $10\overline{)430}$ 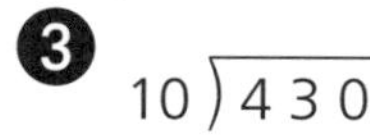

❹ Josie replaced sets of horseshoes for 253 horses this year. How many shoes did she replace? ______

❺ **a** 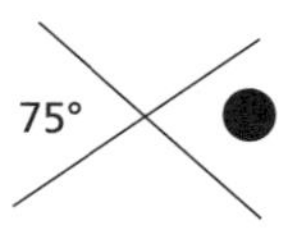

b 100°

● = ______ ▲ = ______

❻ I bought eight 336 mL containers of kombucha. How many litres did I buy? ______

❼ **a** $\frac{1}{3}$ of 15 ______

b $\frac{2}{3}$ of 15 ______

c $\frac{1}{5}$ of 15 ______

d $\frac{4}{5}$ of 15 ______

❽ Order these decimals from smallest to largest.

1·2122 1·2132 1·1201 2·12

______

❾ Write the decimal for:

a $\frac{8}{10}$ ______ **b** $\frac{35}{100}$ ______

❿ Write the decimal for:

a 8 tenths ______ **b** 9 hundredths ______

c 8 and 5 hundredths ______

⓫ Each day I ride 1270 m to get to school. How many kilometres do I ride to school and back in 1 school week? ______

❶ 6 rolls of silk each contain a 24 m length of silk, while 2 other rolls each contain 86 m. What is the total length of silk? ______

❷ Adam cuts 2 slices of bread like this to make four sandwiches. A loaf of bread contains 24 slices. How many sandwiches can Adam make from 3 loaves of bread? ______

❸ How many zeros has the product of 3 thousand and 16 thousand? ______

❹ Find the estimate by rounding each number to the nearest 10.

a 21 × 99 ______

b 48 × 121 ______

c 504 × 21 ______

❺ Mia rode 3546 m four times this week and Jiyu rode 3157 m five times this week.

a Who rode the furthest? ______

b What was the difference between the total distances? ______

❻ **a** 128 ÷ ______ = 32 **b** 586 − ______ = 259

Challenge

Write number sentences that are equal to 24

______

______

______

______

______

Heather is the youngest person in her family. This drawing has a scale of 1:50. Measure the heights in this picture using millimetres, and then find, correct to the nearest 5 cm, the real height of:

a Heather ______ **b** her mother ______

c her brother ______ **d** her father ______

e Heather's dog, Shasta ______

© PEARSON AUSTRALIA 2024 ISBN 978 0 6557 0913 8

13:1

out of 13

1. 4×600 ______
2. 800×5 ______
3. $\frac{4}{10} + \frac{1}{10}$ ______
4. $647 - 29$ ______
5. $\begin{array}{r} 76590 \\ \times \quad 2 \\ \hline \end{array}$
6. $3 \times 5 + 199$ ______
7. $(3 + 4) \times 8$ ______
8. $298 - 32$ ______
9. $21 \div 3 + 89$ ______
10. $\begin{array}{r} 95624 \\ \times \quad 4 \\ \hline \end{array}$

11. Andrew worked 5 days each week for 67 weeks. For how many days did he work? ______

12. On Makayla's first day at her new school, she studies the map at the front gate. Fill in the distance and directions using the scale.

Start
metres 0 5 10 15 20
Year 6 | Year 5 | Library | Year 4 | N | Canteen | Office | Year 3 | Toilets | Year 2 | Year 1 | Kindergarten

   a She walks ______ m south to order her lunch.

   b She then walks 15 m ______ to the office.

   c She then walks 15 m in a ______ direction to rest under a shady tree.

   d If she then walks south to her classroom, what year is she in? ______

13. The opposite direction to north is ______.

13:2

out of 15

1. 8×25 ______
2. $0{\cdot}6 \times 100$ ______
3. $4 - \frac{3}{4}$ ______
4. $17 - 72 \div 9$ ______
5. $\begin{array}{r} 46388 \\ + \quad 3 \\ \hline \end{array}$
6. Multiply 19 by 7. ______
7. $\frac{7}{8} - \frac{1}{4}$ ______
8. $6 \times (73 - 43)$ ______
9. $72 \div 9 \times 14$ ______
10. $\begin{array}{r} 80478 \\ \times \quad 7 \\ \hline \end{array}$

11. A photographer allows 10 minutes to take one family portrait. How many families can be photographed from 9am to 12:30pm? ______

12. A bus travels east for 4 blocks, north for 2 blocks, west for 2 blocks, then stops.

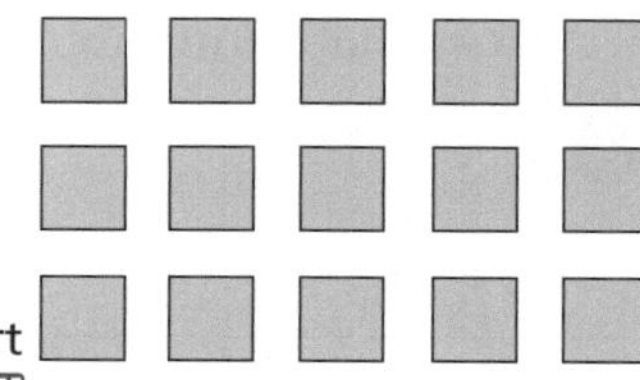

   a What direction is it now facing? ______

   b What direction is it now from the starting point? ______

13. If I blink 16 000 times a day, estimate how many times I blink in a week. ______

14. a

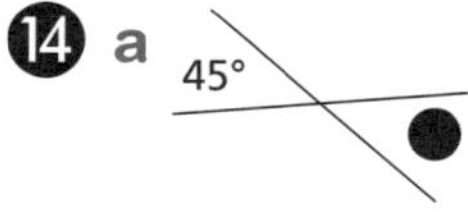

● = ______

b

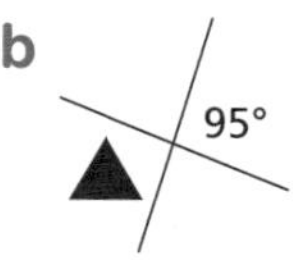

▲ = ______

15. a $1000 - 20 \times (5 \times 3)$ ______

    b $(49 + 36) \div (45 \div 9)$ ______

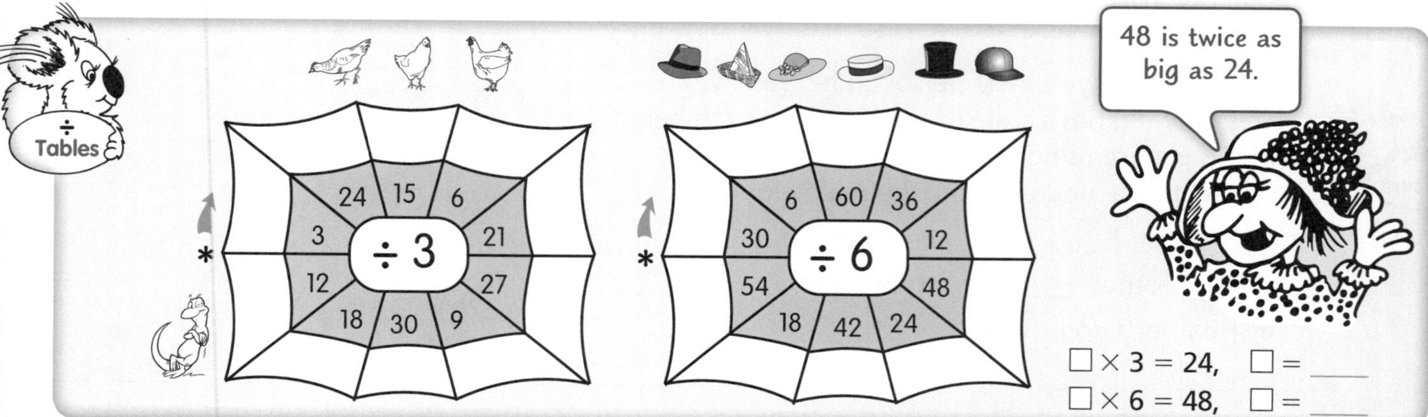

© PEARSON AUSTRALIA 2024 • *AUSTRALIAN SIGNPOST MATHS NSW 6 MENTALS* • ISBN 978 0 6557 0913 8

13:3 out of 11

1.  $8\overline{)586}$
2. $5\overline{)947}$
3. $9\overline{)476}$
4. a If I need to drink 2200 mL a day, how many litres should I drink in a week? ______
   b If I only drank 12 800 mL this week, how much more did I need? ______
5. Use the scale to find the distance from Sydney to:
   a Hobart ______
   b Perth ______

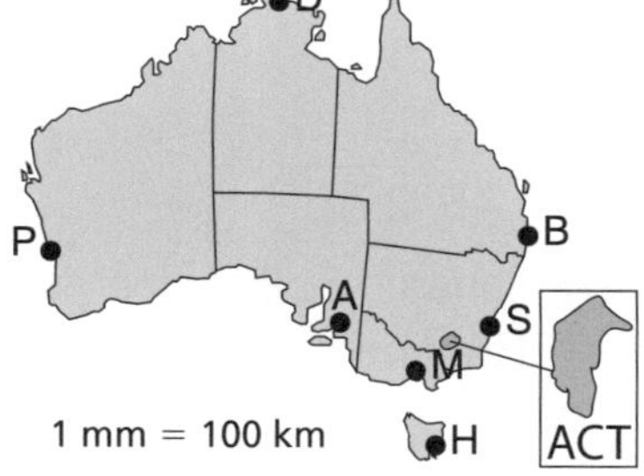

   c List the states and territories shown on this map in order of area size.
   ACT, ______
6. Adua drives 1·25 km on a sealed road and 1·25 km on a dirt road. How far has she driven altogether? ______

7. What is the size of angle ▲? ______

8. 48 grapes are shared fairly among 4 children. How many grapes were given to each child? ______
9. $8000 is shared equally between 7 adults. How much does each receive? (Round off correct to the nearest 5 cents.) ______
10. 700 + 90 + 3 + 0·06 ______
11. Does 54 354 767 round off to 54 000 000 or 55 000 000? ______

13:4 Extension out of 6

1. If I take about 22 500 breaths a day, how many breaths less than 1 million would I take in:
   a a week? ______
   b April? ______
2. 3 lunches cost $8.70. How much would:
   a 12 lunches cost? ______
   b 1 lunch cost? ______
3. The shortest distance by road from:
   a A to **F** ______ **b C** to **D** ______

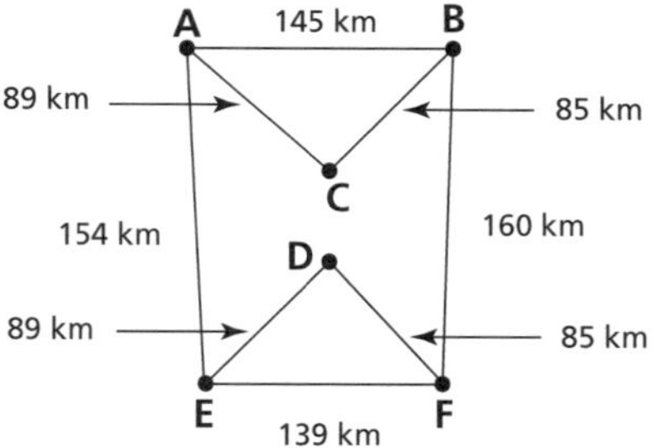

4. If $10^3 = 1000$ and $10^2 = 100$ and $10^1 = 10$, what is the value of 10^0? ______
5. If I blink 16 000 times a day, when awake, estimate how many times I blink in an hour. ______
6. What is the size of angle ▲? ______

Challenge

Describe the position of items on this grid, e.g. the pentagon is north-east of the triangle.

A	⬡	○
⯃	+	B
C	☆	⬠
□	△	↗

______
______
______

× Tables

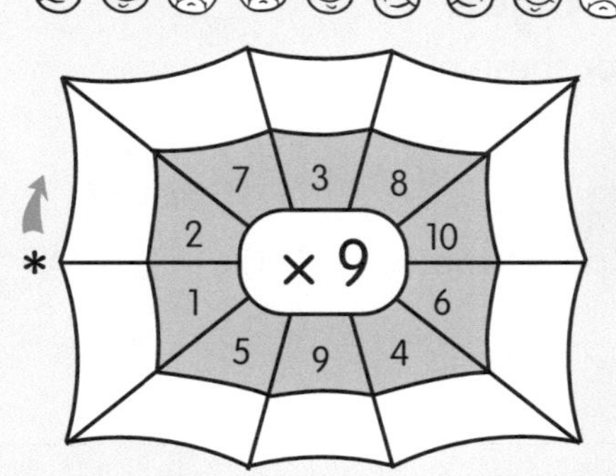

The digits in each number add up to 9.

9	18	27	36	45
54	63	72	81	90

14:1 — ☐ out of 13

1. 300 − 43 ______
2. $\frac{4}{6} + \frac{1}{6}$ ______
3. 849 − 427 ______
4. 0·5 × 10 ______
5. $\begin{array}{r} 2647 \\ +\ 5638 \\ \hline \end{array}$
6. 8 × (56 − 52) ______
7. Multiply 3 by 60. ______
8. 45 + 36 = ______ + 40
9. 76 − 23 = ______ − 20
10. $\begin{array}{r} 3750 \\ \times\ \ \ \ 4 \\ \hline \end{array}$
11. **a** $4\overline{)49}$ r **b** $7\overline{)62}$ r
12. **a** In which direction does a compass needle always point? ______

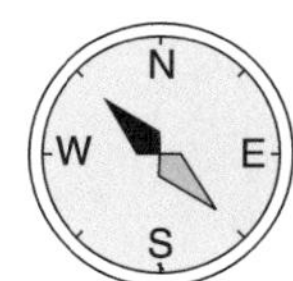

    b The angle between the compass directions, south and east? ______
13. 

    What is found at the coordinates:
    a **F3**? ______
    b **J4**? ______
    c **A5**? ______
    d **F5**? ______
    e **C2**? ______

14:2 — ☐ out of 17

1. 7 + 5 × 62 ______
2. 6 × 48 ______
3. $7 - \frac{1}{3}$ ______
4. (3 + 6) × 9 ______
5. $\begin{array}{r} 8465 \\ +\ 2859 \\ \hline \end{array}$
6. $9^2 \times 8$ ______
7. $\frac{5}{6} + \frac{2}{3}$ ______
8. 845 + 298 ______
9. 345 + 456 = ______ + 450
10. $\begin{array}{r} 97860 \\ \times\ \ \ \ \ 7 \\ \hline \end{array}$
11. **a** $5\overline{)27}$ r **b** $4\overline{)27}$ r
12. I shared 5684 mL equally into 7 drink bottles. How much did I put in each bottle? ______
13. **a** Draw a dot at (2, 3), (1, −2), (−1, 3) and (−2, −2).
    b Join the dots to make a shape.
    c What shape did you draw?
    ______

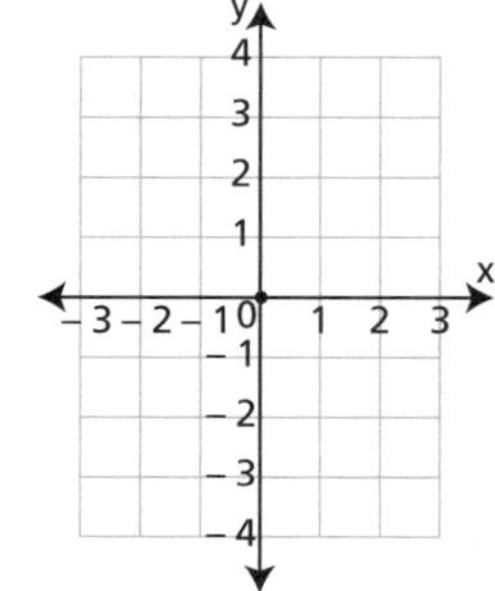

14. Four friends shared $6574 equally. How much did each receive? ______
15. I pay an average of $3569 in rates for each year. What is the total cost of rates over 5 years? ______
16. What is the distance from Hobart to:
    a **A**? ______
    b **B**? ______
    c **C**? ______
    d **D**? ______

    B
    C
    D
    A
    HOBART

    Scale: 1 mm = 18 km
17. 4 × 7 + 2 + 57 ______

Turn to ID card C on page 8.
Give the answers for these numbers.

(14) ______ shapes (15) ______ shapes
(16) ______ (17) axis of ______
(20) ______ of symmetry (21) ______
(22) ______ (23) ______
(24) ______ (25) ______

Flip, slide or turn?

© PEARSON AUSTRALIA 2024 • *AUSTRALIAN SIGNPOST MATHS NSW 6 MENTALS* • ISBN 978 0 6557 0913 8

14:3 ☐ out of 12

❶ $4\overline{)291}$ ❷ $7\overline{)704}$ ❸ $8\overline{)302}$

❹ $7\overline{)927}$ ❺ $4\overline{)285}$ ❻ $8\overline{)809}$

❼ How many seeds are in a packet if half are used to plant 5 rows of 9 seeds? ______

❽ Which object is:

a north of **A** and west of **B**? ______

b east of **D** and south of **C**? ______

N ↑

		C	
D			B
⑤	A		E

❾ If I had $35, how many of these books could I buy?

$7.50

______

❿ **a** Draw a dot at (1, 1), (3, −3), (−3, −3) and (−1, 1).

b Join the dots to make a shape.

c What shape did you draw?

______

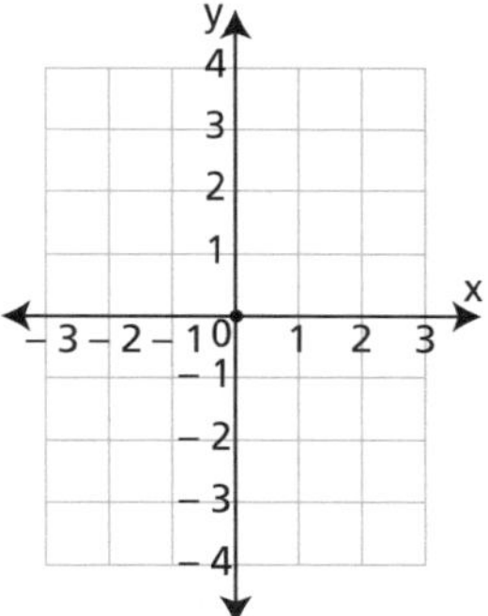

⓫ What is:

a one third of 12? ______

b one sixth of 12? ______

⓬ **a** 6·8 kg = ______ g

b 67 mm = ______ cm

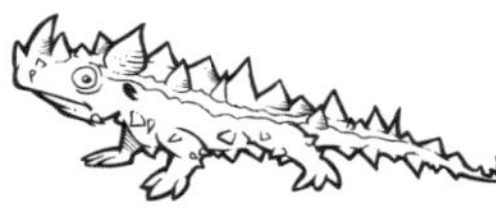

14:4 Extension ☐ out of 5

❶ A girl was born in 5 BCE and died 89 years later. Her great grandchild was born 16 years after she died. In what year was the grandchild born? (There is no 'zero' as a year date.) ______

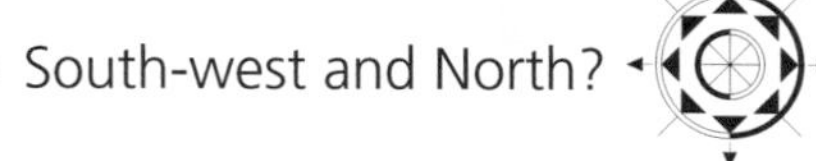

❷ The angle between the compass directions:

a North and North-east? ______

b South-west and North? ______

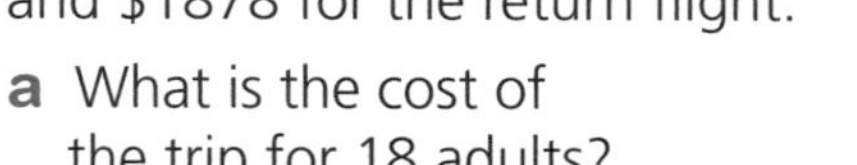

❸ A plane ticket cost $2867 to India and $1878 for the return flight.

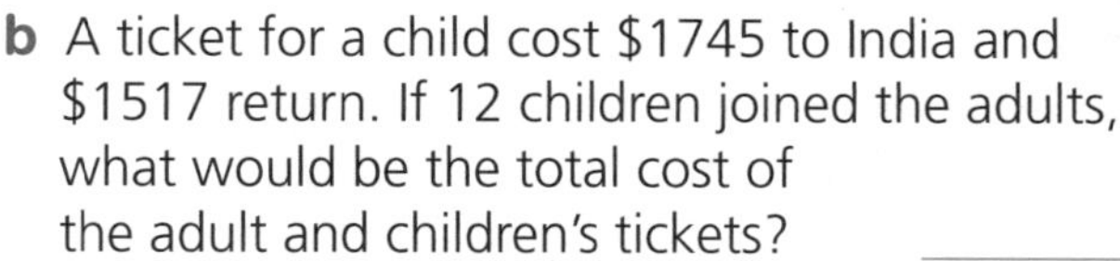

a What is the cost of the trip for 18 adults? ______

b A ticket for a child cost $1745 to India and $1517 return. If 12 children joined the adults, what would be the total cost of the adult and children's tickets? ______

❹ Insert grouping symbols to make this number sentence true.

18 − 5 × 3 = 39

❺ An octagon with the head of a tiger inside it represents 128 tigers. What number is represented below?

______

Challenge

Write facts about the number 78 504 536.

______

______

______

Turn to ID card C on page 8.
Give the answers for these numbers.

(4) ______ (5) ______
(6) ______ (7) ______
(8) ______ (9) ______
(10) ______ (11) ______
(12) ______ (13) ______

Make a study card:
Put questions on one side
and answers on the other.

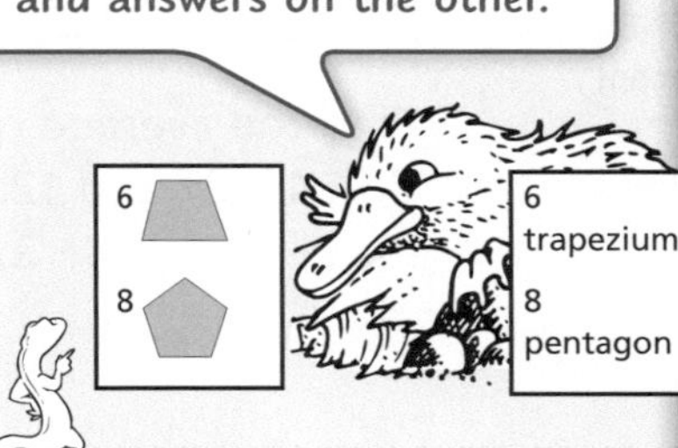

15:1   ☐ out of 14

1. 8×12 ______
2. 700×4 ______
3. $0{\cdot}3 \times 100$ ______
4. $15 \div 3 + 9$ ______
5. $\begin{array}{r} \$8354 \\ +\ \$1097 \\ \hline \end{array}$
6. \$4.80 − 23c ______
7. \$10 minus \$5.20 ______
8. \$3.15 − ______ = \$2.85
9. $\frac{1}{4} + \frac{3}{4}$ ______
10. $\begin{array}{r} \$1087 \\ \times \quad 5 \\ \hline \end{array}$

11. How big is this acute angle? ______

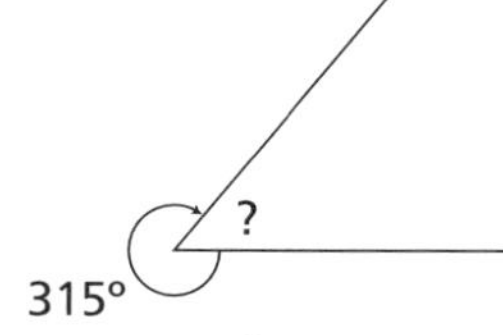

12. Name these 3D shapes.

a 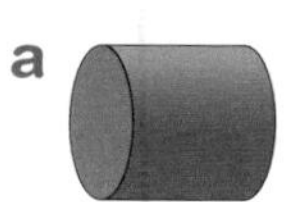 ______

b  ______

13. These are the results of our soccer matches.

							Totals
Our team	5	4	2	0	8	7	
Our opposition	2	0	5	2	2	3	

a Write the total number of goals for each team.
b What was our average goals scored? ______
c What was the average number of goals scored by our opposition? ______
d How many games did our team win? ______

14. Write the letter used to name the point:

a (0, 3) ______
b (2, 1) ______
Write the coordinates for:
c K ______
d N ______

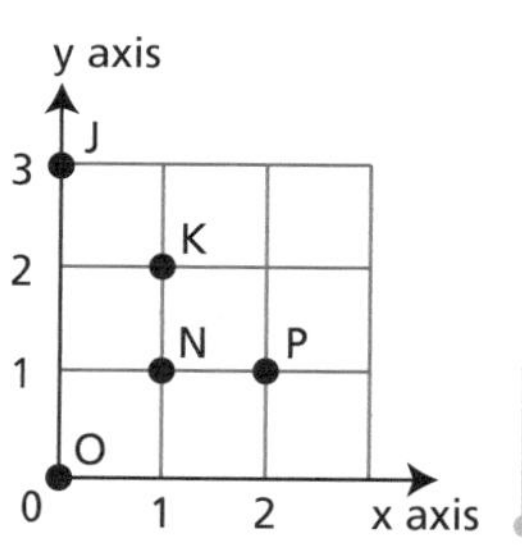

15:2   ☐ out of 16

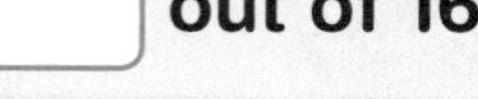

1. $5 \times (46 + 56)$ ______
2. $354 - 276$ ______
3. $\frac{4}{8} - \frac{1}{2}$ ______
4. $\$68 \times 7$ ______
5. $\begin{array}{r} 7483 \\ +\ 1987 \\ \hline \end{array}$
6. ______ + 78 = 145
7. 82 + ______ = 245
8. 200 − ______ = 63
9. 75 − 43 = ______ −40
10. $\begin{array}{r} 3649 \\ \times \quad 8 \\ \hline \end{array}$

11. What is the average of these lengths?
67 cm, 82 cm, 94 cm, 45 cm ______

12. On a cube, what is the number of:
a faces? ______
b corners? ______

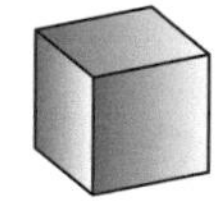

13. I had 4 cucumbers. The length of each was 355 mm, 376 mm, 329 mm and 340 mm. What was the average length in centimetres? ______

14. One watermelon cost \$16. How many could be bought for \$100? ______

15. a 90° ● b

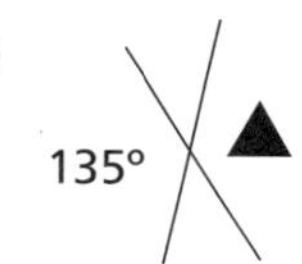

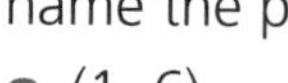

● = ______ ▲ = ______

16. Write the letter used to name the point:

a (1, 6) ______
b (6, 4) ______
Write the coordinates for:
c C ______
d B ______

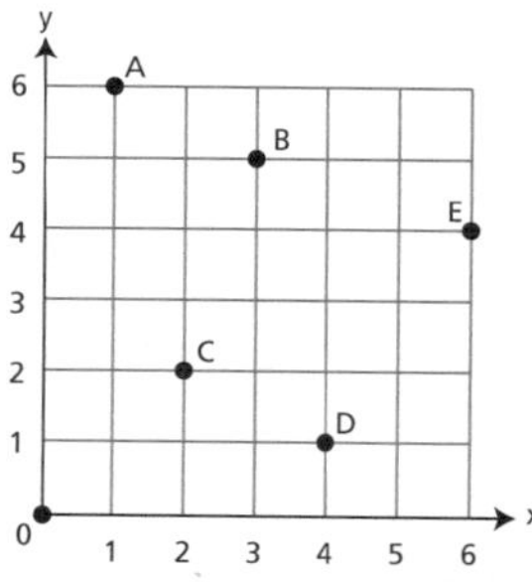

Average

$= \frac{\textbf{sum of the items}}{\textbf{number of items}}$

Find the average of 8, 7, 11, 27 and 12.
= (8 + 7 + 11 + 27 + 12) ÷ 5
= 13

Find the average of:
a 6 m, 15 m, 8 m and 7 m ______
b 71 g, 132 g and 88 g ______
c 463, 684 and 671 ______
d 7, 9, 1, 4 and 9 ______
e 81, 43, 70 and 58 ______

Add the numbers, then divide.

© PEARSON AUSTRALIA 2024 • *AUSTRALIAN SIGNPOST MATHS NSW 6 MENTALS* • ISBN 978 0 6557 0913 8

15:3 out of 10

1. Write each answer as a mixed number.

   a $5\overline{)43}$ b $8\overline{)34}$ c $6\overline{)835}$

   d $4\overline{)782}$ e $9\overline{)546}$ f $10\overline{)736}$

2. An angle of 360° is a ________________.

3. How much would each person receive if 6 students equally shared 8 apples? (Write your answer as a mixed number.) ________

4. Draw a triangular pyramid. How many:

   a faces? ________

   b edges? ________

   c vertices? ________

5. At an average speed of 80 km/h, how far would I travel in 3 hours? ________

6. Write the letter found at:

   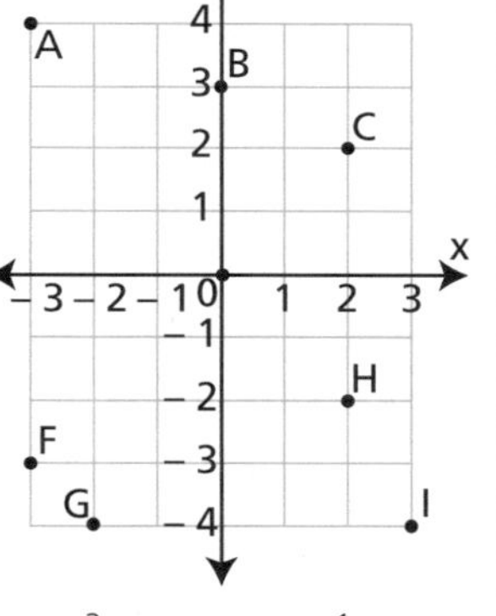

   a (0, 3) ________

   b (3, – 4) ________

   Write the coordinates for:

   c C ________

   d G ________

   e F ________

   f A ________

7. $(1 \times 10^4) + (8 \times 10^3) + (9 \times 10^2) + (9 \times 10^1) + 5$
   = ________

8. Write as an improper fraction:

   a $2\frac{1}{4}$ ________ b $3\frac{3}{5}$ ________

9. The value of 5 in 98·895. ________

10. Write the decimal for 87 hundredths. ________

15:4 out of 6

Extension

1.

   Give the approximate value at the letter:

   a **A** ________ b **B** ________

   c **C** ________ d **D** ________

2. A mug contained 235 mL of water. A glass held three times as much and a bucket contained 6·54 L more than the glass. What was the total capacity of the containers? ________

3. Tickets to the show cost $169 per adult and $138.50 per child. Find the cost for our family if there are 2 adults and 6 children. ________

4. What must we add to $771 952.38 to make $900 000? ________

5. Which factor of 64 can be added to 69 to make a total of 101? ________

6. My bench top has a sink and hotplates on it. The bench top is 3·9 m by 90 cm. The sink is 85 cm by 51 cm and the hotplates cover an area 930 mm by 450 mm. How much bench space is left on the bench top? ________

Challenge

List groups of numbers and record the average of each group.

____

____

____

____

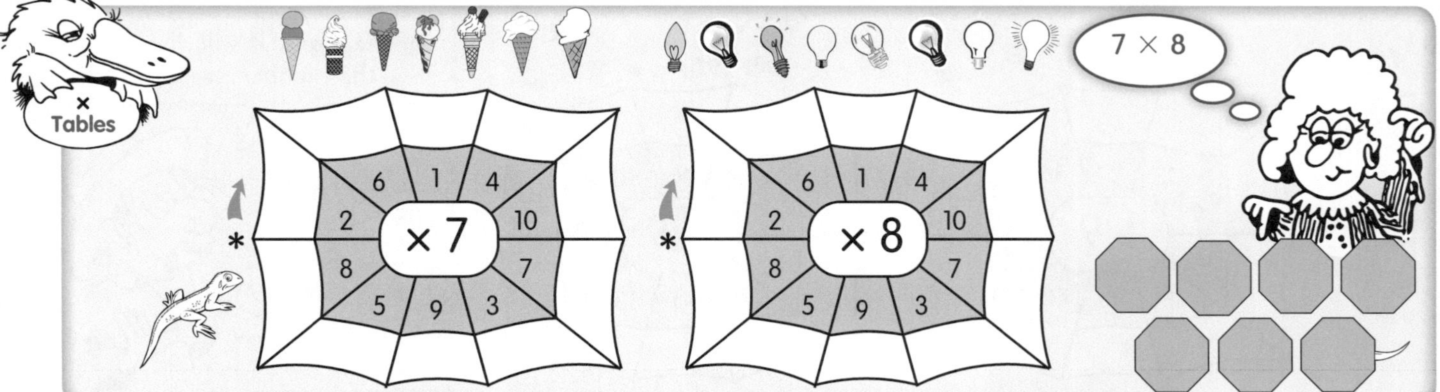

1. 7×80
2. $42 \div 7$
3. $3 \times 7 - 8$
4. $0{\cdot}6 \times 100$
5. $57487 + 20729$
6. Triple 29.
7. $\frac{1}{2}$ of 86
8. $45 + 298$
9. $\frac{6}{2} + \frac{1}{2}$
10. $30586 + 18474$
11. How much would each receive if six students equally shared 10 cucumbers? (Write your answer as a mixed number.)
12. At an average speed of 60 km/h, how far would I travel in 2 hours?
13. Join:
1 and 5, 5 and 9, 9 and 1,
2 and 6, 6 and 10, 10 and 2,
3 and 7, 7 and 11, 11 and 3,
4 and 8, 8 and 12, 12 and 4.
What have you drawn?

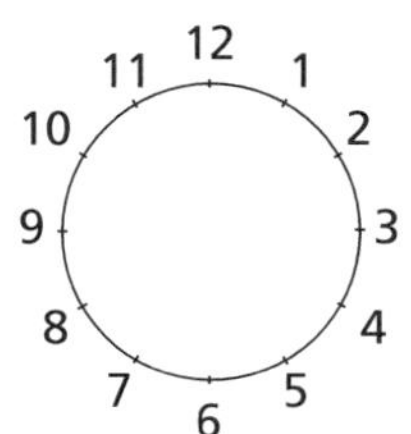

14. a How many faces on a cube?
b How many edges on a cube?
15. a Which solid does this model represent?
b What is the cross-section of this solid?
c List all vertical lines.
d List all horizontal lines.

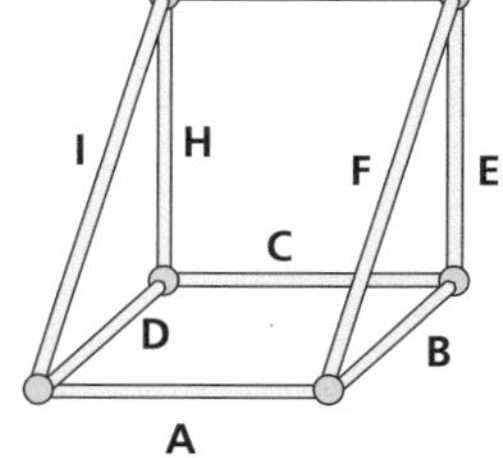

1. $763 + 157$
2. $465 - 156$
3. $56 \div 8 + 9$
4. $42 \div 7 - 6$
5. $419676 + 36849$
6. $\frac{9}{12} - \frac{1}{4}$
7. $365 + 927$
8. $\frac{1}{8}$ of 24
9. $84 + 43 = 87 +$ ____
10. $435790 - 56841$
11. How far can a kangaroo travel if it moves at an average speed of 46 km/h for half an hour?

12. $(9 \times 10^4) + (2 \times 10^3) + (7 \times 10^2) + (4 \times 10^1) + 6$
$=$ ____
13. Draw a copy of each solid.
a

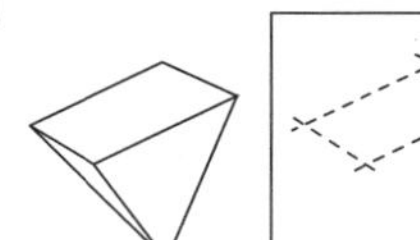
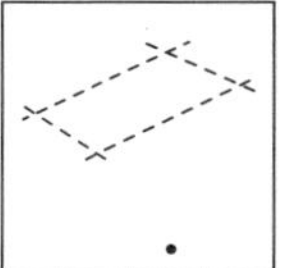

b

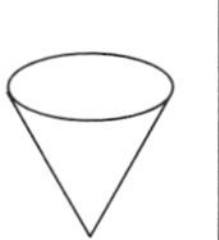
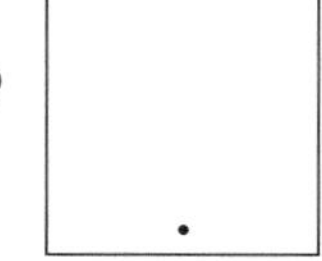

14. A triangular prism has _____ faces, _____ edges and _____ vertices.
15. A supermarket purchased 465 475 apples this month and sold 287 365 in the first 10 days.
a How many have not been sold?
b Is it likely that they will all be sold by the end of the month?
16. These pears weighed 197 g, 218 g and 188 g. What was the average mass?

17. Name solids that have a square cross-section.

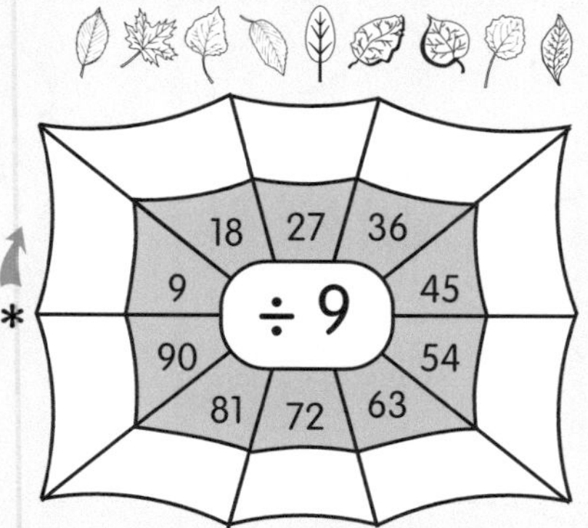

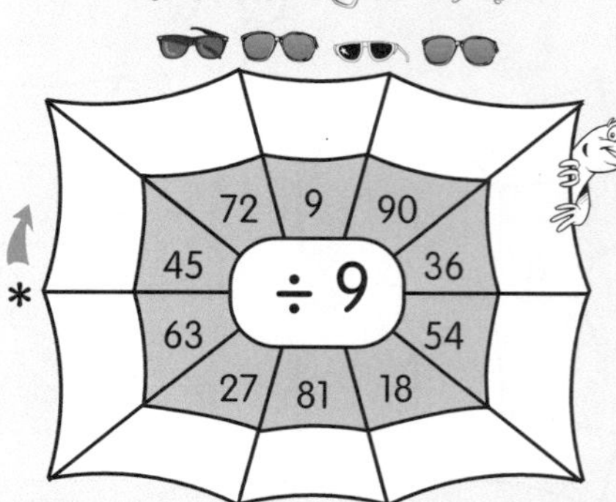

If 9 will divide the sum of the digits, it will divide the number itself.

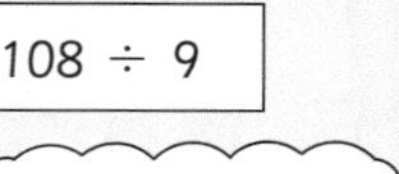

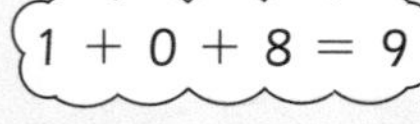

© PEARSON AUSTRALIA 2024 • *AUSTRALIAN SIGNPOST MATHS NSW 6 MENTALS* • ISBN 978 0 6557 0913 8

16:3 ☐ out of 10

1 Write each answer as a mixed number.

a $7\overline{)57}$ **b** $5\overline{)94}$ **c** $3\overline{)695}$

d $6\overline{)693}$ **e** $8\overline{)639}$ **f** $10\overline{)392}$

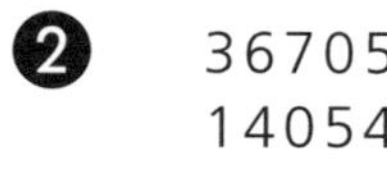

2
```
  36705
  14054
+ 23109
```

3
```
  73000
  14000
   3100
+  1053
```

4 How far would a dog travel if it ran at an average speed of 12 km/h for 10 minutes? ______

5 How much would each person receive if 3 students equally shared 11 slices of bread? ______

6 I had 4 bananas with a mass of 105 g, 129 g, 116 g and 106 g. What is the average mass? ______

7 Sophie bought a house for $568 000 and sold it for $934 550. What was the difference between the purchase and sale price? ______

8 There were 46, 52 and 73 fish in each of three fish tanks. What was the average number of fish in the tanks? ______

9 A cube has ______ faces and ______ edges.

10 Draw a:

a cube **b** triangular prism

16:4 ☐ out of 7

Extension

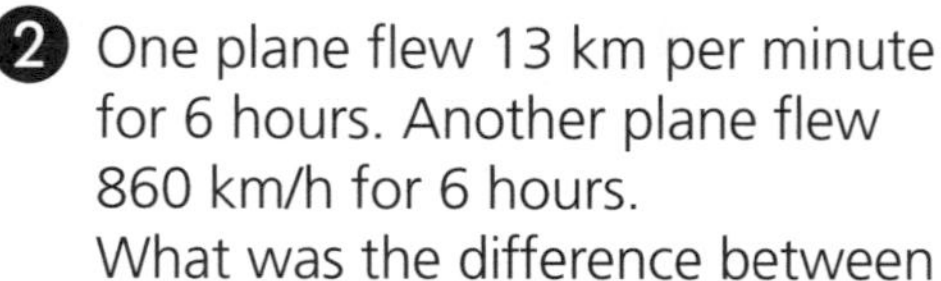

1 Toothpicks and Blu Tack were used to make triangular prisms. What is the greatest number of separate triangular prisms you could create with:

a 19 toothpicks? ______

b 27 toothpicks? ______

2 One plane flew 13 km per minute for 6 hours. Another plane flew 860 km/h for 6 hours. What was the difference between the total distance they flew? ______

3 I used square pieces of wood 4 cm long to construct open cubes. How many open cubes could I make using 79 of the square pieces? ______

4 If # stands for 7356 and ~ stands for 193, what is 2 × (8000 − # − ~) − (4 × ~). ______

5 **a** 266 × 34 ______

b 675 × 26 ______

6 The teachers set out 29 rows of 34 chairs for the assembly. If 896 people sat in the chairs during the assembly, how many chairs were not used? ______

7 If the time is 3:42 pm, how long is it until I start school at 9am tomorrow? ______

Challenge

Make your own rule to complete each table.

Rule = × ______ + ______

1st number	1	2	3	4	5	6	7
2nd number							

Rule = × ______ − ______

1st number	1	2	3	4	5	6	7
2nd number							

Profit and loss

When we sell something for more than we paid for it, we make a **profit**. When we sell something for less than we paid for it, we make a **loss**.

Give the profit or loss, if an item:

a bought for $137.50 is then sold for $150. Profit of ______

b bought for $18 250 is then sold for $10 850. ______ of ______

c bought for $9380 is then sold for $16 250. ______ of ______

17:1

out of 19

1. 600 − 38 ____
2. 200 − 152 ____
3. 36 ÷ 6 + 3 ____
4. 27 ÷ 9 + 6 ____
5. $\begin{array}{r} 507484 \\ +\ 28018 \\ \hline \end{array}$
6. $\frac{1}{2}$ of 362 ____
7. 0·6 × 100 ____
8. Multiply 90 by 7. ____
9. Divide 100 by 4. ____
10. $\begin{array}{r} 809230 \\ -\ 28560 \\ \hline \end{array}$
11. Three friends equally shared $4656. How much did each receive? ____
12. This is the net of a ____________.
13. What is the cross-section of a square pyramid parallel to the base? ____
14. What is the probability of spinning G:
    a as a fraction? ____
    b as a decimal? ____
    c as a percentage? ____

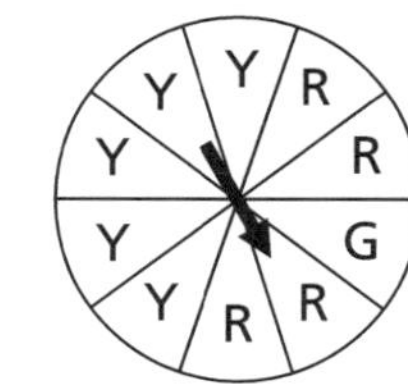

15. Jessica wins if a Y is spun, Felicity wins if an R is spun and Lachlan wins if a G is spun.
    a Is this a fair game? ____
    b Who has the best chance of winning? ____
16. 0·8, 1·0, 1·2, ____, ____, ____, ____
17. Write $3\frac{4}{5}$ as an improper fraction. ____
18. a How many halves in $2\frac{1}{2}$? ____
    b How many quarters in 3? ____
19. The value of 6 in 857·786. ____

17:2

out of 17

1. 5198 − 36 ____
2. 1000 − 79 ____
3. 800 − 156 ____
4. 560 ÷ 7 ____
5. $\begin{array}{r} 800000 \\ -\ 13648 \\ \hline \end{array}$
6. $\frac{1}{5}$ of 45 ____
7. 50% of $62. ____
8. 0·8 as a fraction. ____
9. 0·65 as a percentage. ____
10. $\begin{array}{r} 900000 \\ -\ 26478 \\ \hline \end{array}$
11. I scored 91% in Maths, 82% in English, 82% in Science. What was the average of my 3 scores? ____
12. A plane can fly at 14 km per minute. How far can it fly in one hour? ____
13. My odometer now shows 39 873 km. How far must I travel until my next service which is at 50 000 km? ____
14. a Complete the drawing of this shape.

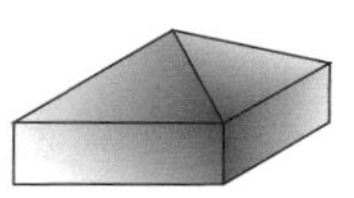

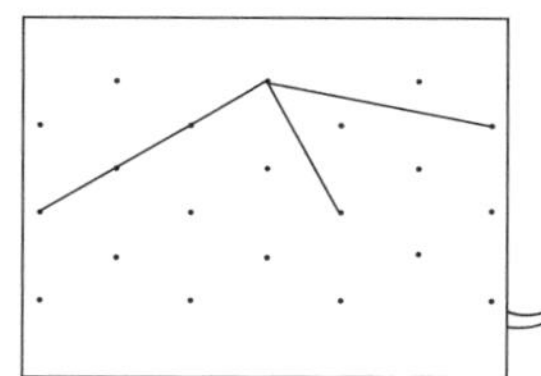

This shape has:

b ____ vertices   c ____ faces

d Describe the cross-sections of this shape that are parallel to the base. ____

15. This is the net of a ____________

16. What is the cross-section of a triangular prism parallel to the base? ____
17. The value of 9 in 3546·893 ____

PEARS
$2.95 per kg

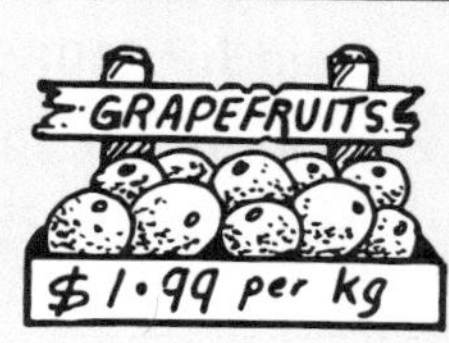

© PEARSON AUSTRALIA 2024 • *AUSTRALIAN SIGNPOST MATHS NSW 6 MENTALS* • ISBN 978 0 6557 0913 8

17:3 ☐ out of 11

1
```
    576476
     64769
   3568401
+     3567
```

2
```
  900000
−  35975
```

3 The aeroplane was at a height of 10 232 m. An hour later it was at a height of 12 588 m. What was the difference between the heights? ______

4 This is the net of a ______________.

5 What is the cross-section of a hexagonal prism, parallel to the base? ______

6 What is the probability of spinning Y:

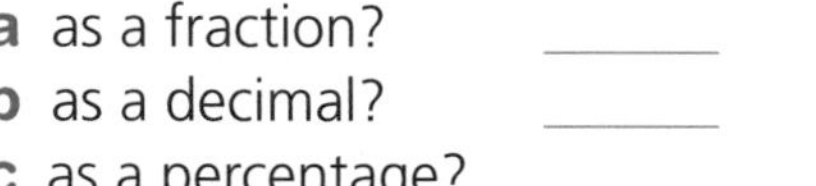

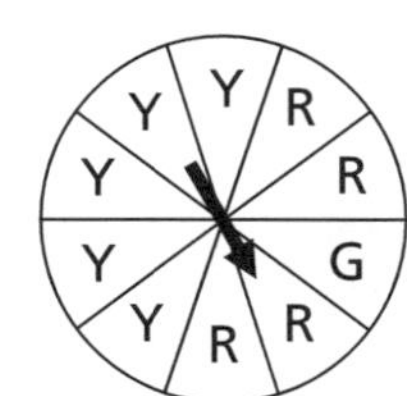

a as a fraction? ______
b as a decimal? ______
c as a percentage? ______

7 100 tickets are sold at a raffle. Harvey bought 4. What is his chance of winning as a:

a percentage? ______ **b** fraction? ☐
c decimal? ______

8 Complete each pattern.
a 0·2, 0·8, 1·4, ____, ____, ____, ____
b 0·3, 0·6, 0·9, ____, ____, ____, ____

9 The value of the 9 in 4657·97. ______

10 (4 × 900) + (3 × 600) = ______

11

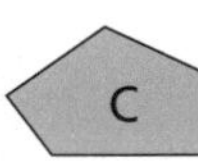

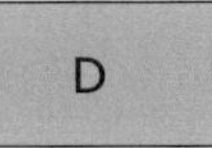

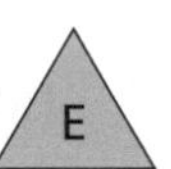

a Which shapes are regular? ______
b Which shapes have all angles obtuse? ______

17:4 ☐ out of 6

Extension

1 What is the smallest number of matchsticks needed to make:

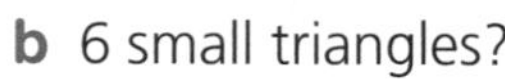

a 7 small hexagons? ______
b 6 small triangles? ______

2 The number of faces plus the number of corners minus the number of edges on 19 triangular prisms. ______

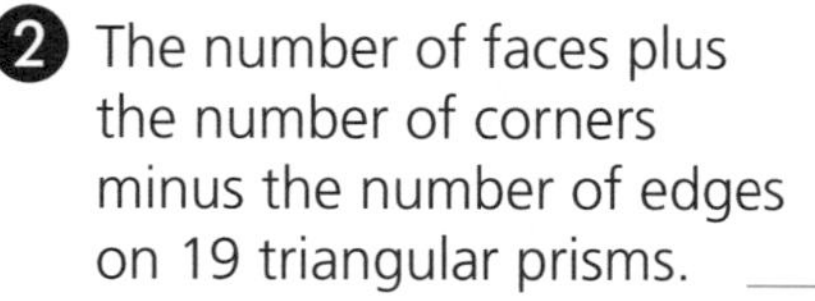

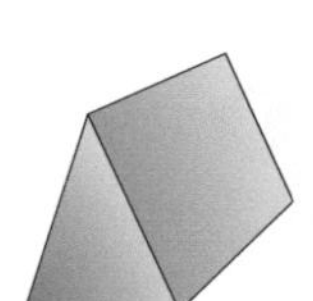

3 I used square pieces of wood 8 cm long to construct open cubes. How many open cubes could I make using 127 of the square pieces? ______

4 True or false?

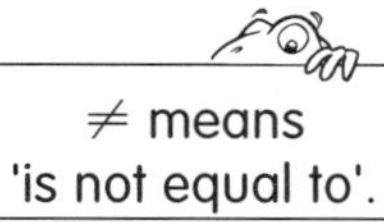

a 0·60 ≠ 0·06 ______
b 0·70 = $\frac{7}{10}$ ______

5 I stands for 1, V stands for 5, X stands for 10 L stands for 50 and C stands for 100.
Write the number for:

a LXXXI ______ **b** CLXII ______
c CCXVI ______ **d** CCVI ______

6 If # stands for 887·978 and ~ stands for 168·99, what is 9 × (# + ~) − (2 × ~). ______

Challenge

Write questions that are equal to:

a 987 765 + 786 543	**b** 987 675 + 235 432
= ______	= ______
= ______	= ______
= ______	= ______
= ______	= ______
= ______	= ______

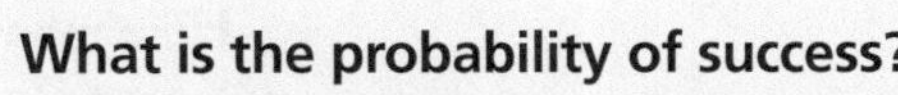

Chance

What is the probability of success?

Estimate the place for each letter and write it above the scale.

A The next baby born in Melbourne will be a girl.
B It will rain tomorrow.
C I will go to the movies next month.
D I will get a 6 if I throw a dice once.
E Our teacher will become prime minister tomorrow.

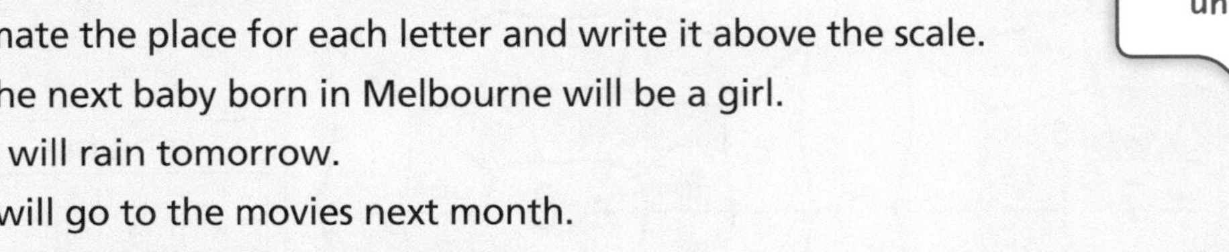

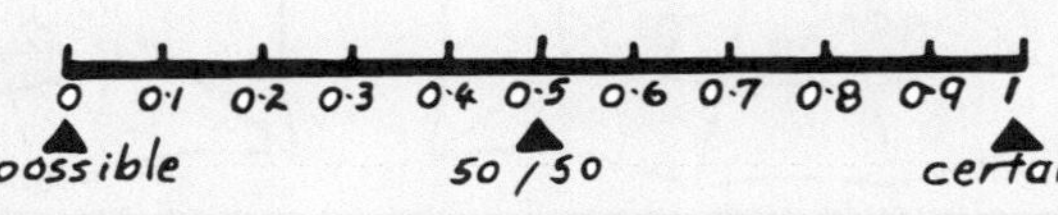

© PEARSON AUSTRALIA 2024 • *AUSTRALIAN SIGNPOST MATHS NSW 6 MENTALS* • ISBN 978 0 6557 0913 8

18:1 ☐ out of 16

1. 18 ÷ 3 ____
2. 42 ÷ 6 ____
3. 18 ÷ 2 − 7 ____
4. 0·7 × 100 ____
5. 354657 + 36509
6. 40 ÷ 10 + 76 ____
7. 36 divided by 6. ____
8. $\frac{1}{3}$ of 63 ____
9. 7 × $93 ____
10. 809780 − 47293

11. For this spinner, which colour's chance of occurring is:

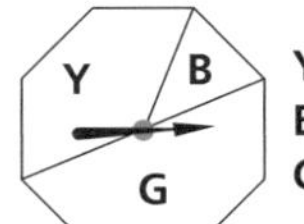

Y = yellow
B = blue
G = green

   a least likely? ____
   b an even chance? ____
   c a 50% chance? ____
   d a $\frac{1}{8}$ chance? ____
12. How many 20c coins have the same value as $5.40? ____
13. Five friends shared 3657 mL of water. How much water did each get? ____
14. Heidi began with $30 and bought these items.

$2.80 $1.70 $1.40

Total spent = ____

Amount left = ____

15. a $\frac{4}{6} + \frac{1}{6}$ ____ b $\frac{10}{12} - \frac{5}{12}$ ____
16. Write 8:23 am using 24-hour time. ____

18:2 ☐ out of 15

1. 820 ÷ 9 ____
2. $\frac{1}{9}$ of 45 ____
3. 0·8 × 100 ____
4. $\frac{3}{4}$ of 80 ____
5. 400000 − 89977
6. 467 + 635 = ____ + 640
7. 587 − 227 = ____ − 30
8. $645 − 80c ____
9. $56.30 − $5.85 ____
10. $8000·00 −$7987·90

11. Two heads, two tails, or a head and a tail could result from tossing two coins. What is the most likely result? ____
12. Which letter has a 25% chance that the spinner will land on it? ____

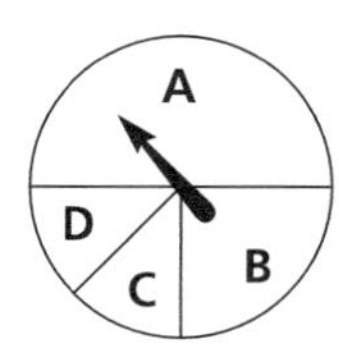

13.

Income	Gabby	Priscilla	Ilya
Mowing lawns	$30	0	$10
Babysitting	0	$28	$12
Washing cars	$18	$8	$12
Odd jobs	$16	$23	$25
TOTAL	$ ____	$ ____	$ ____

   a How much was earned by Gabby, Priscilla and Ilya altogether? ____
   b Round this total to the nearest ten dollars. ____
14. Find the total of these amounts, rounded off to the nearest 5 cents. ____

$ 5.30
$ 9.00
$ 2.50
$ 8.26

15. 63 ÷ (16 − 7) = ____

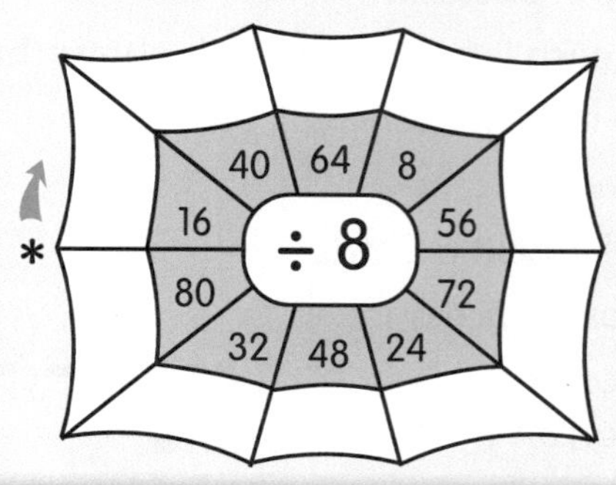

© PEARSON AUSTRALIA 2024 • AUSTRALIAN SIGNPOST MATHS NSW 6 MENTALS • ISBN 978 0 6557 0913 8

Answers

ID card answers

ID card A

1 millimetres **2** centimetres **3** metres **4** kilometres **5** scale **6** grams **7** kilograms **8** tonnes **9** millilitres **10** litres **11** square centimetres **12** square metres **13** 1 square metre **14** hectares **15** 10 000 m^2 **16** square kilometres **17** cubic centimetres **18** 1 cm^3 **19** 1 mL **20** cubic metres **21** seconds **22** minutes **23** hours **24** before noon **25** after noon **26** 5:40 am **27** 19:30 **28** degrees Celsius **29** thermometer **30** tape measure

ID card B

1 integers **2** prime number **3** composite number **4** 7 **5** 2 and 4 **6** 5 **7** remainder **8** square numbers **9** digits **10** 4 ones, 3 tenths, 9 hundredths, 5 thousandths **11** 19 out of 100 **12** vertical line **13** horizontal line **14** interval **15** ray **16** parallel lines **17** perpendicular lines **18** corner **19** arm of an angle **20** acute angle **21** right angle **22** obtuse angle **23** straight angle **24** reflex angle **25** revolution **26** 90° **27** 180° **28** 360° **29** A = C, B = D **30** protractor

ID card C

1 circle **2** oval **3** triangle **4** square **5** rectangle **6** rhombus **7** parallelogram **8** trapezium **9** kite **10** quadrilateral **11** pentagon **12** hexagon **13** octagon **14** regular shapes **15** irregular shapes **16** diagonals **17** axis of symmetry **18** cubic centimetres **19** rotational symmetry **20** tessellation **21** reflection **22** translation **23** rotation **24** coordinates **25** number plane **26** P = W + W + L + L (or P = 2W + 2L) **27** A = L × W **28** A = S^2 **29** rectangle **30** area = base × height

ID card D

1 face **2** corner or vertex **3** edge **4** cube **5** rectangular prism **6** triangular prism **7** hexagonal prism **8** triangular pyramid **9** square pyramid **10** rectangular pyramid **11** base **12** cylinder **13** cone **14** sphere **15** net of a cube **16** net of a cone **17** net of a cylinder **18** net of a square pyramid **19** cross-section **20** picture graph **21** tally **22** column graph **23** line graph **24** dot plot **25** sector graph **26** divided bar graph **27** median **28** mode **29** range **30** average

1:1

1 54 **2** 9 **3** $18 **4** 4 **5** 8048 **6** 667 **7** 21 **8** 3 **9** 1 **10** 8506 **11** a $\frac{1}{6}$ b $\frac{4}{6}$ **12** 49 300 000 **13** $\frac{4}{8}$ or $\frac{1}{2}$ **14** a 48% b 29% **15** a 32, 36, 40, 44 b 24, 27, 30, 33 c 37, 42, 47, 52 **16** 12 **17** a 2 m 56 cm b 4·6 cm c 4000 g d 4·75 kg **18** $175

1:2

1 8 **2** $42 **3** 551 **4** 43 **5** 5706 **6** 9 **7** $32 **8** 386 g **9** 50 mL **10** 26 540 **11** 6500 **12** $\frac{8}{12} - \frac{1}{3} = \frac{8}{12} - \frac{4}{12} = \frac{4}{12}$ **13** a 0·51, 0·5, 0·49 b subtract 0·01 **14** 4 × 164 = (4 × 100) + (4 × 60) + (4 × 4) = 400 + 240 + 16 = 656 **15** $6.30 or 630c **16** a 1200 b 1200 c 1500 d 4200 **17** $5\frac{4}{6}, 5\frac{5}{6}, 5\frac{6}{6}$ (or 6) **18** 300 minutes **19** $\frac{9}{10}$ **20** 68%

Activity

26, 79, 20, 44, 33, 55, 31, 42, 47, 58
28, 81, 22, 46, 35, 57, 33, 44, 49, 60
even + odd = odd
odd + odd = even

1:3

1 108 **2** 127 **3** 167 **4** 745 321 **5** 7, 14, 21, 28, 35, 42 **6** 97 774 421 **7** 40 **8** 6 **9** 36 m^2 **10** 67 – 45 = 62 – 40 = 22 **11** 5 square kilometres **12** 1, 2, 3, 4, 6, 12 **13** 60 squares will be coloured red, and 30 squares will be coloured blue. $\frac{90}{100}$ or $\frac{9}{10}$ **14** a 376 b 699 c 999 **15** 36 **16** a 155, 145, 135 b 40, 48, 56, 64 **17** 77 **18** 9

1:4

1 135th **2** a 64 × 3 = 192 b 3)387 = 129 **3** 810 **4** a 160 b 460 c 35 460 **5** 24 **6** $\frac{15}{24}$ **7** a 7 b 9 **8** a 5 b 9

Challenge

Answers may vary. E.g. It has 5 digits. It becomes 43·83 when rounded to the nearest hundredth.

Activity

Answers will vary.

2:1

1 6 **2** 18 **3** 80 **4** 100 **5** 8912 **6** 222 **7** 10 **8** $28 **9** 4 **10** 7160 **11** 24 **12** 5:56 am **13** $15 will be circled. **14** Answers will vary. **15** 8 781 344, 8 780 033, 8 768 367 **16** 46 400 **17** 35 483 **18** a 5 L b 7300 mL c 7·365 km d 5538 mL **19** a 36, 42, 48, 54 b 42, 49, 56, 63

2:2

1 32 **2** 30 **3** 5 **4** 5 **5** 2816 **6** 109 **7** 409 **8** $72 **9** 9 **10** 11 253 **11** $\frac{1}{6}$ **12** 52 000 000 **13** $\frac{65}{100}$ **14** nine million, seven hundred and fifty-six thousand. **15** a 49 squares will be shaded. b 51 **16** 2·63 **17** a 3 b 9 **18** a 250 cm b 25 mm **19** 24 m

Activity

60, 56, 85, 93, 88, 71, 85, 67, 39, 72
58, 48, 63, 41, 79, 86, 78, 65, 77, 70
even – even = even
odd – even = odd

2:3

1 109 **2** 203 **3** 96 **4** 2456 **5** a 6·09 b 19·3 **6** 137 **7** 9 o'clock and 3 o'clock **8** 16 cm **9** 16:03 **10** a 1300 mL or 1 L 300 mL b 700 mL **11** 2 hundreds, 0 tens, 1 one, 7 tenths, 9 hundredths **12** a $\frac{3}{4}$ b $\frac{1}{4}$

2:4

1 a 10 b 12 **2** 5 **3** 9 **4** a $870 b $1044 **5** a 435 + 297 = 432 + 300 = 732 b 824 – 392 = 822 – 390 = 432 c 725 – 409 = 726 – 410 = 316 **6** a 81 b 486

Challenge

Answers will vary.
E.g. 30 + 6 = 36, 42 – 6 = 36, 3 × 12 = 36, etc.

Activity

(1) face (2) corner or vertex (3) edge (12) cylinder (13) cone (14) sphere (15) net of a cube (16) net of a cone (17) net of a cylinder (18) net of a square pyramid

3:1

1 20 **2** 15 **3** 3 **4** 4 **5** 2919 **6** 141 **7** 864 **8** 40
9 $62 **10** 16 126 **11** **a** G = 8, S = 12, B = 16 **b** Bronze **c** 8
12 46 m **13** **a** C **b** A **14** 7 050 321

3:2

1 25 **2** $496 **3** 3 **4** 4 **5** 8280 **6** 178 **7** $56

8 6 **9** 7 **10** 50 776

11 **a**

3:04 am

b

7:22 pm

12 36 **13** 87 – 35 = 92 – 40 = 52 **14** **a** 3:02 pm **b** 5:39 pm
c 7:53 am **d** 4:28 am

15

Pentagons	1	2	3	4	5
Sides	5	**10**	**15**	**20**	**25**

16 15 **17** 45 **18** 171

Activity

8, 40, 24, 80, 56, 32, 64, 16, 72, 48
5, 25, 15, 50, 35, 20, 40, 10, 45, 30

3:3

1 166 **2** 117 r 6 **3** 94 **4** 32 **5** 14 **6** 75 **7** 16·25
8 1·2, 0·99, 0·8, 0·67 **9** true **10** 56
11

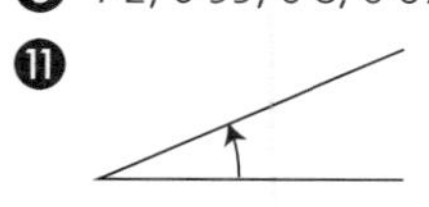

acute

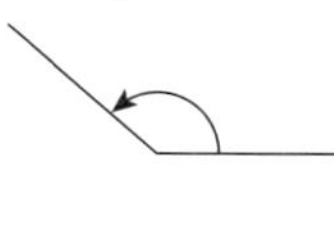

obtuse

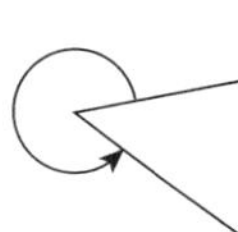

reflex

12 4002·21 **13** 2 033 469

3:4

1 44 407 kg **2** **a** 10 min **b** 20 min **3** 2 **4** 5 **5** 5
6 1281

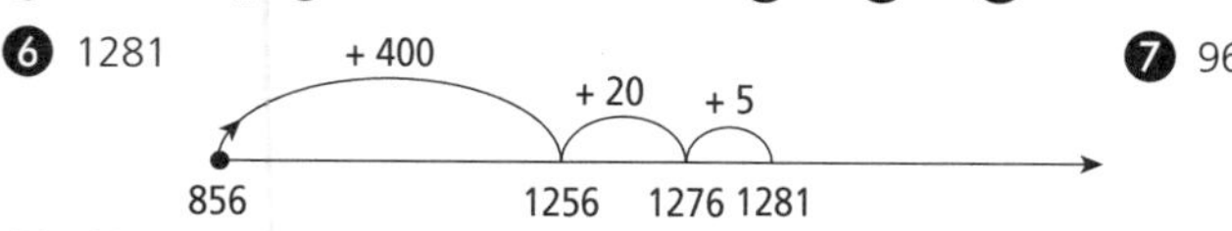

7 964

Challenge

Answers may vary.
E.g. **a** 740 + 276, 808 + 208, etc. **b** 204 + 447, 300 + 351, etc.
c 3000 + 5360, 2678 + 5682, etc.

Activity

a $37.45 **b** $43.90 **c** $30.00 **d** $84.65 **e** $117.10 **f** $265.15
g $630.95 **h** $365.30 **i** $289.10 **j** $836.35

4:1

1 16 **2** 32 **3** 4 **4** 8 **5** 8027 **6** 796 **7** 30 **8** 50 **9** 846
10 18 624 **11** 1, 3, 5, and 15. **12** 6, 12, 18, 24, 30, 36, 42, 48, 54, 60
13 **a** 16 **b** 64 **14** one share = 3 **15** **a** 9 **b** 7 **16** 80 eggs **17** 35
18 85 cm **19** 3 000 000 **20** 6 tenths or 0·6 **21** 0·51 **22** 4

4:2

1 25 **2** 2 **3** 9 **4** 27 **5** 5608 **6** 40 **7** 72 **8** 240 **9** 300
10 59 704 **11** 9 **12** **a** 7 **b** 7 **13** 7 **14** 2625 mL or 2·625 L **15** 36
16 **a** 24 **b** 8 **17** 480 **18** **a** 1 **b** 2 **19** **a** 0·3 **b** $\frac{3}{10}$
20 3, 4, and 6 will be circled.

Activity

124, 116, 174, 190, 180, 146, 174, 138, 82, 148
208, 96, 324, 196, 212, 272, 296, 392, 228, 184

4:3

1 109 **2** 271 **3** 181 **4** 73 **5** 1, 24, 2, 12, 3, 8, 4 and 6.
6 8, 16, 24, 32, 40, 48, 56, 64, 72, 80 **7** **a** 9 **b** 81 **8** 6 **9** 18
10 **a** 7 **b** 7 **11** **a** 14 cm or 0·14 m **b** 96·81 kg **12** 9
13 14, 12, 9 and 7.

4:4

1 72 and 73. **2** 115 **3** 25 h 15 min **4** 4 **5** 5036 g or 5·036 kg
6 **a** 30 **b** 36 **7** 39

Challenge

Answers will vary.
E.g. **a** 900 – 289, 614 – 3, etc. **b** 700 – 302, 474 – 76, etc.
c 7159 – 4000, 7659 – 4500, etc.

Activity

762, 126, 103, 434, 169, 231, 150, 79, 768, 147
164, 933, 100, 355, 947, 854, 642, 71, 659, 778
even + even = even
odd + even = odd

5:1

1 21 **2** $12 **3** 3 **4** 5 **5** 993 **6** 4 **7** 4 **8** 35 **9** 70
10 7944 **11** 1, 12, 2, 6, 3 and 4. **12** 3 **13** 6 **14** **a** 12 **b** 4
15 31 763 116, 33 761 301, 37 631 713 **16** **a** cylinder **b** cone
17 20 **18** 100 **19** 9 **20** 98% **21** 7277

5:2

1 54 **2** $\frac{2}{6}$ or $\frac{1}{3}$ **3** $5 **4** 9 **5** 8753 **6** 25 **7** 45 **8** $9
9 900 **10** 17 670 **11** 7, 14, 21, 28, 35, 42, 49, 56, 63, 70
12 **a** 4 groups 2 left **b** 5 groups 1 left **13** **a** 7 **b** 9 **14** **a** 8 **b** 6
15 **a** 700 **b** 1200 **16** 420 cm or 4·2 m **17** 8
18

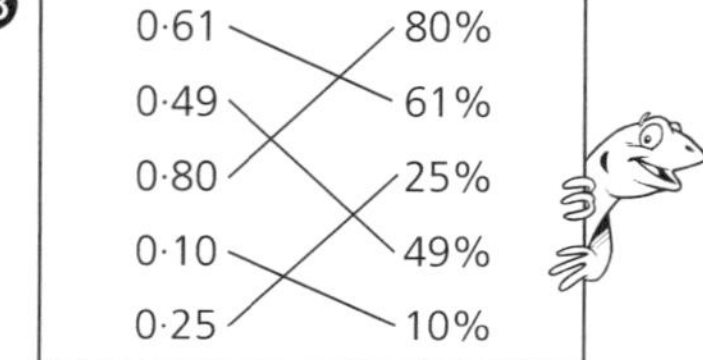

Activity

a 20% **b** 12%

© PEARSON AUSTRALIA 2024 • *AUSTRALIAN SIGNPOST MATHS NSW 6 MENTALS* • ISBN 978 0 6557 0913 8

5:3

1 144 **2** 309 **3** 102 r 5 **4** 9063 **5** 32 599
6 Books each = 5, Remainder = 2 **7** 1, 2, 3, 4, 6, 9, 12, 18, and 36.
8 **a** 7 **b** 7 **9** **a** 15 and 60 **b** 1 and 49 **10** 15 **11** $396
12 **a** 4208 **b** 4734 **13** 114 + 425 = 539 or □ + 114 = 539.
14 1% **15** **a** 1 **b** 2

5:4

1 16 **2** $2^2 + 3^2 + 4^2$ **3** **a** 14 **b** 36 **4** 110 **5** 40
6 **a** yes **b** no **7** $83.10 **8** 294 **9** 370

Challenge

Answers will vary.

Activity

	$\frac{3}{10}$	$\frac{30}{100}$	0·3	30%
	$\frac{6}{10}$	$\frac{60}{100}$	0·6	60%

The shaded part is 70%.

6:1

1 47 **2** 4 **3** 6 **4** 4 **5** 6342 **6** 10 **7** 33 **8** 54 **9** 47
10 4269
11

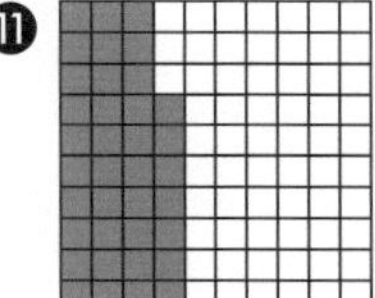

0·37	$\frac{37}{100}$	37%

12 67 747 324, 67 647 324, 67 541 234 **13** 95 747 013 **14** 35 000 000
15 **a** 24 **b** 43 **16** rectangle **17** obtuse angle **18** 18
19 4·8, 4·5, 4·25

6:2

1 37 **2** 36 **3** 8 **4** 6 **5** 1877 **6** $\frac{5}{12}$ **7** 532 **8** 162
9 162 **10** 14 588 **11** 600 000 **12** 76 out of 100 = $\frac{76}{100}$ = 0·76 = 76%
13 53 803 **14** reflection **15** 1, 42, 2, 21, 3, 14, 6 and 7.
16 73 000 000 **17** **a** 12 **b** 29 **18** A **19** A was reflected.

Activity

a 6 **b** 4 **c** 16 **d** 4 **e** 17 **f** 17 **g** 4 **h** 16 **i** 12 **j** 16 **k** 63

6:3

1 46 **2** 156 **3** 68 r 3 **4** 2137 **5** 19 045 **6** 8
7

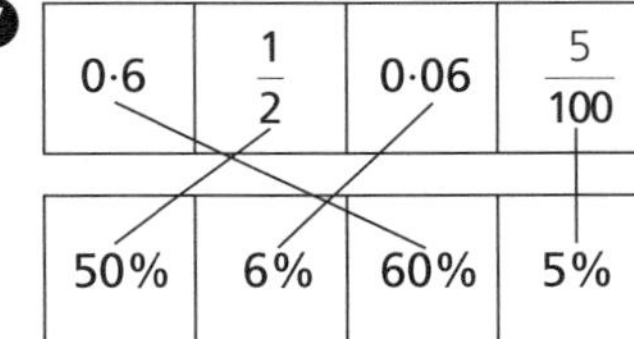

0·6	$\frac{1}{2}$	0·06	$\frac{5}{100}$

50%	6%	60%	5%

8 **a** B **b** A **9** 56 499 **10** 89 000 000 **11** **a** 5 **b** 13
12 A was translated to the right. **13** 4 tenths or 0·4 **14** 56·35

6:4

1 **a** 7 equal sides **b** 3 equal angles **2** **a** yes **b** yes **3** 1470
4 1502 **5** **a** 20 cm **b** 60 cm

Challenge

Answers will vary.

Activity

1 4, 16, 100, 36, 81, and 49.
2 **a** 4, 16, 100, 36, and 14. **b** 45, 100, and 35.
c 21, 35, 49, and 14.

7:1

1 27 **2** 28 **3** 25 **4** 42 **5** 10 052 **6** 28 **7** 3 **8** 50
9 1 **10** 20 652 **11** **a** 0·59 **b** 0·857 **12** **a** 16 **b** 9 **13** $\frac{3}{2}$
14 **a** 72% **b** 9%
15

16 **a** 70° **b** acute **17** 04:53

7:2

1 7 **2** 99 **3** 5 **4** 40 **5** 5408 **6** 162 **7** 475 **8** $79
9 29 **10** 8296 **11** **a** 60% **b** 30% **12** 96 408 **13** **a** 1 **b** 0
14 4·11, 4·142, 4·4142, 4·444 **15** **a** 0·892 **b** 0·46 **16** **a** 64 **b** 36
17 $\frac{7}{5}, 1\frac{2}{5}$ **18** square pyramid **19** **a** 35% **b** 25%

Activity

a 7 **b** 8 and 3 **c** 14

7:3

1 312 **2** 68 **3** 65 **4** True **5** 92 485 **6** **a** 81 **b** 49
7

8

Number of years	1	2	3	4	5
Number of months	12	24	36	48	60

a *number of years* × 12 **b** 360

9 **a**

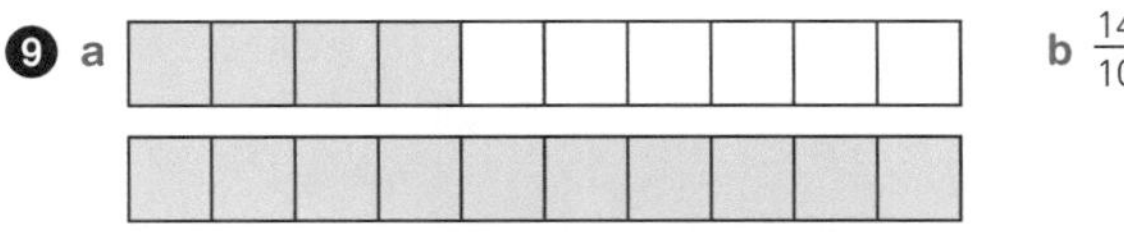

b $\frac{14}{10}$

10 $\frac{5}{4}$ **11** **a** 56% **b** $\frac{56}{100}$

7:4

1 49, 16, and 49 – 13 will be circled.
2 **a** $\frac{1}{10}$ **b** 0·1 **c** 10% **d** 90% **3** D **4** **a** C **b** B **c** D **d** E **5** D

Challenge

Answers will vary.

Activity

a 10 o'clock **b** no **c** no **d** no

8:1

❶ 22 ❷ 48 ❸ 39 ❹ 71 ❺ 5954 ❻ 8 ❼ 37 ❽ $88 ❾ 9
❿ 9280 ⓫ 45% ⓬ **a** 25 **b** 36 ⓭ square (or rectangular) pyramid
⓮ 0·78 ⓯ $6\frac{1}{3}$ ⓰ −17°C ⓱ **a** 10 **b** Rachel **c** Heather

8:2

❶ 80 ❷ 27 ❸ 27 ❹ $\frac{17}{10}$ or $1\frac{7}{10}$ ❺ 10 456 ❻ −7, −6
❼ 134 ❽ 44 ❾ $90 ❿ 21 632 ⓫ 78 318
⓬ 1, 4, 9, 16, 25, 36, 49, 64, 81, 100
⓭ **a** 83% **b** 0·83 ⓮ 12 ⓯ $\frac{7}{4}$ ⓰ −19°C
⓱ 1, 56, 2, 28, 4, 14, 7 and 8. ⓲ 12

⓳

Squares	1	2	3	4	5
Sides	4	8	**12**	**16**	**20**

⓴ −4, −3, −2, −1, 0

Activity

a 25 **b** 9 **c** 100 **d** 16 **e** 64 **f** 1 **g** 81 **h** 4 **i** 36

8:3

❶ 149 ❷ 175 r 2 ❸ 118 ❹ $3\frac{4}{5}$ ❺ 27 671
❻ 68, Rule: 1st number + 15 ❼ −8, −2, 0, 2, 4 ❽ 25, 36, 49, 64
❾ **a** 70% **b** 10% **c** 7% **d** 1% ❿ 807, <u>813</u>, 819, 825, <u>831</u>, 837
⓫ 17 ⓬ −0·8, −0·6, −0·4, −0·2, 0
⓭ −23°C ⓮ 1, 81, 3, 27 and 9. ⓯ **a** 0·38 **b** 38% ⓰ 242

8:4

❶ 25 ❷ **a** 12 **b** 15 ❸ **a** 21 cm **b** 84 cm

❹

□	15	25	35	44	54
△	54	64	74	83	93

❺ **a** 13 and 16 **b** 89

Challenge

Answers may vary. See ID card D, Cards 4–14 for examples.

Activity

a 21 **b** 2 **c** 0 **d** 18 **e** 11 **f** 3 **g** 25 **h** 7 **i** 48 **j** 2 **k** 24

9:1

❶ 77 ❷ 132 ❸ 60 ❹ 43 ❺ 2926 ❻ 10 ❼ 69 ❽ $9
❾ 5 ❿ $26 840
⓫ −20%, −15%, −10%, −5%, 0 ⓬ −12°C
⓭ **a** $105 **b** $465
⓮ The diagonal lines will be traced over in red. Two of the horizontal lines will be traced over in blue.

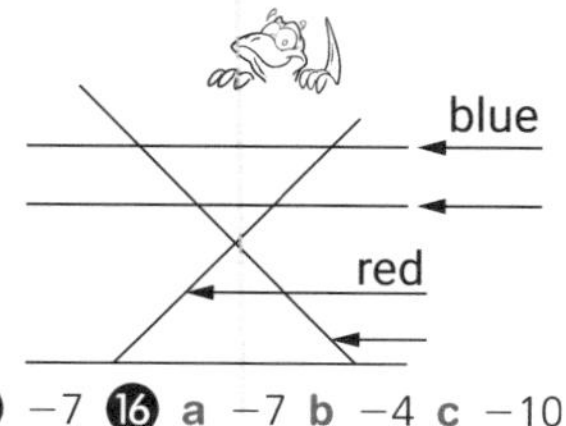

⓯ −7 ⓰ **a** −7 **b** −4 **c** −10

9:2

❶ 9 ❷ $9 ❸ 76 ❹ $243 ❺ $8373 ❻ 165 ❼ 52 ❽ 356
❾ −2 ❿ $19 428 ⓫ 63 929 ⓬ −49°C
⓭ **a** 10 **b** Monday and Thursday ⓮ **a** A and B **b** E and D
⓯ −9, −7, −2, 4, 8 ⓰ $4\frac{4}{5}$ ⓱ $0{\cdot}29 = 29\% = \frac{29}{100}$ ⓲ 53

Activity

(16) parallel lines (17) perpendicular lines (18) corner (19) arm of an angle (20) acute angle (21) right angle (22) obtuse angle (23) straight angle (24) reflex angle (25) revolution

9:3

❶ 121 ❷ 324 r 1 ❸ 46 ❹ 3
❺ **a** 4 > −5 **b** −8 < 3 **c** −3 > −21 **d** −7 < −1
❻

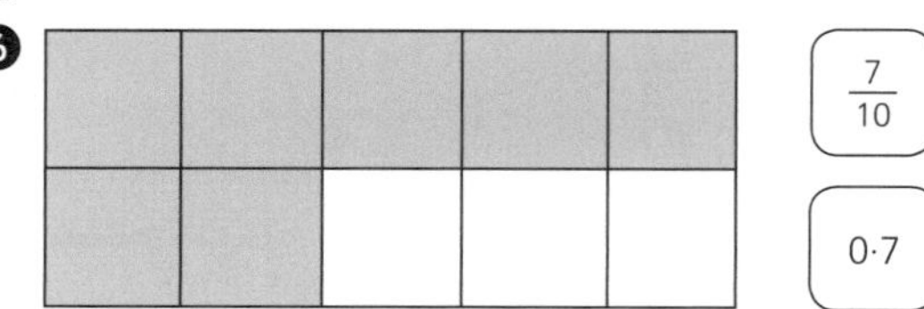

❼ **a** $\frac{20}{100}$ or $\frac{1}{5}$ **b** 27% **c** 120 ❽ **a** 0·51 **b** 51% ❾ **a** 3 squares will be coloured red. **b** 4 squares will be coloured blue. **c** no

9:4

❶ 4020 min ❷ 8 ❸ **a** B and C. **b** A, B, C, and D. ❹ 74 ❺ 70°
❻ 11 ❼ 8 ❽ Yes ❾ 76

Challenge

Answers will vary. E.g. 40 + 16, 7^2 + 7, etc.

Activity

23, 14, 47, 29·5, 35·5, 29, 18, 21, 27, 36
18, 15, 23·5, 24, 17, 19, 13, 12, 14, 16

10:1

❶ 50 ❷ 11 ❸ 7 ❹ 25 ❺ 7939 ❻ 600 ❼ 250 ❽ 158
❾ 8 ❿ 24 188
⓫ **a** There are 6 possible answers (see pairs of dots below) **b** There are 2 possible answers (see pairs of dots below)

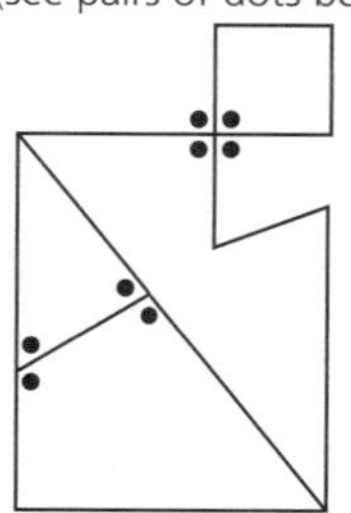
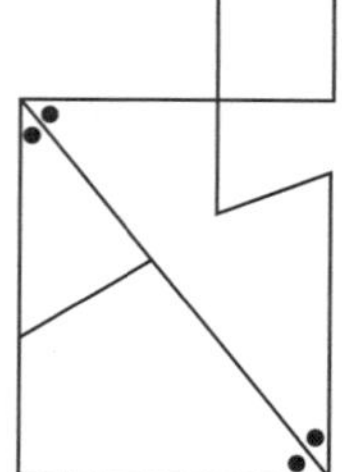

⓬ 56 350 356, 56 480 093, 56 798 453
⓭ 3/5

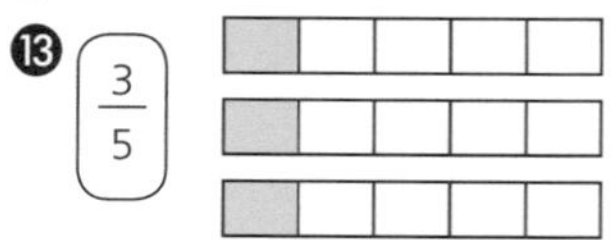

⓮ **a** 3 **b** 5 ⓯ **a** −2 **b** 1 **c** −5 ⓰ 503 054 ⓱ 3

© PEARSON AUSTRALIA 2024 • *AUSTRALIAN SIGNPOST MATHS NSW 6 MENTALS* • ISBN 978 0 6557 0913 8

10:2

❶ 902 ❷ 680 ❸ 12 ❹ 6 ❺ 50 178 ❻ $3 ❼ 281 ❽ 27
❾ 22 ❿ $42 399 ⓫ 180° ⓬ **a** 135° **b** 50°
⓭ **a** About 22¥ **b** About 52¥ **c** About 46c **d** About 69c
⓮ **a**

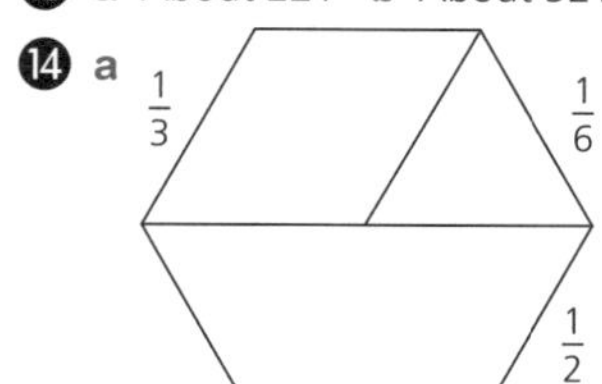

b yes **c** no

⓯ **a** 3 **b** 4

Activity

(1) integers (2) prime number (3) composite number (4) 7 (5) 2 and 4 (7) remainder (8) square numbers (9) digits (10) 4 ones, 3 tenths, 9 hundredths, 5 thousandths

10:3

❶ 124 ❷ 121 ❸ 94 ❹ 34 067 ❺ $3\frac{1}{2}$
❻ **a** $-3 > -7$ **b** $6 > -5$ **c** $0 > -1$ **d** $-10 < -8$
❼ **a** 0 **b** 1 **c** $-1\frac{1}{2}$ ❽ **a** 12 **b** 20 **c** 18 **d** 16 ❾ **a** 142° **b** 55°
❿ **a** −40% **b** 0% **c** −100% ⓫ 67 864 ⓬ 15:27

10:4

❶ 8 ❷ 156 BCE ❸ 26 ❹ **a** 260 **b** 10 ❺ 240
❻ **a** 9 **b** 12 **c** 150

Challenge

Answers may vary. E.g. This is an acute angle. Its size is between 0° and 90°. An open pair of scissors might have an acute angle.

Activity

41, 15, 18, 30, 5, 39, 14, 36, 23, 57
15, 42, 55, 43, 21, 34, 24, 30, 9, 29
even – odd = odd
odd – odd = even

11:1

❶ 240 ❷ 270 ❸ 132 ❹ 6 ❺ 4921 ❻ 2400 ❼ 1500
❽ 72 ❾ $\frac{7}{9}$ ❿ 4212 ⓫ $\frac{6}{10}$, 0·6 ⓬ $1800
⓭ **a** 6 **b** 12 **c** 3 **d** 15 ⓮ **a** 45° **b** 60° ⓯ 1111
⓰ 48 265 980, 48 376 098, 48 576 386 ⓱ 5:23 am

11:2

❶ 1400 ❷ 70 ❸ 90 ❹ 919 ❺ 7343 ❻ 64 ❼ $\frac{2}{10}$ or $\frac{1}{5}$ ❽ 88
❾ 115 ❿ 30 952 ⓫ **a** 6 **b** 3 **c** 15 **d** yes ⓬ $17.70 ⓭ **a** 55° **b** 125° ⓮ 57·521, 57·352, 57·239 ⓯ 0·007 or 7 thousands
⓰ $3\frac{3}{4}$ ⓱ $\frac{3}{4}$

Activity

6, 21, 12, 18, 3, 30, 27, 9, 24, 15
12, 42, 24, 36, 6, 60, 54, 18, 48, 30

11:3

❶ 194 ❷ 78 ❸ 34 ❹ 1652 ❺ **a** 25° **b** 95°
❻ 91·711, 91·709, 91·699 ❼ **a** 4 **b** 12 **c** 2 **d** 14 ❽ −2°C
❾ 600 000 ❿ 367 ⓫ **a** 7·686 **b** 465·78
⓬ 9 teams of six, with 5 children remaining.

11:4

❶ **a** $2.75 **b** $46.75 ❷ 5 weeks
❸ 800 m ❹ **a** 20 **b** $16\frac{1}{2}$
❺ ❻ 9

Challenge

Answers will vary.
E.g. $5^2 + 5^2 + 50$, $164 - (8 \times 8)$, etc.

Activity

a 1500 **b** 5600 **c** 2400 **d** 2500 **e** 4500 **f** 5000 **g** 4000 **h** 12 000 **i** 2500 **j** 640 000

12:1

❶ 93 ❷ 1 ❸ 48 ❹ 56 ❺ 8644 ❻ 60 ❼ 10 ❽ 81 ❾ 53
❿ 5120 ⓫ 768 L ⓬ 676 000 000 ⓭ **a** 82 576 354 < 82 586 739 **b** 98 735 089 < 98 735 900 ⓮ **a** 130° **b** 90°
⓯ **a** 108 **b** 77 **c** 6000 ⓰ **a** 6000 **b** 14 000 **c** 970 **d** 18 000 **e** 670 **f** 6000

12:2

❶ 536 ❷ 440 ❸ 536 ❹ $\frac{7}{6}$ or $1\frac{1}{6}$ ❺ 5622 ❻ 700 ❼ 63
❽ 1134 ❾ 439 ❿ 14 686 ⓫ **a** 310° **b** 145°
⓬ **a** 6 after 4 **b** 28 to 10
⓭ **a** $1\frac{2}{3}$ **b** $\frac{5}{3}$ ⓮ **a** 140° **b** 125° ⓯ 46 ⓰ North

Activity

2, 6, 4, 8, 10, 5, 9, 3, 7, 1
3, 8, 5, 2, 7, 4, 1, 9, 6, 10

12:3

❶ 99 ❷ 32 ❸ 43 ❹ 1012 ❺ **a** 75° **b** 100° ❻ 2·688 L
❼ **a** 5 **b** 10 **c** 3 **d** 12 ❽ 1·1201, 1·2122, 1·2132, 2·12
❾ **a** 0·8 **b** 0·35 ❿ **a** 0·8 **b** 0·09 **c** 8·05 ⓫ 12·7 km

12:4

❶ 316 m ❷ 144 ❸ 6 ❹ **a** 2000 **b** 6000 **c** 10 000
❺ **a** Jiyu **b** 1601 m ❻ **a** 4 **b** 327

Challenge

Answers will vary.
E.g. $6 \times 8 \div 2$, $4^2 + 2^2 + (9 - 5)$, etc.

Activity

a 100 cm **b** 175 cm **c** 130 cm **d** 190 cm **e** 60 cm
Answers may vary. Here we measure from the base of the heel to the top of the head (not including hat or dog's ears, etc.)

13:1

1 2400 **2** 4000 **3** $\frac{5}{10}$ or $\frac{1}{2}$ **4** 618 **5** 153 180 **6** 214 **7** 56 **8** 266 **9** 96 **10** 382 496 **11** 335 **12** **a** about 20 m **b** east **c** south-westerly **d** Year 1 **13** south

13:2

1 200 **2** 60 **3** $3\frac{1}{4}$ **4** 9 **5** 46 391 **6** 133 **7** $\frac{5}{8}$ **8** 180 **9** 112 **10** 563 346 **11** 21 **12** **a** west **b** north-east **13** 112 000 **14** **a** 45° **b** 95° **15** **a** 700 **b** 17

Activity

1, 8, 5, 2, 7, 9, 3, 10, 6, 4

5, 1, 10, 6, 2, 8, 4, 7, 3, 9

□ = 8

□ = 8

13:3

1 73 r 2 **2** 189 r 2 **3** 52 r 8 **4** **a** 15·4 L **b** 2600 mL **5** **a** 1000 km **b** 3300 km **c** ACT, Tas, Vic, NSW, SA, NT, Qld, WA **6** 2·5 km **7** 102° **8** 12 **9** $1142.86 **10** 793·06 **11** 54 000 000

13:4

1 **a** 842 500 **b** 325 000 **2** **a** $34.80 **b** $2.90 **3** **a** 293 km **b** 330 km **4** 1 **5** around 1000 times (if I sleep for 8 hours). **6** 110°

Challenge

Answers may vary. E.g. the square is south-west of the star.

Activity

12, 42, 18, 48, 60, 36, 24, 54, 30, 0

18, 63, 27, 72, 90, 54, 36, 81, 45, 9

14:1

1 257 **2** $\frac{5}{6}$ **3** 422 **4** 5 **5** 8285 **6** 32 **7** 180 **8** 41 **9** 73 **10** 15 000 **11** **a** 12 r 1 **b** 8 r 6 **12** **a** north **b** 90° **13** **a** the person in the aisle **b** the exit **c** the spider **d** the movie screen **e** the audience

14:2

1 317 **2** 288 **3** $6\frac{2}{3}$ **4** 81 **5** 11 324 **6** 648 **7** $\frac{9}{6}$ or $1\frac{1}{2}$ **8** 1143 **9** 351 **10** 685 020 **11** **a** 5 r 2 **b** 6 r 3 **12** 812 mL **13** **a** and **b**

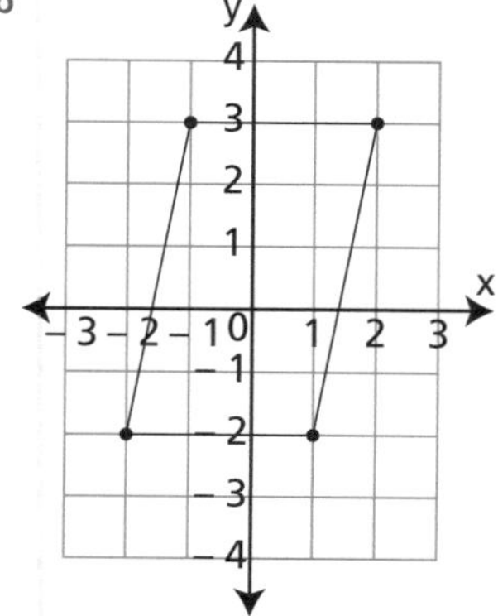

c parallelogram

14 $1643.50 **15** $17 845 **16** Approximately: **a** 216 km **b** 306 km **c** 360 km **d** 252 km **17** 87

Activity

(14) regular shapes (15) irregular shapes (16) diagonals (17) axis of symmetry (20) tessellation (21) reflection (22) translation (23) rotation (24) coordinates (25) number plane

14:3

1 72 r 3 **2** 100 r 4 **3** 37 r 6 **4** 132 r 3 **5** 71 r 1 **6** 101 r 1 **7** 90 **8** **a** the flower **b** the tree **9** 4 **10** **a** and **b**

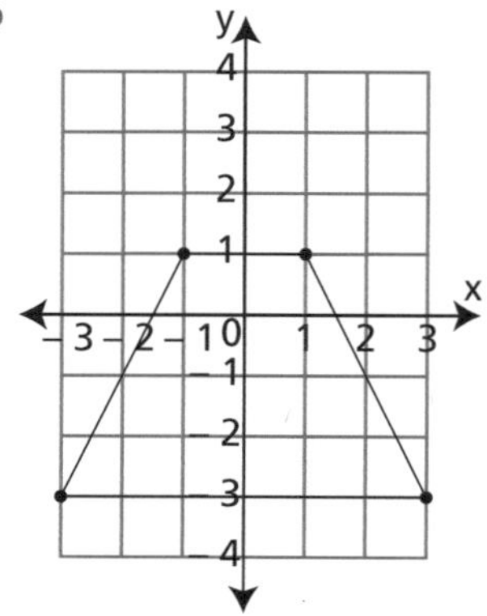

c trapezium

11 **a** 4 **b** 2 **12** **a** 6800 g **b** 6·7 cm

14:4

1 101 CE **2** **a** 45° **b** 135° **3** **a** $85 410 **b** $124 554 **4** (18 – 5) × 3 = 39 **5** 624

Challenge

Answers may vary. E.g. It is an eight-digit even number. It becomes 79 000 000 when rounded to the nearest million.

Activity

(4) square (5) rectangle (6) rhombus (7) parallelogram (8) trapezium (9) kite (10) quadrilaterals (11) pentagons (12) hexagons (13) octagon

15:1

1 96 **2** 2800 **3** 30 **4** 14 **5** $9451 **6** $4.57 **7** $4.80 **8** $0.30 **9** 1 **10** $5435 **11** 45° **12** **a** cylinder **b** sphere **13** **a** Our team total = 26, Our opposition total = 14 **b** $4\frac{2}{6}$ or $4\frac{1}{3}$ **c** $2\frac{2}{6}$ or $2\frac{1}{3}$ **d** 4 **14** **a** J **b** P **c** (1, 2) **d** (1, 1)

15:2

1 510 **2** 78 **3** 0 **4** $476 **5** 9470 **6** 67 **7** 163 **8** 137 **9** 72 **10** 29 192 **11** 72 cm **12** **a** 6 **b** 8 **13** 35 cm **14** 6 **15** **a** 90° **b** 135° **16** **a** A **b** E **c** (2, 2) **d** (3, 5)

Activity

a 9 m **b** 97 g **c** 606 **d** 6 **e** 63

15:3

1 **a** $8\frac{3}{5}$ **b** $4\frac{1}{4}$ **c** $139\frac{1}{6}$ **d** $195\frac{1}{2}$ **e** $60\frac{2}{3}$ **f** $73\frac{3}{5}$ **2** revolution **3** $1\frac{2}{6}$ or $1\frac{1}{3}$ **4** [pyramid] **a** 4 **b** 6 **c** 4 **5** 240 km **6** **a** B **b** I **c** (2, 2) **d** (−2, −4) **e** (−3, −3) **f** (−3, 4) **7** 18 995 **8** **a** $\frac{9}{4}$ **b** $\frac{18}{5}$ **9** 0·005 or 5 thousandths **10** 0·87

© PEARSON AUSTRALIA 2024 • *AUSTRALIAN SIGNPOST MATHS NSW 6 MENTALS* • ISBN 978 0 6557 0913 8

15:4

1 a $6\frac{1}{3}$ b 7 c $7\frac{1}{2}$ d $8\frac{1}{3}$ **2** 8185 mL or 8·185 L **3** $1169
4 $128 047.62 **5** 32 **6** 2·658 m²

Challenge

Answers will vary.
E.g. Group: $13, $84, $56, $17, $35
Average: $41

Activity

14, 42, 7, 28, 70, 49, 21, 63, 35, 56
16, 48, 8, 32, 80, 56, 24, 72, 40, 64

16:1

1 560 **2** 6 **3** 13 **4** 60 **5** 78 216 **6** 87 **7** 43 **8** 343
9 $\frac{7}{2}$ or $3\frac{1}{2}$ **10** 49 060 **11** $1\frac{2}{3}$ or $1\frac{4}{6}$ cucumbers **12** 120 km
13

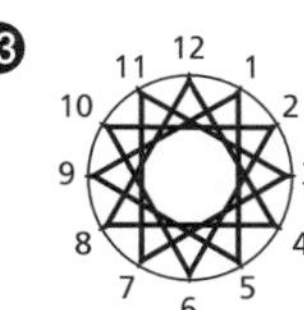

A 12-point star

14 a 6 b 12 **15** a triangular prism b triangle c H and E
d A, C, G, D and B

16:2

1 920 **2** 309 **3** 16 **4** 0 **5** 456 525 **6** $\frac{6}{12}$ or $\frac{1}{2}$ **7** 1292
8 3 **9** 40 **10** 378 949 **11** 23 km **12** 92 746
13 a The shape will be copied. b The shape will be copied.
14 A triangular prism has 5 faces, 9 edges, and 2 vertices.
15 a 178 110 b yes **16** 201 g **17** Cube and square pyramid, square prism.

Activity

1, 2, 3, 4, 5, 6, 7, 8, 9, 10
5, 8, 1, 10, 4, 6, 2, 9, 3, 7

16:3

1 a $8\frac{1}{7}$ b $18\frac{4}{5}$ c $231\frac{2}{3}$ d $115\frac{1}{2}$ e $79\frac{7}{8}$ f $39\frac{2}{10}$ **2** 73 868
3 91 153 **4** 2 km **5** $3\frac{2}{3}$ slices **6** 114 g **7** $366 550 **8** 57
9 A cube has 6 faces and 12 edges.
10 a

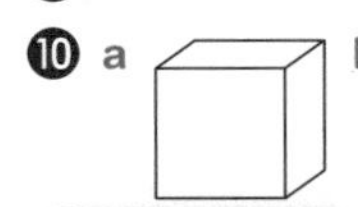

b

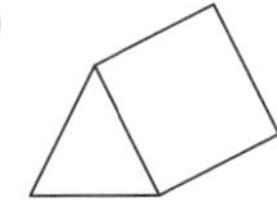

16:4

1 a 2 b 3 **2** 480 km **3** 15 **4** 130 **5** a 9044 b 17 550
6 90 **7** 17 h 18 min

Challenge

Answers will vary.
E.g. **Rule** = × 16 + 17

1st number	1	2	3	4	5	6	7
2nd number	33	49	65	81	97	113	129

Activity

a $12.50 b Loss of $7400 c Profit of $6870

17:1

1 562 **2** 48 **3** 9 **4** 9 **5** 535 502 **6** 181 **7** 60
8 630 **9** 25 **10** 780 670 **11** $1552
12 This is the net of a square pyramid. **13** a square
14 a $\frac{1}{10}$ b 0·1 c 10% **15** a no b Jessica **16** 1·4, 1·6, 1·8, 2·0
17 $\frac{19}{5}$ **18** a 5 b 12 **19** 0·006 or $\frac{6}{1000}$

17:2

1 5162 **2** 921 **3** 644 **4** 80 **5** 786 352 **6** 9 **7** $31
8 $\frac{8}{10}$ or $\frac{4}{5}$ **9** 65% **10** 873 522 **11** 85% **12** 840 km **13** 10 127 km
14 a Students will copy the shape. b 9 vertices c 9 faces d squares
15 This is the net of a cone. **16** a triangle **17** 0·09 or $\frac{9}{100}$

Activity

Answers will vary.
E.g. 2·5 kg of Apples + 1 kg of Pears + 1 Kiwi Fruit + 3 kg of Oranges + 0·5 kg of Bananas

17:3

1 4 213 213 **2** 864 025 **3** 2356 m **4** This is the net of a cube.
5 a hexagon **6** a $\frac{5}{10}$ or $\frac{1}{2}$ b 0·5 c 50%
7 a 4% b $\frac{4}{100}$ or $\frac{1}{25}$ c 0·04
8 a 2·0, 2·6, 3·2, 3·8 b 1·2, 1·5, 1·8, 2·1 **9** 0·9 or $\frac{9}{10}$ **10** 5400
11 a B and E. b B

17:4

1 a 30 (the hexagons will be attached in a group) b 12
2 95 + 114 – 171 = 38 **3** 25 **4** a true b true
5 a 81 b 162 c 216 d 206 **6** 9174·732

Challenge

Answers will vary.
a 988 308 + 795 000, 1 024 308 + 750 000, etc.
b 980 000 + 243 107, 1 173 107 + 50 000, etc.

Activity

a about 0·5 b about 0·1 c Estimates will vary. d about 0·17 e 0

18:1

1 6 **2** 7 **3** 2 **4** 70 **5** 391 166 **6** 80 **7** 6 **8** 21
9 $651 **10** 762 487 **11** a Blue b Green c Green d Blue **12** 27
13 $731\frac{2}{5}$ mL or 731·4 mL **14** Total spent = $5.90, Amount left = $24.10
15 a $\frac{5}{6}$ b $\frac{5}{12}$ **16** 08:23

18:2

1 $91\frac{1}{9}$ **2** 5 **3** 80 **4** 60 **5** 310 023 **6** 462 **7** 390
8 $644.20 **9** $50.45 **10** $12.10 **11** A head and a tail. **12** B
13 a $182 b $180 **14** $25.05 **15** 7

Activity

2, 6, 3, 9, 7, 4, 10, 8, 5, 1
2, 5, 8, 1, 7, 9, 3, 6, 4, 10
How many weeks? 4

18:3

1 13 841 429 **2** \$324.60 **3** **a** G **b** B or Y **4** 280 km

5 \$14.30 **6** **a** 18 **b** 41 **c** 59 **d** 0 **e** 1 **f** 6 **g** 11 **h** $\frac{1}{2}$ **i** $\frac{5}{2}$ or $2\frac{1}{2}$

7 Answers may vary. There is a skew towards the lower scores.

18:4

1 16 **2** **a** 19 cm **b** 57 cm **3** 1980 km **4** 769·5 km

5 **a** 156 **b** 386 **c** 116 **d** 277 **6** 33 h 11 min

Challenge

Answers will vary.

E.g.
There is a 50% chance of tossing a head on a coin.

Activity

Answers will vary.

E.g.
1500 g of Crumpets + 1200 g of Honey + 2000 g of Jam + 510 g of Cheese Spread

19:1

1 210 **2** 3200 **3** 32 **4** 6 **5** 0·85 **6** 5 **7** 0·7 **8** 0·9

9 23 **10** 6·60 **11** **a** \$6 will be circled. **b** \$10.80 **c** \$15 will be circled.

12 2, 2, 2, 3, 5, 6, 8 **a** 6 **b** 3 **c** 2 **d** 4 **13** 7·21, 8·9, 54, 67·25

19:2

1 \$456 **2** \$1560 **3** 496 **4** 40 **5** 101·519 **6** 20 **7** 8

8 32 **9** 26 **10** 2·2 billion **11** \$163.10 **12** 336 km **13** **a** 13

b 6 **c** 7 **d** $9\frac{1}{7}$ **14** **a** 1 **b** 2 **15** **a** Wiping benches **b** 35

Activity

Alan's age = 51

19:3

1 13·037 **2** 11·443 km

3 Total amount spent = \$52.20, Amount left = \$17.80

4 **a** 12 **b** 40 **c** 39 **d** 39 **5** \$10.2 million

6

Cups of water we drank		Number
Jasmine	𝍸 IIII	9
Matilda	𝍸 𝍸 II	12
Lydia	𝍸 II	7
Isaac	𝍸 𝍸 𝍸 I	16

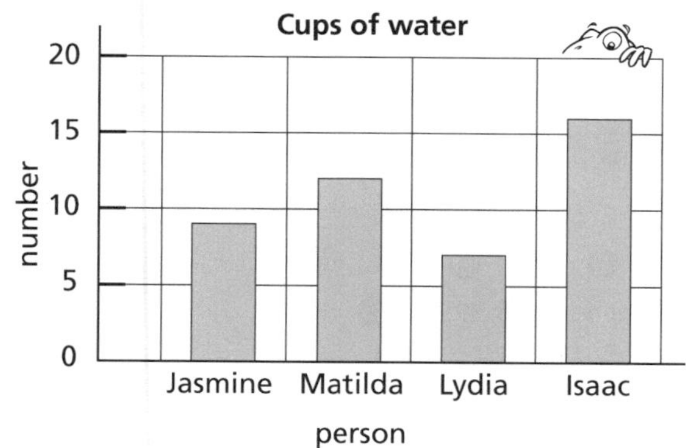

19:4

1

```
    7 · [3] 7 5
+ [9] · 8 [0] 6
  1 7 · 1 8 1
```

2

```
    2 · 9 5 [7]
+ [7] · 4 [9] 6
  1 0 · 4 5 3
```

3 48 **4** **a** New Zealand **b** 10 medals **c** 0·57 **d** 3·31

5 265 BCE

Challenge

Answers may vary. E.g. The title implies that all Australians were represented in the survey.

Activity

a

1			
2	3	4	5
6	7	8	9
10	11	12	13
14	15	16	17
18	19	20	21
22	23	24	25
26	27	28	29
30	31	32	33

b Which numbers are left? 1, 2, 4, 8, 16, 32.
What kind are they? Powers of 2.

20:1

1 5 **2** 10 **3** 9 **4** 5 **5** 493·09 **6** 44 **7** 33 **8** 2 **9** 90

10 93·482 **11** \$5.2 million **12** \$5

13 **a** 8000 m **b** 7·655 L **c** 4·5 cm **d** 3·56 m **14** **a** 12·4 m **b** 2·8 m

15 32·23 kg **16** 995·5 g **17** $5\frac{1}{4}$, 4, $3\frac{1}{8}$, $1\frac{3}{8}$ **18** 17:45

20:2

1 373 **2** 549 **3** 21 **4** 25 **5** 192·496 **6** 20 **7** \$18

8 8500 cm **9** 1234 **10** 88·113 **11** 71 **12** 201 **13** 81 r 5

14 \$176.25 **15** 62·302 L

16 Answers may vary. E.g. The title doesn't show that only the cricket team were surveyed.

17 This object is a triangular prism. **18** 12 m

Activity

66, 44, 59, 38, 52, 47, 31, 25, 20, 42
70, 56, 52, 55, 48, 51, 27, 29, 51, 73

20:3

1 9·875 **2** 0·1195 km **3** **a** 10·214 km **b** 0·48 km

4 **a** B **b** 0·5 **c** 0·25 **5** 3·88 kg **6** **a** $\frac{1}{2}$ **b** $\frac{1}{6}$ **c** $\frac{2}{6}$ or $\frac{1}{3}$ **d** $\frac{3}{4}$

7 

8 998·6 m **9** 34927

20:4

1

```
    3 · [5] 9 7
+ [5] · 1 [3] 4
    8 · 7 3 1
```

2

```
    5 · 6 4 [8]
+ [6] · 5 [3] 9
  1 2 · 1 8 7
```

3 52 **4** 4995·455 kg **5** 310 **6** 0·545 kg or 545 g

© PEARSON AUSTRALIA 2024 • *AUSTRALIAN SIGNPOST MATHS NSW 6 MENTALS* • ISBN 978 0 6557 0913 8

7 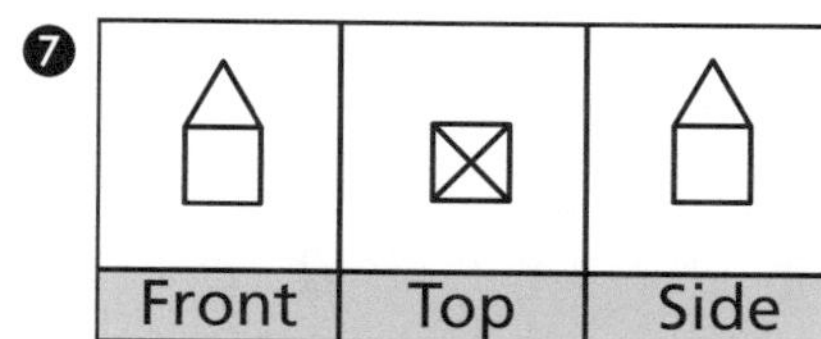

Challenge

The mystery number is 48.

Activity

65, 29, 56, 37, 68, 34, 53, 32, 71, 50
37, 36, 39, 68, 50, 57, 45, 54, 62, 81
even + odd = odd
odd + even = odd

21:1

1 1 **2** $350 **3** 3 **4** 4 **5** 16·117 **6** 97·5 m **7** 6400
8 0 **9** 12 **10** 45·80 **11** 98·9 cm **12** **a** $\frac{3}{4}$ **b** $1\frac{1}{8}$ **c** $1\frac{1}{2}$ **d** $2\frac{3}{8}$
13 **a** 9, 9·343 **b** 8, 7·893 **14** **a** $56.90 **b** $57 **15** 9·9
16 **a** 10 **b** 20 **17** $\frac{3}{6}$ or $\frac{1}{2}$

21:2

1 90 **2** 6 **3** 70 **4** $\frac{3}{10}$ **5** $903.23 **6** $3920 **7** 69
8 1935 **9** 56 **10** $33 474 **11** 56 **12** 64 **13** 64
14 triangular prism **15** 15·35 m **16** **a** 14, 14·065 **b** 12, 12·064
17 $\frac{3}{6}$ or $\frac{1}{2}$ **18** **a** 5600 **b** 6900

Activity

(21) tally (22) column graph (23) line graph (24) dot plot
(25) sector graph (26) divided bar graph (27) median (28) mode
(29) range (30) average

21:3

1 **a** 6, 6·278 **b** 13, 12·329 **2** −3, −2, 5 **3** 5
4 0·06, 0·36, 0·63 **5** 108 **6** 67 **7** 298·11
8 **a** south-west **b** north-east **9** 1·85 **10** 33 **11** −12°C
12 **a** $\frac{75}{100}$ or $\frac{3}{4}$ **b** 0·75

21:4

1

	4 · 7 0 2
+	8 · 4 5 9
	1 3 · 1 6 1

2

	9 · 2 4 7
+	2 · 9 6 7
	1 2 · 2 1 4

3 **a** 15 **b** 30 **4** 325 BCE **5** 5 **6** 36 **7** **a** 355·6 km **b** 2133·6 km
8 39

Challenge

a n – 5 = 87, n = 92 **b** 2 × n – 2 = 28, n = 15 **c** n × 6 = 90, n = 15

Activity

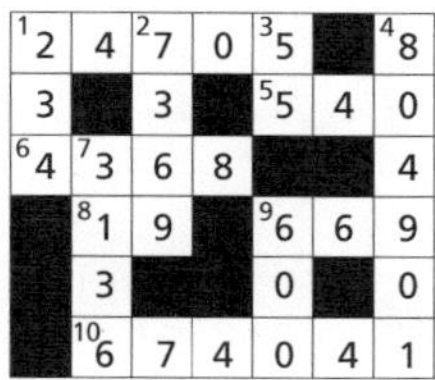

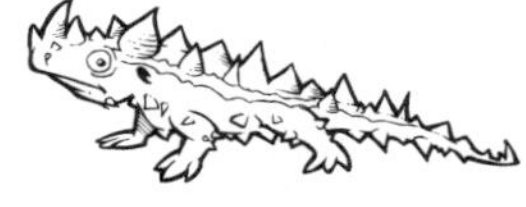

Across:
1. 24 705 **5.** 540 **6.** 4368 **8.** 19 **9.** 669 **10.** 674 041
Down:
1. 234 **2.** 7369 **3.** 55 **4.** 804 901 **7.** 3136 **9.** 600

22:1

1 11·8 **2** 132 **3** 30 **4** 16 **5** $74.34 **6** 6300 **7** 24 **8** 70
9 $\frac{7}{10}$ **10** $137.70 **11** **a** 2 (counting numbers)
b 5 (counting numbers) **12** **a** 3·6 **b** $3\frac{6}{10}$ or $3\frac{3}{5}$ **13** 4·2 L
14 2, 3, 4, 5, 6, 7, 8, 9, 10, 11, and 12. **15** **a** $\frac{9}{4}$ **b** $\frac{18}{5}$
16 75 921 977, 75 241 119, 75 124 911 **17** 62·45, 64·48

22:2

1 594 **2** 50 **3** 571 **4** 70 **5** $101.46 **6** 6700 km **7** 1
8 $\frac{17}{12}$ or $1\frac{5}{12}$ **9** 891 **10** 319·14 **11** 162 **12** 133 r 5 **13** 96 r 5
14 6·4 m **15** 50% **16** 4108 paces. **17** 43·6 m
18 1, 18, 2, 9, 3 and 6. **19** **a** 10, 10·091 **b** 11, 10·986 **20** $450

Activity

a

8	3	4
1	5	9
6	7	2

b

9	4	5
2	6	10
7	8	3

c

8	3	10
9	7	5
4	11	6

22:3

1 **a** 10, 10·005 **b** 10, 9·673 **2** 407 cm or 4·07 m
3 **a** 0·02 or $\frac{2}{100}$ **b** 0·2 or $\frac{2}{10}$ **4** 330° **5** 4·2 L
6 **a** $61.70 **b** $33.80 **c** $31.15 **7** 38 kg **8** 36

22:4

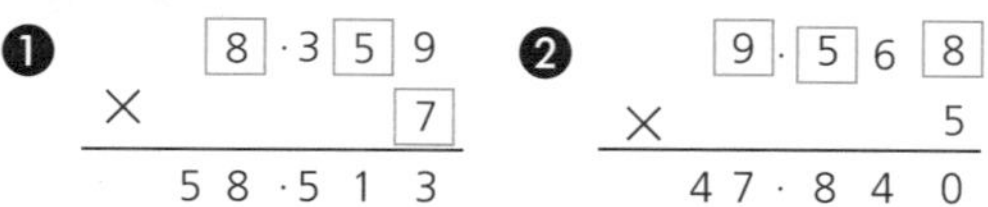

3 120 h **4** 14 **5** 20 **6** $49 **7** Estimates will be around 8967.

Challenge

Answers will vary.
E.g.
a 3 × 3, (6 × 3) – 3^2, etc. **b** 6 × 10 + 4, 8^2, etc.

Activity

1: 2	3	2: 5	6	3: 2	■	4: 5
4	■	1	■	5: 5	4	6
6: 4	7: 5	9	3	■	■	9
■	8: 1	3	■	9: 8	6	5
■	8	■	■	0	■	4
■	10: 4	5	5	6	2	5

Across:
1. 23 562 **5.** 546 **6.** 4593 **8.** 13 **9.** 865 **10.** 455 625
Down:
1. 244 **2.** 5193 **3.** 25 **4.** 569 545 **7.** 5184 **9.** 806

23:1

1 1 **2** 4·5 **3** $\frac{2}{4}$ or $\frac{1}{2}$ **4** 37 **5** 5·534 **6** 620 **7** 7 **8** 522
9 81 **10** 8·096 km **11** 430 r 5 **12** 6651 r 2 **13** 7·17 **14** 37
15 **a** $\frac{19}{5}$ **b** $\frac{17}{8}$ **16** 7 000 000 **17** **a** 6500 **b** 7535 **18** **a** false **b** true
19 9 **20** 56 cm **21** 83 **22** 0·06 or $\frac{6}{100}$

23:2

1 $\frac{12}{10}$ or $1\frac{2}{10}$ **2** 18 **3** 3819 **4** 3366 **5** 43·848 m **6** 0·25 **7** 255
8 290 **9** $120 **10** 42·534 cm **11** 9689 **12** 1161 **13** $1\frac{1}{4}$ **14** 2
15 Monday **16** 56 499 **17** 310° **18** 1501 **19** 345·6 cm **20** 5686

Activity

5, 7, 1, 12, 9, 17, 15, 21, 25, 27
1, 20, 32, 11, 3, 6, 4, 39, 28, 24
10, 14, 7, 32, 41, 24, 0, 19, 8, 30

23:3

1 **a** 16, 15·963 **b** 14, 13·887 **2** 2546 **3** 3012
4 **a** 3·56 **b** 7·893 **c** 8·342 **5** 25 mL **6** 125 mL **7** 356·7 cm
8 540 **9** $458 **10** **a** 467 000 m **b** 5·763 kg **c** 7800 kg
d 4·657 m **e** 8·674 L **f** 60 000 m² **g** 78 400 m **11** $43·65

23:4

1 1600 and 420 will be circled. **2** 59·8 **3** **a** $576 **b** $460·80
4 44 km **5** 504 times. **6** Thursday **7** 286 **8** 250

Challenge

Answers will vary.

Activity

8·375 km	8 km 375 m	8375 m
2·914 km	**2 km 914 m**	2914 m
5·446 km	**5 km 446 m**	**5446 m**
9·125 km	9 km 125 m	**9125 m**
3·546 km	**3 km 546 m**	3546 m
9·897 km	**9 km 897 m**	**9897 m**

24:1

1 833 **2** 38 **3** 26 **4** 25 **5** 5·226 **6** $\frac{3}{10}$ **7** 376 **8** 8
9 44 **10** 21·072 **11** 745·9 **12** 9·03 **13** **a** 45·643 **b** 934·5
c 0·0706384 **d** 4656·78 **14** 3456 **15** 57 mm or 5·7 cm
16 **a** 45 mm **b** 7·8 cm **c** 4·3 km **d** 6800 m **17** B

24:2

1 45 **2** 16 **3** 75 **4** 0·7896 **5** 24·472 m **6** 2 **7** $11.33
8 $\frac{2}{10}$ or $\frac{1}{5}$ **9** 599 **10** 47·912 cm **11** 37 500·8 **12** 12·72
13 **a** $4\frac{3}{10}$ **b** $\frac{43}{10}$ **c** 4·3 **14** **a** 2·1 cm **b** 21 mm **15** 22·5 km
16 **a** 87·645 **b** 57 893·4 **17** **a** 500 m **b** 1750 m **18** 89 km/h

Activity

a Rachel **b** Rhonda **c** Heather

24:3

1 6 669 085 **2** 29·945 m **3** 265·8 **4** 2·99
5 **a** 62·4721 **b** 46 567·8 **6** **a** 3·4 cm **b** 34 mm **7** 123 km/h
8 4·35 km or 4350 m **9** **a** 9700 m **b** 36·7 cm **c** 8·47 km
d 137 mm **e** 5400 m **10** 14
11 24 × 20 = (20 × 20) + (4 × 20) = 400 + 80 = 480

24:4

1 6000 **2** 30 min **3** 5 **4** 4·533 km or 4533 m **5** 9 **6** 8

Challenge

1st column: 6378·9, 4·9028, 8703·4, 941·6, 310·8, 9·0023, 832·5, 79·32
2nd column: 10·23, 324·1, 3·4098, 4·2937, 3000·2, 5112·3, 9·0076, 23·1

Activity

a 100

b

Thickness	10 mm	1 mm	0·1 mm
Number of sheets	100	10	1

c 0·8 cm or 8 mm

25:1

1 21 **2** 741 **3** 2 **4** 26 **5** 269·98 **6** $\frac{3}{12}$ or $\frac{1}{4}$
7 367 km **8** −4°C **9** 52 **10** 783·03
11

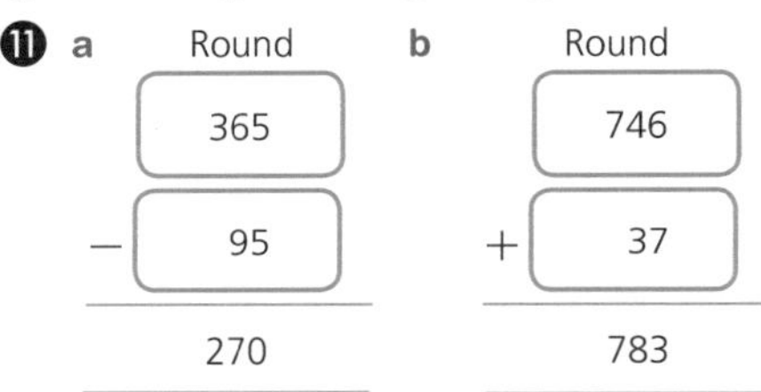

12 **a** 50 ÷ 5 = 10 **b** 49 ÷ 7 = 7
13 **a** Estimates will vary, between 40–50 mm
b Measure = 45 mm or 4·5 cm **14** **a** 624·721 **b** 4656·78
15 **a** 599 mm **b** 876·9 cm **c** 2500 m **d** 8200 m

25:2

1 54 **2** 20 L **3** 4·59 **4** $7\frac{1}{5}$ **5** 289 556 **6** $\frac{5}{12}$ **7** 4588
8 6 **9** $3.55 **10** 222 879 **11** 5·86 m
12 **a** 90 ÷ 3 = 30 **b** 36 ÷ 6 = 6 **13** **a** 39 **b** 5
14 **a** 3·566 **b** 948 230
15 **a** Estimates will vary, between 70–80 mm **b** Measure = 73 mm or 7·3 cm
16 **a** 5690 cm **b** 87·654 km **c** 375·6 cm **d** 27 cm 9 mm **e** 8846 m

Activity

a 2 m **b** 8 cm **c** 10 m **d** 2 cm **e** 20 cm **f** 75 cm **g** 4 m **h** 0·5 cm

25:3

1 4 234 915 **2** $3141.65 **3** 9·26 m **4** 43·7 m
5 **a** 64 ÷ 8 = 8 **b** 27 ÷ 9 = 3 **6** **a** 16 **b** 9 **7** $\frac{1}{12}$, $\frac{1}{6}$, $\frac{1}{4}$, $\frac{1}{3}$, $\frac{1}{2}$
8 **a** 89·289 **b** 79 254 **9** **a** 3·527 **b** 8·721 **c** 9·138
10 **a** 38 cm 2 mm **b** 36 670 m **11** 3810

© PEARSON AUSTRALIA 2024 • *AUSTRALIAN SIGNPOST MATHS NSW 6 MENTALS* • ISBN 978 0 6557 0913 8

25:4

1 15 564 **2** 330 mm

3 a 13 152 m (The path taken will be E, B, A, C, D and E.)
b 13 minutes **4** 30

Challenge

Answers will vary.

Activity

1, 12, 2, 6, 3 and 4.

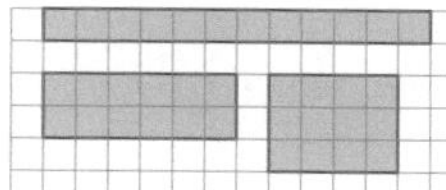

26:1

1 599 **2** 514 **3** 70 **4** $4\frac{1}{2}$ **5** 66 **6** 31 **7** 24 **8** $13
9 9·42 **10** 35465·7 **11** a Estimates will vary, between 50–60 mm
b Measure = 57 mm or 5·7 cm **12** a 5 cm 6 mm b 78 km 720 m
13 4 **14** $\frac{7}{12}$ **15** a $\frac{3}{4}$ b $\frac{4}{4} = 1$ **16** a 54·621 b 86 734
17 a 57 b 8684 **18** 360

26:2

1 49 **2** 37 L **3** $\frac{1}{12}$ **4** $38 **5** 51 **6** 52 **7** 84 **8** 42 mL
9 18·31 **10** 7108·9 **11** 3·75 m **12** 79·2 cm **13** 86·734
14 8 cm 3 mm **15** a Estimates will vary, between 20–30 mm
b Measure = 26 mm or 2·6 cm **16** 23 cm **17** a 54 ÷ 9 = 6
b 56 ÷ 7 = 8 **18** a 30 b 8 **19** $\frac{6}{8}$ or $\frac{3}{4}$

Activity

a 4 b $\frac{3}{4}$ c $\frac{5}{8}$ d $\frac{4}{8}$ or $\frac{1}{2}$ e $\frac{3}{8}$ f $\frac{9}{8}$ or $1\frac{1}{8}$ g $\frac{1}{8}$ h $1\frac{5}{8}$ i $1\frac{7}{8}$ j $\frac{7}{8}$

26:3

1 6288·32 **2** 209·88 **3** 161·2 cm or 1·612 m **4** a 80 b 7
5 0% **6** 167 **7** 3·677 **8** a $3\frac{1}{2}$ b $6\frac{1}{2}$ **9** 9
10 a 62 973 b 83 497 **11** 12 **12** 410·3 **13** a $\frac{1}{5} < \frac{3}{10}$ b $\frac{7}{10} > \frac{2}{5}$
14 78 984

26:4

1 528 cm or 5·28 m **2** $94.95 **3** $3 086 800
4 1 and 14; 2 and 7 **5** 978
6 This route will be coloured (11 m + 17 m + 7 m).

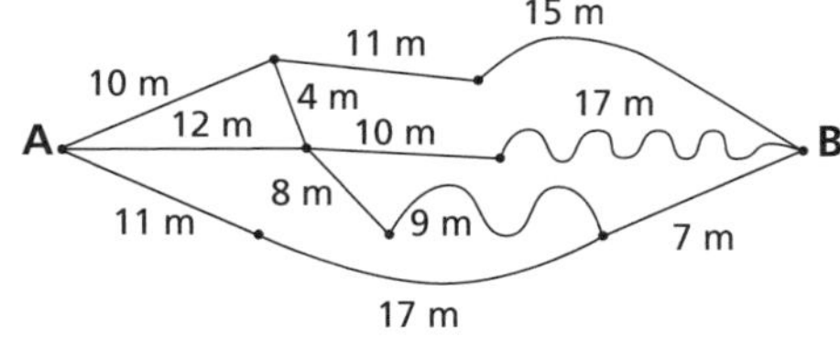

Challenge

Answers may vary. E.g. It has 1 ten, 3 ones, 4 tenths, 5 hundredths, and 2 thousandths. It becomes 13 when rounded to the nearest whole number.

Activity

a $3\frac{1}{2}$ b $1\frac{1}{2}$ c $2\frac{1}{4}$ d $2\frac{3}{4}$ e $\frac{3}{4}$ f $\frac{1}{4}$ g $3\frac{1}{2}$ h $1\frac{1}{4}$

27:1

1 7 **2** 2 **3** 300 **4** 560 **5** 12 **6** 27 m **7** 60 **8** 7200
9 9·41 **10** 83 456·9 **11** a 893 mm b 8·345 km c 297·8 cm
d 7200 m e 3750 m **12** a 66 cm b 28 cm **13** a B b B
14 a $\frac{5}{6}$ b $\frac{5}{12}$ **15** a 1·53 b 17 476·2 c 8·1346

27:2

1 1080 **2** 519 **3** 32 **4** 45 L **5** 6 **6** 54 **7** 60 **8** 13
9 17·19 **10** 29 076·8 **11** 16 **12** 750 mL
13 a $\frac{17}{100}$ b $\frac{9}{100}$ c $\frac{11}{100}$ d $\frac{89}{100}$ **14** Area = 55 cm^2, Perimeter = 36 cm
15 a $\frac{3}{5}$ (Answers may vary) b $\frac{2}{8}$ (Answers may vary)
c $\frac{1}{3}$ (Answers may vary) **16** a 15 b 4 c 8 d 16 **17** 829 m

Activity

a 0·5 b 0·6 c 0·35 d 0·52 e 0·875 f 0·0625 g 0·625 h 0·1875
i 0·28 j 0·03125 k 0·015625 l 0·984375

27:3

1 4755·97 **2** 277 217 **3** Area = 88 m^2, Perimeter = 46 m
4 a $\frac{63}{100}$ b $\frac{43}{100}$ c $\frac{21}{100}$ d $\frac{47}{100}$ **5** a 21 b 63 c 14
6 1, 42, 2, 21, 3, 14, 6 and 7
7 a $\frac{4}{10}$ (Answers may vary) b $\frac{8}{10}$ (Answers may vary)
c $\frac{2}{10}$ (Answers may vary) **8** 5 oranges **9** $20

27:4

1 a 4·5 cm^2 b 4·5 cm^2 **2** 6 cm **3** Peter **4** 4 pizzas
5 a 900 b 90 000

Challenge

$\frac{1}{2}$				$\frac{1}{2}$			
$\frac{1}{4}$		$\frac{1}{4}$		$\frac{1}{4}$		$\frac{1}{4}$	
$\frac{1}{8}$	$\frac{1}{8}$	$\frac{1}{8}$	$\frac{1}{8}$	$\frac{1}{8}$	$\frac{1}{8}$	$\frac{1}{8}$	$\frac{1}{8}$

Activity

8, 32, 48, 24, 40, 64, 16, 72, 56, 80
6, 24, 36, 18, 30, 48, 12, 54, 42, 60

28:1

1 56 **2** 511 **3** 827 **4** 3500 **5** $\frac{11}{12}$ **6** 55 **7** 320 **8** 6
9 44 334 **10** 14·73 **11** 20 mm
12 a $\frac{4}{5}$ (Answers may vary) b $\frac{2}{5}$ (Answers may vary)
c $\frac{3}{5}$ (Answers may vary) **13** a 69 mm b 2·947 km
c 545·6 cm d 3700 m e 1400 m **14** 357·2 m **15** 24 m^2

28:2

1 213 **2** 171 **3** 14 **4** $\frac{5}{10}$ or $\frac{1}{2}$ **5** 20 **6** 52 **7** 4800 L
8 12 **9** 56 866 **10** 9·44 **11** a 4·4 m b 13·2 m **12** a $\frac{4}{5}$ b $\frac{4}{8}$ or $\frac{1}{2}$

13 $2\frac{3}{4}$ **14** a $\frac{3}{4}$ b $\frac{3}{4}$ **15** a $\frac{2}{5}$ b $\frac{6}{18}$ **16** 1156 m²

17 $\frac{2}{3}-\frac{1}{6}=\frac{4}{6}-\frac{1}{6}=\frac{3}{6}$ **18** a 24 m² b 28 m

Activity

(1) millimetres (2) centimetres (3) metres (4) kilometres (24) before noon (25) after noon (26) 5:40 am (27) 19:30 (28) degree Celsius (29) thermometer

28:3

1 5 772 233 **2** 111 229 **3** $\frac{3}{10}$ **4** 1, 32, 2, 16, 4, 8.

5 9, 18, 27, 36, 45, 54, 63, 72, 81, 90 **6** a 25 b 49

7 a $\frac{5}{8}$ b $\frac{5}{6}$ c $\frac{7}{10}$ d $\frac{5}{12}$

8 a $\frac{2}{12}$ (Answers may vary.) b $\frac{1}{4}$ (Answers may vary.)
c $\frac{2}{5}$ (Answers may vary.) d $\frac{1}{1}$ (Answers may vary.)
e $\frac{2}{6}$ (Answers may vary.) f $\frac{8}{10}$ (Answers may vary.)

9 0·008 or $\frac{8}{1000}$ **10** a A = 32 m² b A = 15 m² **11** a 120° b 180°

28:4

1 a 1963 b 1942 **2** Area = 95 m², Perimeter = 58 m **3** 6 L

4 □= 14 ,△ = 4

5 a 64 m b 84 m² **6** a 279 b 12

Challenge

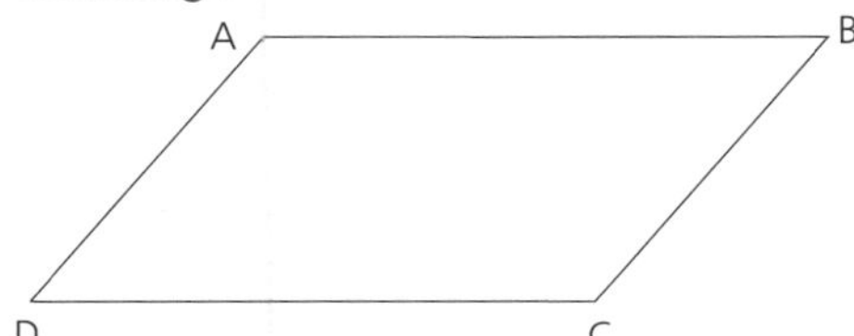

It is a quadrilateral. It has two pairs of parallel sides that are equal in length. Its opposite angles are equal in size.

Activity

a 3 vans b kangaroos: 12, cows: 19

29:1

1 63 **2** 560 **3** 45 **4** 22 **5** 1 and 17. **6** 4 **7** 45 **8** $\frac{1}{8}$

9 285 677 r 1 **10** 12·25

11 a $\frac{4}{10}$ (Answers may vary.) b $\frac{2}{4}$ (Answers may vary.)
c $\frac{6}{8}$ (Answers may vary.) **12** 10 **13** $1\frac{2}{4}$ or $1\frac{1}{2}$

14 a A = 15 m² b A = 6 m² **15** a $\frac{2}{4}$ or $\frac{1}{2}$ b $\frac{3}{4}$ **16** 54 m² **17** 12

29:2

1 168 **2** 27 L **3** 17 **4** 34 **5** $\frac{10}{12}$ or $\frac{5}{6}$ **6** 252 **7** 4900

8 $6 **9** 40 811 r 1 **10** 3·19 **11** a $\frac{1}{2}<\frac{4}{6}$ b $\frac{3}{4}>\frac{3}{8}$ **12** $15

13 26 **14** a A = 36 m² b A = 40·5 m² **15** $\frac{3}{10}+\frac{1}{2}=\frac{3}{10}+\frac{5}{10}=\frac{8}{10}$

16 $\frac{1}{4}$ **17** a 8·7 b 0·897 **18** 225·6 cm **19** 48 **20** 81 m² **21** 66

Activity

a 20 m per second b 48 km per hour c 245 km per day d 12 mm per second

29:3

1 9 883 055 **2** 406 151 **3** a $\frac{18}{20}$ (Answers may vary.)
b $\frac{2}{6}$ (Answers may vary.) c $\frac{1}{1}$ (Answers may vary.) **4** 36 m²

5 $\frac{3}{6}+\frac{1}{3}=\frac{3}{6}+\frac{2}{6}=\frac{5}{6}$ **6** a 6546 g b 4·795 km c 8·8 cm

7 a 40 000 b 50 c 0·008 **8** a kite b yes **9** $28 **10** a $\frac{7}{8}$ b $\frac{1}{8}$

11 a 3·52 m² b 8 m 60 cm or 8·6 m

29:4

1 a 18 b 27 **2** a 2040 b 840 c 1080 d 880

3 a 0·6 m or 60 cm b 5·4 m² **4** Ty

Challenge

Answers may vary. E.g. It is a 9-digit odd number. It becomes 356 000 000 when rounded to the nearest million. 712 934 906 is double this number.

Activity

Put a tick for YES ✓

Put a cross for NO ✗

	Drama	Gym	Tennis	Monday	Tuesday	Friday
Heather	✗	✓	✗	✓	✗	✗
Naomi	✓	✗	✗	✗	✓	✗
Luke	✗	✗	✓	✗	✗	✓

Answers	Club	Day
Heather	Gym	Monday
Naomi	Drama	Tuesday
Luke	Tennis	Friday

30:1

1 787 **2** 614 **3** 75 **4** $\frac{5}{12}$ **5** 20 **6** $\frac{7}{10}$ **7** 21 **8** 650 cm

9 a 20 b 8 c 7 d 21 **10** a 320° b 240° **11** a 30 cm b 56 cm²

12 a A = 10·5 m² b A = 7·5 m² **13** $28 **14** 72

15 a 296 mm b 2·98 km

30:2

1 17 **2** 104 **3** 540 L **4** $\frac{5}{6}$ **5** 553 566 **6** 12·5 **7** 40 **8** 15

9 40 **10** 840 975 **11** a 24 cm²

12 $\frac{4}{5}-\frac{2}{10}=\frac{4}{5}-\frac{1}{5}=\frac{3}{5}$ or $\frac{4}{5}-\frac{2}{10}=\frac{8}{10}-\frac{2}{10}=\frac{6}{10}$ **13** 40%

14 a 64 m b 202 m² **15** 17·5 m² **16** 25% **17** a $\frac{1}{2}+\frac{1}{3}=\frac{3}{6}+\frac{2}{6}=\frac{5}{6}$
b $\frac{3}{4}+\frac{1}{5}=\frac{15}{20}+\frac{4}{20}=\frac{19}{20}$ **18** 7·25 h

Activity

1 a 25 b 13 c 3 **2** a 15 b 6

30:3

1 5 235 363 **2** 75 968 **3** $1 **4** a $\frac{1}{10}<\frac{4}{5}$ b $\frac{5}{6}>\frac{2}{3}$

5 a A = 84 m² b A = 27 m² **6** 31

7 a $\frac{3}{5}-\frac{1}{2}=\frac{6}{10}-\frac{5}{10}=\frac{1}{10}$ b $\frac{3}{4}-\frac{1}{3}=\frac{9}{12}-\frac{4}{12}=\frac{5}{12}$

8 a −0·05 b 0·05 c −0·2 **9** 20% **10** $\frac{1}{4}$

11 a 34 mm b 8·937 km c 84·5 cm d 2800 m

© PEARSON AUSTRALIA 2024 • *AUSTRALIAN SIGNPOST MATHS NSW 6 MENTALS* • ISBN 978 0 6557 0913 8

30:4

❶ $\frac{5}{12}$ ❷ \$3302 ❸ 12 ❹ \$801 ❺ My number is 738.
❻ **a** 65·95 kg **b** 34·05 kg

Challenge

Answers will vary. See 30:4, Question 5 for an example.

Activity

Answers may vary. True is =384, False is ?17\$4

31:1

❶ 6 ❷ 12 ❸ 3 ❹ 30 ❺ 5039·9 ❻ $\frac{5}{8}$ ❼ 100 ❽ 8 ❾ 33
❿ 331·94 ⓫ \$104 ⓬ 30 km ⓭ A ⓮ **a** 12 m^2 **b** 42 m^2
⓯ **a** $\frac{1}{5}+\frac{4}{10}=\frac{1}{5}+\frac{2}{5}=\frac{3}{5}$ **b** $\frac{3}{6}+\frac{2}{12}=\frac{3}{6}+\frac{1}{6}=\frac{4}{6}$ or $\frac{2}{3}$
⓰ **a** 3000 mL **b** 9261 mL **c** 2734 mL

31:2

❶ 10 ❷ 4 ❸ 700 ❹ 6 ❺ 250 ❻ 13 ❼ 55 ❽ 273
❾ 71 291 ❿ 12·23 ⓫ 6 ⓬ 15
⓭ **a** $\frac{8}{10}-\frac{1}{2}=\frac{8}{10}-\frac{5}{10}=\frac{3}{10}$ **b** $\frac{5}{7}+\frac{2}{10}=\frac{50}{70}+\frac{14}{70}=\frac{64}{70}$
⓮ \$10 ⓯ 3 h 21 min ⓰ **a** 2 **b** 1

Activity

a 25 **b** 14 **c** 33 **d** 0 **e** 24 **f** 10 **g** 12 **h** 26 **i** 15 **j** 3 **k** 40

31:3

❶ 21 164 ❷ 4·32 ❸ 175 min ❹ 2068 ❺ **a** 3 **b** 20
❻ **a** 8 L **b** 9·465 L **c** 7·234 L ❼ **a** 1200 **b** 3600 **c** 15 000
❽ **a** 8000 mL **b** 4·839 L ❾ 9 ❿ 24

31:4

❶ 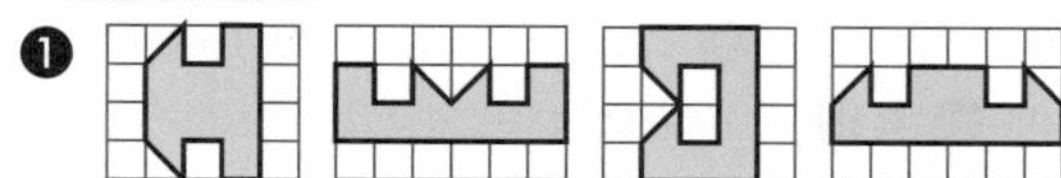

❷ 1260 minutes, or 21 h ❸ Answers will vary. ❹ 22 seconds

Challenge

Answers will vary.

Activity

a Answers will vary.

b

	a	e	i	o	u
Tally	𝍸 II	𝍸 𝍸 𝍸	𝍸 𝍸 II	𝍸 𝍸 III	𝍸 I

c e

32:1

❶ 37 ❷ 164 ❸ 2400 ❹ 39 ❺ 10 313·7 ❻ $\frac{1}{10}$ ❼ 522
❽ 3 ❾ 49 ❿ 687·14 ⓫ 15 ⓬ $0{\cdot}7=\frac{70}{100}=70\%$ ⓭ 48
⓮ **a** $\frac{2}{10}+\frac{3}{4}=\frac{4}{20}+\frac{15}{20}=\frac{19}{20}$ **b** $\frac{3}{4}+\frac{1}{3}=\frac{9}{12}+\frac{4}{12}=\frac{13}{12}$
⓯ **a** 6846 mL **b** 7278 mL ⓰ $\frac{98}{100}$
⓱ **a** 490 **b** 49 000 **c** 350 000

32:2

❶ 300 L ❷ 7 ❸ 980 ❹ 9

❺
```
    3 5
  × 7 6
  2 1 0   (6 × 35)
2 4 5 0   (70 × 35)
2 6 6 0
```
❻ \$4 ❼ 17 400 ❽ 46 ❾ 365

❿
```
    9 3
  × 6 7
  6 5 1   (7 × 93)
5 5 8 0   (60 × 93)
6 2 3 1
```
⓫ 16 ⓬ 4935

⓭ **a** $\frac{6}{7}-\frac{3}{10}=\frac{60}{70}-\frac{21}{70}=\frac{39}{70}$ **b** $\frac{3}{10}+\frac{1}{3}=\frac{9}{30}+\frac{10}{30}=\frac{19}{30}$
⓮ 7 cm^2 ⓯ **a** 0·846 L **b** 0·058 L

Activity

120, 60, 300, 480, 600, 240, 540, 360, 180, 420
140, 280, 350, 420, 700, 70, 630, 560, 210, 490
720, 400, 160, 320, 800, 640, 560, 240, 80, 480

32:3

❶ 6349 ❷ 7·87

❸
```
    2 3
  × 4 5
  1 1 5   (5 × 23)
  9 2 0   (40 × 23)
1 0 3 5
```
❹
```
    8 6
  × 6 7
  6 0 2   (7 × 86)
5 1 6 0   (60 × 86)
5 7 6 2
```

❺ **a** $\frac{8}{12}-\frac{1}{4}=\frac{8}{12}-\frac{3}{12}=\frac{5}{12}$ **b** $\frac{3}{4}+\frac{1}{10}=\frac{15}{20}+\frac{2}{20}=\frac{17}{20}$
❻ **a** 0·298 L **b** 0·046 L **c** 0·007 L
❼ \$1560 ❽ **a** 2000 **b** 6000 **c** 10 000 ❾ **a** 15 000 mL
b 4250 mL **c** 76 300 g **d** 3500 g **e** 57 750 m ❿ 73

32:4

❶ **a** 200 **b** 2400 ❷ \$72 ❸ **a** 350 m **b** 2800 m or 2·8 km ❹ 90
❺ 7585

Challenge

Answers will vary.

Activity

16, 21, 14, 22, 15, 18, 17, 20, 19, 23
a 18 **b** 24 **c** 32

33:1

❶ 86 ❷ 561 ❸ 3000 ❹ 6 ❺ 536 ❻ $\frac{1}{10}$ ❼ \$8 ❽ 6434 m
❾ 2400 L ❿ 378 ⓫ **a** 5926 mL **b** 2978 mL **c** 6750 mL
⓬ 175 km ⓭ g and kg will be underlined. ⓮ **a** mm **b** mL **c** t
⓯ **a** 6000 kg **b** 3 t ⓰ **a** yes **b** yes **c** $\frac{7}{10}$ **d** $\frac{7}{10}$

33:2

❶ 860 ❷ 540 ❸ 62 ❹ \$9

❺
```
    5 9
  × 4 6
  3 5 4   (6 × 59)
2 3 6 0   (40 × 59)
2 7 1 4
```
❻ $\frac{9}{10}$ ❼ \$13·27 ❽ 377 ❾ 435

© PEARSON AUSTRALIA 2024 • *AUSTRALIAN SIGNPOST MATHS NSW 6 MENTALS* • ISBN 978 0 6557 0913 8

❿
$$\begin{array}{r l} 71 & \\ \times\ 53 & \\ \hline 213 & (3 \times 71) \\ 3550 & (50 \times 71) \\ \hline 3763 & \end{array}$$

⓫ 78 291 ⓬ **a** $290 **b** $180

⓭ **a** 0·298 L **b** 0·084 L **c** 0·019 L ⓮ **a** 7400 kg **b** 90 t

⓯ **a** 75 kg **b** 210 kg

Activity

72, 23, 50, 77, 61, 65, 39, 54, 28, 86

91, 28, 49, 73, 16, 35, 70, 82, 54, 67

33:3

❶
$$\begin{array}{r l} 83 & \\ \times\ 76 & \\ \hline 498 & (6 \times 83) \\ 5810 & (70 \times 83) \\ \hline 6308 & \end{array}$$

❷
$$\begin{array}{r l} 926 & \\ \times\ 78 & \\ \hline 7408 & (8 \times 926) \\ 64820 & (70 \times 926) \\ \hline 72228 & \end{array}$$

❸ **a** 140 t **b** 1800 kg ❹ **a** 2970 kg **b** 30 t ❺ **a** 14:44 **b** 15:02

❻ **a** 60 **b** 43 **c** 22 **d** 126 ❼ **a** 0·289 L **b** 0·037 L **c** 0·106 L

❽ **a** 3600 mL **b** 9250 mL **c** 0·627 L **d** 0·092 L ❾ **a** 0·65 **b** 14%

33:4

❶ 5·75 t

❷

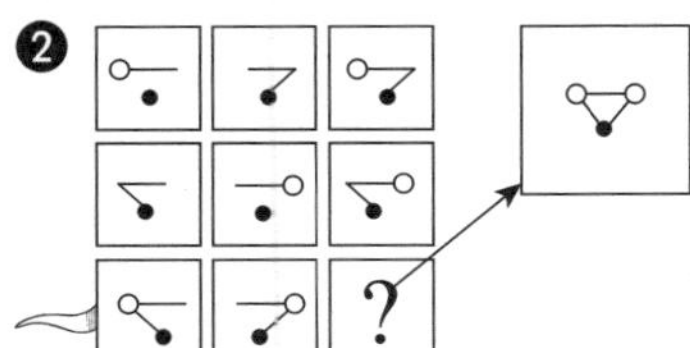

❸ **a** 100 **b** 20 ❹ 8

Challenge

Answers will vary. E.g. Semitrailer: 50 t.

Activity

❶ **a** 96 **b** 160 **c** 610 **d** 204 **e** 66 **f** 36

❷ **a** LXXV **b** CCCLXXX **c** CCCLXXVIII **d** MMDLXVII

e DCXXXV **f** MMMCMXCIX

34:1

❶ 2 ❷ 12 ❸ $\frac{5}{8}$ ❹ 30 ❺ 522 ❻ $32 ❼ 8475 m ❽ 421

❾ $3.50 ❿ 672

⓫

Tonnes	Kilograms
7 t	7000 kg
70 t	70 000 kg
7·546 t	7546 kg

Litres	Millilitres
9 L	9000 mL
2 L	2000 mL
8·3 L	8300 mL

⓬ 14:30 ⓭ 127 ⓮ 0·678 ⓯ **a** 4:35 pm **b** 4:09 am

⓰ **a** kilograms (kg) **b** tonnes (t) **c** grams (g) ⓱ triangular pyramid

34:2

❶ 53 ❷ 36 ❸ 7 ❹ $\frac{11}{12}$ ❺ 3738 ❻ $21.40 ❼ 975 ❽ 27

❾ 174 ❿ 47 652 ⓫ 115·0 ⓬ 222·3 ⓭ 251·6 ⓮ 30 min

⓯

Tonnes & kilograms	Tonnes
7 t 300 kg	7·3 t
9 t 546 kg	9·546 t
5 t 476 kg	5·476 t

⓰ 9 ⓱ **a** 4·768 kg **b** 4750 g **c** 67 000 kg **d** 46 800 g **e** 10 250 g

Activity

a 1: 50 **b** 150 cm **c** 100 cm **d** Bed **e** Desk **f** J1 or J2

34:3

❶ 2380 ❷ 1314 ❸ 17 664 ❹ 76·7 ❺ 210·0 ❻ 539·0

❼ **a** 18·2 t **b** 91 t ❽ $\frac{1}{2} = \frac{2}{4} = \frac{4}{8} = \frac{5}{10}$ ❾ **a** 9100 kg **b** 40 t

❿ 852 ⓫ 2·934 kg ⓬ 34 min ⓭ $12 000

⓮ **a** 7:27 pm **b** 4:09 am

34:4

❶ 552 ❷ 1 and 72, 2 and 36, 3 and 24, 4 and 18, 6 and 12, 8 and 9

❸ **a** 8·66 kg or 8660 g **b** 1·34 kg or 1340 g ❹ 37 ❺ 131·25 mg

❻ 8976

Challenge

a 9 **b** 85 **c** 49 **d** 63 **e** 13 **f** 8

Activity

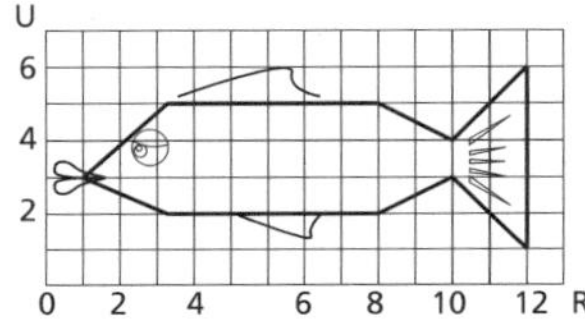

35:1

❶ 76 ❷ 6 ❸ 8 ❹ $\frac{2}{4}$ or $\frac{1}{2}$ ❺ 522 ❻ 77 ❼ 5 ❽ 5498 L

❾ $400 ❿ 308 ⓫ 4 ⓬ **a** 7000 kg **b** 8 t **c** 276 g **d** 7925 g

⓭ □ = ÷, △ = +

⓮

Decagons	1	2	3	4	5
Sides	10	20	30	40	50

⓯ **a** $\frac{4}{5}$ **b** $\frac{3}{12}$

⓰ **a** A prime number has 2 factors, 1 and itself.

b A composite number has more than 2 factors.

⓱ **a**

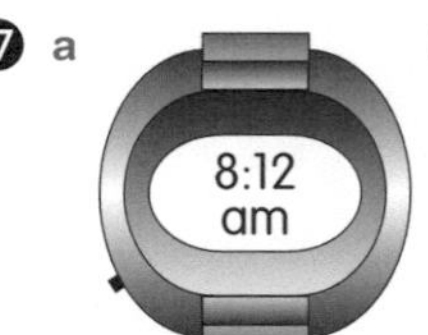

b

35:2

❶ 1099 ❷ 386 ❸ $\frac{8}{10}$ or $\frac{4}{5}$ ❹ $1\frac{3}{5}$ ❺ 18 ❻ 12·5 ❼ 35 ❽ 0

❾ 42·0 ❿ 509·2 ⓫ 660·0 ⓬ **a** 7760 kg **b** 20 t **c** 456 g

d 2487 g **e** 9750 g ⓭ 0·061 kg or 61 g

⓮ 17, 29, 83, and 67 will be circled. ⓯ 2 ⓰ **a** 18 min **b** 27 min

c 1 h 10 min or 70 min

© PEARSON AUSTRALIA 2024 • *AUSTRALIAN SIGNPOST MATHS NSW 6 MENTALS* • ISBN 978 0 6557 0913 8

Activity

a =384 (True) **b** =384 (True) **c** =384 (True)

35:3

❶ 2117 ❷ 205·2 ❸ 8763 ❹ $\frac{3}{4}+\frac{1}{8}=\frac{6}{8}+\frac{1}{8}=\frac{7}{8}$

❺ **a** 4340 kg **b** 50 t **c** 907 g **d** 5264 g ❻ **a** 37 **b** 60 **c** 124

❼ **a** 12·6 t **b** 26·6 t ❽ **a** 2·4 t **b** 4 t ❾ 1 h 27 min or 87 min

❿ 17:26 ⓫ **a** 2:24 am **b** 12:56 pm ⓬ **a** 315 **b** 465

35:4

❶ 105 hours ❷ **a** 2 min **b** 6 min **c** 25 min ❸ 335

❹ **a**

```
    6 · 9 2 7
+   8 · 0 4 9
-------------
  1 4 · 9 7 6
```

b

```
    8 · 7 5 2
+   7 · 8 7 8
-------------
  1 6 · 6 3 0
```

❺ 36 mg

Challenge

Answers will vary. E.g. A grain of rice weighs 21 mg.

Activity

Factors: 1, 3, 5, and 15.

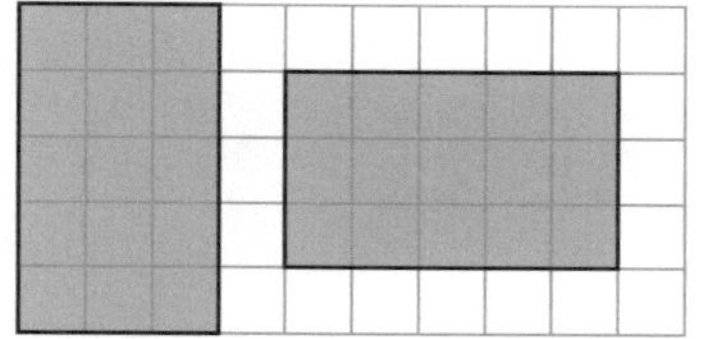

36:1

❶ 765 ❷ 543 ❸ $3600 ❹ 8 ❺ 1233·35 ❻ 1 ❼ 80 ❽ 10

❾ $\frac{6}{10}$ or $\frac{3}{5}$ ❿ $8808.01 ⓫ 9, 12, 6, and 15 will be circled.

⓬ 18 blocks

⓭ 2, 3, 5 and 7 will be ticked.

1	1		
2	1	2	
3	1	3	
4	1	2	4

5	1	5		
6	1	2	3	6
7	1	7		
8	1	2	4	8

⓮ **a**

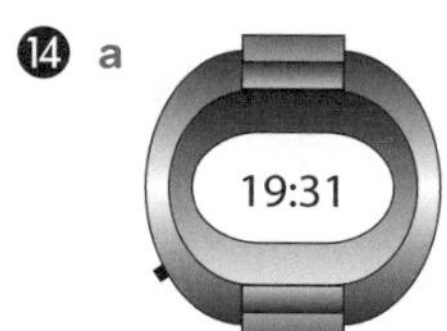

b

⓯ **a** A, C, and E. **b** B and D.

36:2

❶ 84 ❷ 68 ❸ 24 ❹ $\frac{4}{10}$ or $\frac{2}{5}$ ❺ 43·3333 ❻ 100 ❼ 127

❽ $5\frac{1}{6}$ ❾ 5624 m ❿ 853·108 ⓫ 4 ⓬ C

⓭ 790, 685, and 917 080 will be circled. ⓮ **a** 5 **b** 14 **c** 15 **d** 9

⓯ 19, 31, and 47 will be circled. ⓰ 1, 42, 2, 21, 3, 14, 6 and 7

⓱ 16:28 ⓲ 9 h ⓳ **a** 90 **b** 195

Activity

a 3 m **b** 3 m **c** 3·8 m **d** 13·6 m

36:3

❶ 6255·84 ❷ $6021.32 ❸ **a** 10 min **b** 1 h 40 min ❹ 65

❺ 50 ❻ 4·4 cm ❼ 2, 3, 5, 7, 11, 13, 17, 19, 23, and 29

❽ **a** 10:45 pm **b** 6:24 am **c** 2:00 am 1:23 pm

❾ 11 and 13 will be ticked.

9	1	9	3			
10	1	10	2	5		
11	1	11				
12	1	12	2	6	3	4

13	1	13			
14	1	14	2	7	
15	1	15	3	5	
16	1	16	2	8	4

❿ 800 010, 8310, and 7850 will be circled.

⓫ 1, 100, 2, 50, 4, 25, 5, 20, 10

36:4

❶ **a** **b** **c**

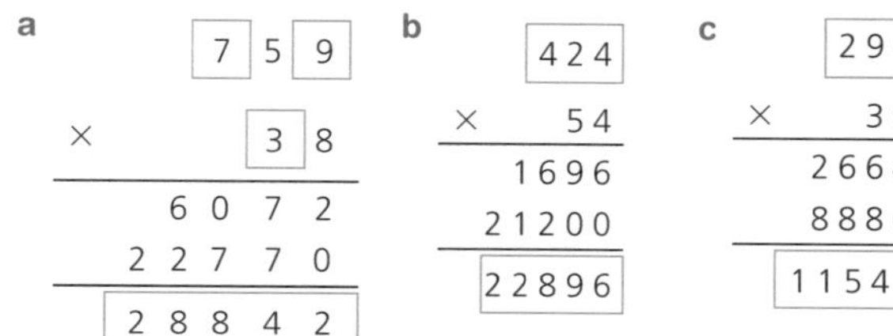

❷ 29 644

❸ ?

❹ These two models represent one cubic metre:

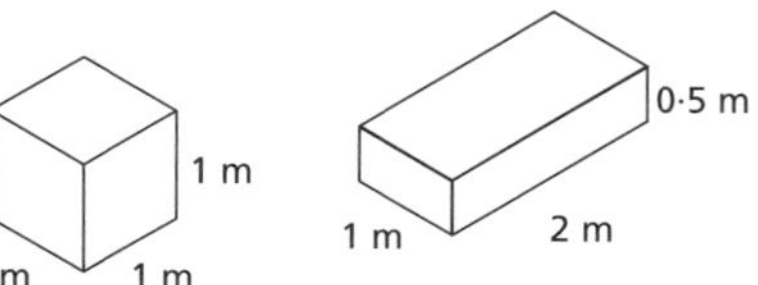

❺ **a** 72 **b** 528 ❻ 140

Challenge

Answers will vary.

Activity

a yes **b** yes **c** yes

37:1

❶ 0·8 ❷ 16 ❸ 12 ❹ $\frac{7}{8}$ ❺ 316 022 ❻ $4.20 ❼ 0·1

❽ 8345 ❾ 43 ❿ 452 513 ⓫ 6578 and 2080 will be circled.

⓬ **a** Eggs **b** $\frac{1}{4}$ **c** 2 **d** Bacon **e** Pastry ⓭ **a** 12 **b** 21

⓮ 48 km ⓯ 0·003 or $\frac{3}{1000}$

37:2

❶ 3·3 ❷ 15 ❸ 17 ❹ $8\frac{3}{8}$ ❺ $1192.49 ❻ 24 ❼ 357 ❽ 58

❾ $\frac{23}{10}$ or $2\frac{3}{10}$ ❿ $6563.07 ⓫ 60 cm^3 ⓬ **a** 122 **b** Male **c** 398
⓭ 36, 100, 812, and 4000 will be circled. ⓮ 160 cm^3

Activity

a (2, 2) **b** (−2, 1) **c** (−2, −2) **d** (0, −1) **e** (2, 0) **f** (0, 0)
Answers may vary. E.g. Triangle : (2, 2), (2, 0), (0, 0)

37:3

❶ 3648 ❷ 792 054 ❸ 56 404

❹

Number of horses	1	2	3	4	5
Number of legs	4	8	12	16	20

a number of horses × 4 = number of legs **b** 2368

❺ 72 m^3 ❻ **a** 24 cm^2 **b** 8 cm^3 ❼ 7 ❽ **a** 10 **b** 2

❾ 2307, 800 010, 410 043, and 8310 will be circled. ❿ 1, 2, and 4

37:4

❶ **a** 525 **b** 869 **c** 78·96 ❷ Svetla ❸ **a** 30% **b** 20%

❹ 60 (packets). Note that each packet must keep its shape.

Challenge

Answers will vary.

Activity

Answers will vary.

© PEARSON AUSTRALIA 2024 • *AUSTRALIAN SIGNPOST MATHS NSW 6 MENTALS* • ISBN 978 0 6557 0913 8

18:3 — out of 7

1.
```
  8456735
    98365
  5260831
+   25498
```

2.
```
  $9000.00
− $8675.40
```

3. If this spinner is spun, which result, **Y**, **B** or **G**,

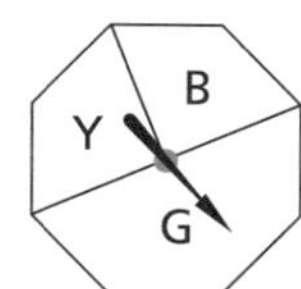

   a is most likely? ______
   b has a 25% chance of occurring? ______

4. How far did I travel if I drove for 5 hours at 56 km/h? ______

5. Find the change from $50 if the total $35.68 is rounded off to the nearest 5 cents. ______

6. This table shows the goals Felicity and Lachlan scored in the first 12 weeks of soccer.

Felicity	0	1	6	1	5	0	4	0	0	0	0	1
Lachlan	3	6	8	5	0	1	0	1	2	3	1	11

How many goals were scored by:

a Felicity? ______ b Lachlan? ______

c both Felicity and Lachlan? ______

What was the mode for:

d Felicity? ______ e Lachlan? ______

What was the range for:

f Felicity? ______ g Lachlan? ______

What was the median for:

h Felicity? ______ i Lachlan? ______

7. Describe the spread of these scores.

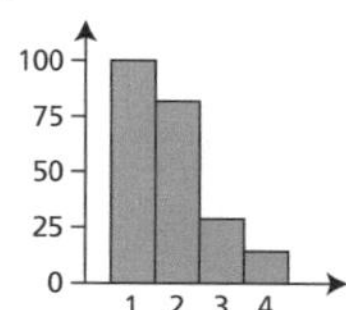

______
______
______

18:4 — out of 6

Extension

1. The number of corners plus the number of faces minus the number of edges for 8 hexagonal prisms. ______

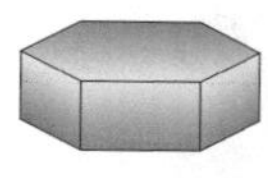

2. This cylinder is 76 cm tall. How high is:

   a one slice? ______
   b three slices? ______

3. One plane flew 12 km per minute for 7 hours. Another plane flew 13 km/h for 9 hours. What was the difference between the total distance they flew? ______

4. On a trip to the Northern Territory, our average speed was 67 km/h for the first part of the trip, 93 km/h for the second part and 85 km/h for the third part.
   If we travelled for 3 hours in the first part of the trip, 2 hours in the second part and $4\frac{1}{2}$ hours in the third part, how far did we travel in total? ______

5. a CLVI ______ b CCCLXXXVI ______
   c CXVI ______ d CCLXXVII ______

6. If the time is 07:34 on Thursday, how long will it be until I leave for my weekend trip at 4:45 pm on Friday afternoon? ______

Challenge

Make a list of events and estimate the probability of each event, as a percentage.

______
______
______
______

Strategy Time

Show what you would buy with $26.

______
______
______
______
______

19:1 out of 13

1. 7×30 ______
2. 8×400 ______
3. $52 - 4 \times 5$ ______
4. $42 \div 7$ ______
5. $\begin{array}{r} 0{\cdot}6 \\ +\ 0{\cdot}25 \\ \hline \end{array}$
6. Divide 35 by 7. ______
7. $0{\cdot}2 + 0{\cdot}5$ ______
8. $0{\cdot}3 + 0{\cdot}6$ ______
9. $83 +$ ______ $= 106$
10. $\begin{array}{r} 5{\cdot}87 \\ +\ 0{\cdot}73 \\ \hline \end{array}$

11.

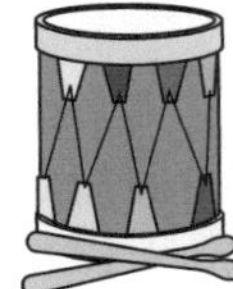

$4.20 $7.60 $1.90

a Circle the best estimate for the cost of 3 ring toys.

$3 $6 $8 $11

b If each item were reduced by fifty cents, what is the total cost of a drum and a toy horse?

______

c Circle the best estimate for the cost of 2 drums.

$10 $13 $15 $18

12. 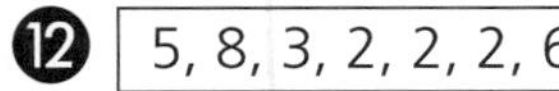
5, 8, 3, 2, 2, 2, 6

Write these scores in order from smallest to largest. ______

Find the:

a range ______ **b** median ______

c mode ______ **d** average ______

13. Arrange from smallest to largest.

67·25 54 7·21 8·9

______

19:2

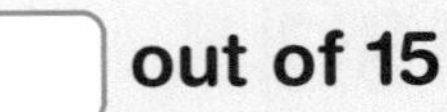

out of 15

1. $57 × 8 ______
2. 4 × $390 ______
3. $670 - 174$ ______
4. $280 \div 7$ ______
5. $\begin{array}{r} 97{\cdot}7 \\ +\ 3{\cdot}819 \\ \hline \end{array}$
6. $\frac{4}{5}$ of 25. ______
7. 80% of 10. ______
8. 80% of 40. ______
9. $57 +$ ______ $= 83$
10. $\begin{array}{r} 4{\cdot}5 \text{ billion} \\ -\ 2{\cdot}3 \text{ billion} \\ \hline \end{array}$

11. Find the total of these amounts, rounded off to the nearest 5 cents. ______

$45.00
$83.00
$35.09

12. How far did I travel if I drove for $3\frac{1}{2}$ hours at 96 km/h? ______

13. For these scores, what is:

5, 6, 6, 7, 9, 13, 18

a the range? ______

b the mode? ______

c the median? ______

d the average score? ______

14. **a** $0{\cdot}7 + 0{\cdot}3 =$ ______ **b** $1{\cdot}2 + 0{\cdot}8 =$ ______

15. **Tally of chores done**

Chore	Tally
Setting table	𝍸 𝍸
Clearing table	𝍸 |
Sweeping floor	𝍸
Wiping benches	𝍸 𝍸 ||||

Isabella kept a tally of the jobs she did during the week.

a Which job did she do 14 times? ______

b How many jobs were recorded altogether? ______

Eliminating possibilities

How old is Alan if:

- reversing the digits of Naomi's age gives Alan's age
- the total of their ages is 66
- Naomi is under 20 years of age.

Alan's age = ______

© PEARSON AUSTRALIA 2024 • *AUSTRALIAN SIGNPOST MATHS NSW 6 MENTALS* • ISBN 978 0 6557 0913 8

19:3 ☐ out of 6

1.
```
  7·867
+ 5·17
```

2.
```
  7·465 km
+ 3·978 km
```

3. Gillian began with this amount. She bought these items.

$15 $35.40 $1.80

Total amount spent: ______ Amount left: ______

4. For these scores, what is:

35, 36, 36, 37, 38, 40, 40, 40, 41, 47

a the range? ______
b the mode? ______
c the median? ______
d the average score? ______

5. Caleb sold three houses for $2·8 million, $3·5 million and $3·9 million. Write the total of these sales, expressed as million. ______

6. Complete the table and graph

Cups of water we drank		Number
Jasmine	𝍸 IIII	
Matilda	𝍸 𝍸 II	
Lydia	𝍸 II	
Isaac	𝍸 𝍸 𝍸 I	

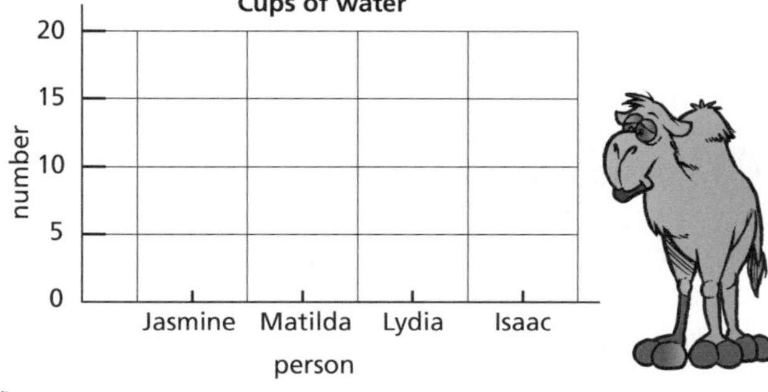

19:4 Extension ☐ out of 5

1.
```
    7·☐75
+   ☐·8☐6
   17·181
```

2.
```
    2·95☐
+   ☐·4☐6
   10·453
```

3. The number of faces plus the number of corners minus the number of edges on 24 square pyramids. ______

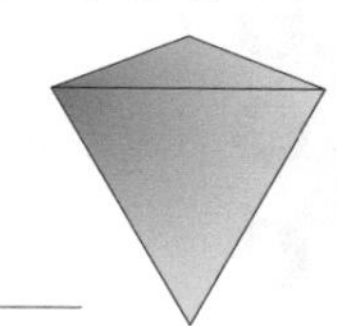

4. The top 5 countries in gold medals per ten million people in the 1996 Atlanta Olympics are shown.

Country	Gold Medals ptmp*
Australia	5·26
Cuba	6·36
Denmark	8
New Zealand	8·57
Switzerland	5·71

*ptmp = per ten million people

a Which country did the best? ______

b Australia's population was 19 million. How many gold medals did we win? ______

By how much did New Zealand beat:

c Denmark? ______ gold medals ptmp

d Australia? ______ gold medals ptmp

5. An 85-year-old Greek woman died in 180 BCE. When was she born? ______

Challenge

I surveyed all the members of my family and created this sector graph. How is this information misleading?

______
______
______
______

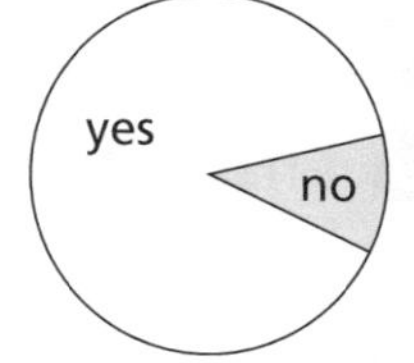

Consecutive numbers follow one another.

4, **5** and **6** are three **consecutive** numbers. Their sum is 15.

a On the list to the right, cross out those numbers that are the sum of 2 consecutive numbers, 3 consecutive numbers etc, up to the sum of 7 consecutive numbers.

b Which numbers are left? ______

What kind are they? ______

1			
2	3	4	5
6	7	8	9
10	11	12	13
14	15	16	17
18	19	20	21
22	23	24	25
26	27	28	29
30	31	32	33

20:1

out of 18

1. $\frac{1}{4}$ of 20. ____
2. 50 ÷ 5 ____
3. 7 × ____ = 63
4. 45 ÷ 9 ____
5. $\begin{array}{r} 457{\cdot}34 \\ +\ \ 35{\cdot}75 \\ \hline \end{array}$
6. 56 + ____ = 100
7. 35 + 78 = ____ + 80
8. 25 × ____ = 50
9. 0·9 × 100 ____
10. $\begin{array}{r} 83{\cdot}536 \\ +\ \ 9{\cdot}946 \\ \hline \end{array}$
11. Lexi bought a house for $1·3 million and sold it for $6·5 million. What is the difference between the buying and selling price, expressed as millions? ____
12. Find the change from $30 if the total is $25. ____
13. a 8 km = ____ m
    b 7655 mL = ____ L
    c 45 mm = ____ cm
    d 356 cm = ____ m
14. I had one 7·6 m length of wood and one 4·8 m length of wood.
    a What is the total length of the wood? ____
    b What is the difference between the lengths of wood? ____
15. My mass is 28·56 kg and my bag is 3·67 kg. When I wear my bag, what is my total mass? ____
16. What is 4·5 grams less than 1 kg? ____
17. Arrange these in descending order:
    $5\frac{1}{4}$, $1\frac{3}{8}$, 4, $3\frac{1}{8}$ ____
18. Write 5:45 pm using 24-hour time. ____

20:2

out of 18

1. 520 − 147 ____
2. 846 − 297 ____
3. $\frac{3}{4}$ of 28 ____
4. 125 ÷ 5 ____
5. $\begin{array}{r} 286{\cdot}478 \\ -\ \ 93{\cdot}982 \\ \hline \end{array}$
6. $\frac{4}{10}$ of 50. ____
7. 50% of $36. ____
8. 8·5 cm × 1000 ____
9. 765 + 449 ____
10. $\begin{array}{r} 79{\cdot}476 \\ +\ \ 8{\cdot}637 \\ \hline \end{array}$
11. $9\overline{)639}$
12. $4\overline{)804}$
13. $9\overline{)734}$
14. Find the total of these amounts, rounded off to the nearest 5 cents. ____

    $28.00
    $61.57
    $86.70

15. I used 26·546 L of water on the garden and 35·756 L of water on the grass. What was my total water usage? ____
16. I surveyed my cricket team for this graph. Explain why this graph is misleading.

    ____
    ____

Australia's favourite sports

17.

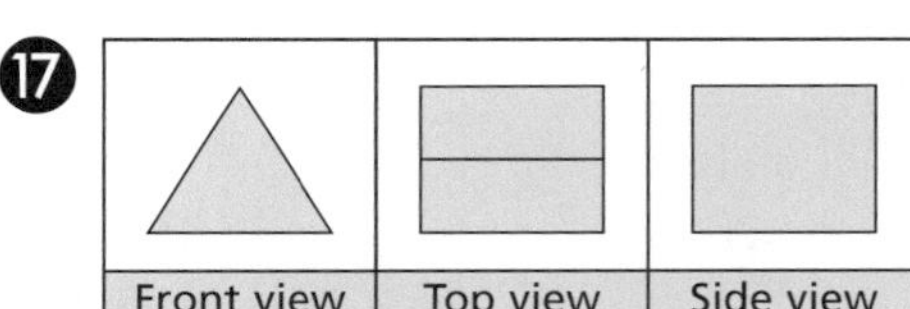

The object is a ____.

18. I painted 5·78 m of my fence on the first day, 2·67 m on the next and 3·55 m to finish. How long is my fence? ____

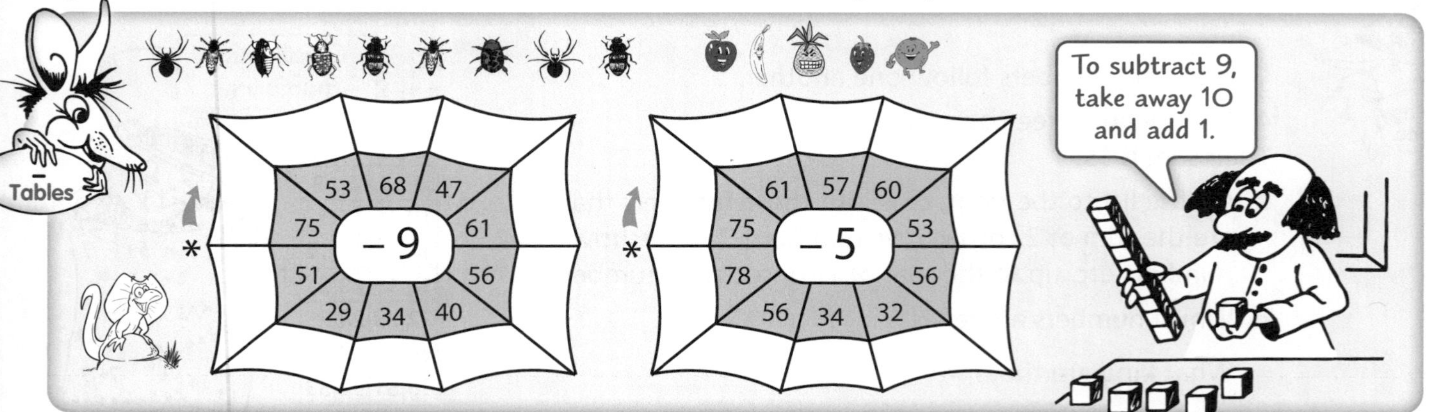

© PEARSON AUSTRALIA 2024 • *AUSTRALIAN SIGNPOST MATHS NSW 6 MENTALS* • ISBN 978 0 6557 0013 8

20:3 [ ] out of 9

1. $\begin{array}{r} 4 \cdot 086 \\ +\ 5 \cdot 789 \\ \hline \end{array}$

2. $\begin{array}{r} 3 \cdot 9988\text{km} \\ -\ 3 \cdot 8793\text{km} \\ \hline \end{array}$

3. On Monday I walked 4·867 km and on Tuesday I walked 5·347 km.

   a What was the total distance I walked? ______
   b What was the difference between the two walks? ______

4. **a** Which letter has a 50% chance that the spinner will land on it? ______
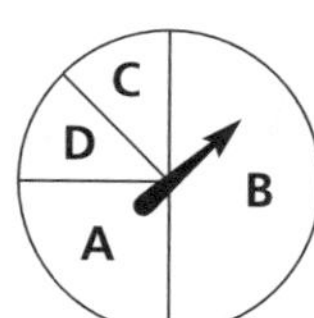

   What is the chance, as a decimal, that the spinner will land on:
   b B? ______ **c** A? ______

5. When wearing my bag, I weighed 33·75 kg. When I took my bag off, I weighed 29·87 kg.
   What was the mass of the bag? ______

6. 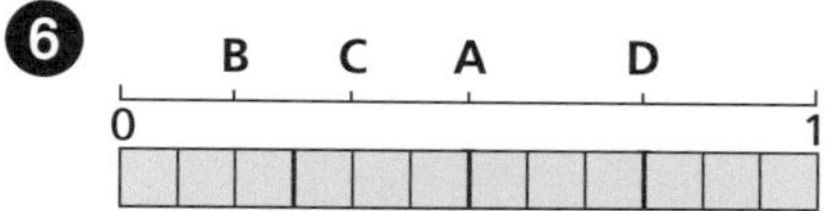

   On this number line what fraction is at:
   a A? ____ **b** B? ____
   c C? ____ **d** D? ____

7. Draw the top, front and side elevations of this solid.
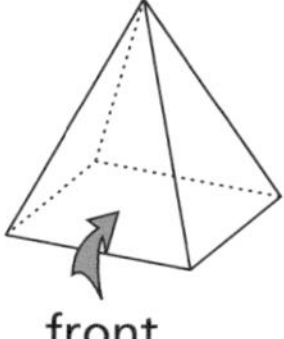

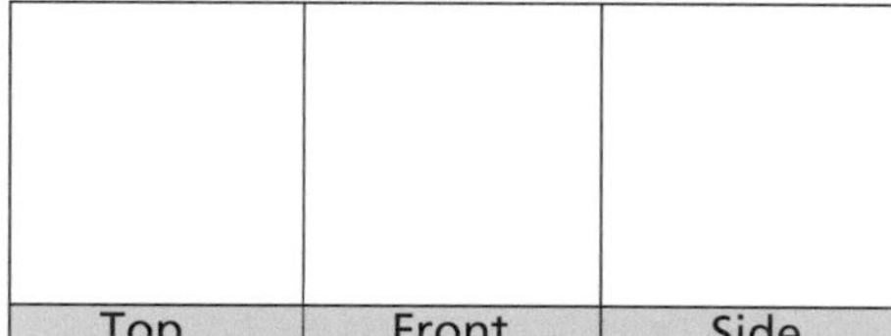

8. What is 1·4 metres less than a kilometre? ______

9. $(3 \times 10^4) + (4 \times 10^3) + (9 \times 10^2) + (2 \times 10^1) + 7$
   = ______

20:4 Extension [ ] out of 7

1. $\begin{array}{r} 3 \cdot \square\, 9\ 7 \\ +\ \square \cdot 1\ \square\, 4 \\ \hline 8 \cdot 7\ 3\ 1 \end{array}$

2. $\begin{array}{r} 5 \cdot 6\ 4\ \square \\ +\ \square \cdot 5\ \square\, 9 \\ \hline 12 \cdot 1\ 8\ 7 \end{array}$

3. The number of faces plus the number of corners minus the number of edges on 26 triangular pyramids. ______
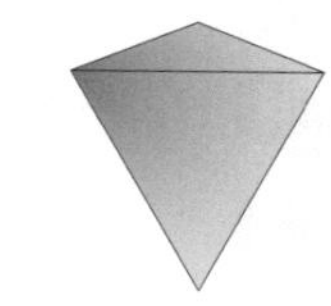

4. What is 4·545 kilograms less than 5 tonnes? ______

5. Jason has five times as many cards as Harvey and 35 less than Jen. How many cards do they have altogether if Harvey has 25? ______

6. I had 5·675 kg of flour in one bag and 3 kg 780 g in another. How much less than 10 kg did I have? ______

7. Draw the elevations for this shape.
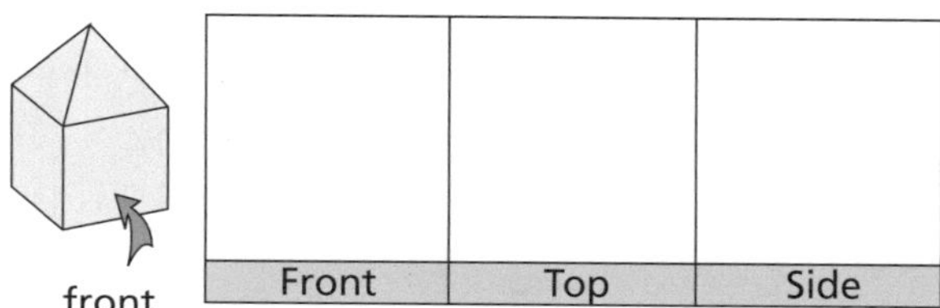

Challenge

Mystery number clues?

I am even. My two digits, when added, make 12. I am less than 60. ______

Make up your own clues for a mystery number.

______

______

______

______

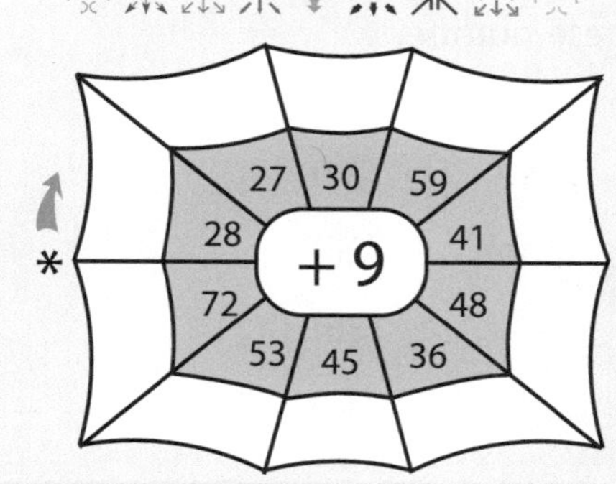

© PEARSON AUSTRALIA 2024 • • ISBN 978 0 6557 0913 8

21:1 out of 17

1. 0·2 + 0·8 ____
2. $5 × 70 ____
3. 24 ÷ 8 ____
4. 32 ÷ 8 ____
5. 35·867 − 19·75
6. 100 m − 2·5 m ____
7. 8 × 800 ____
8. Zero squared. ____
9. $\frac{1}{3}$ of 36. ____
10. 36·87 + 8·93
11. What is 1·1 cm less than 1 m? ____
12. 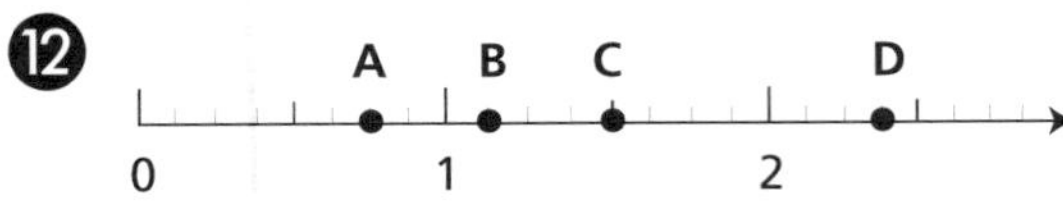

Give the fraction at the letter, as its simplest mixed numeral.
   a A ____ **b** B ____
   c C ____ **d** D ____
13. Write an estimate, to the nearest whole number, in the next algorithm then answer both questions.
   a 3·367 + 5·976 + ____
   b 6·204 + 1·689 + ____
14. Round $56.89 to the nearest:
   a 5 cents ____ **b** dollar ____
15. Round 9·864 to the nearest tenth. ____
16. **a** Halves in 5 wholes. ____
   b Quarters in 5 wholes. ____

17. I throw one standard dice. Write, as a fraction, my chance of rolling a number less than 4. $\frac{\square}{\square}$

21:2 out of 18

1. 720 ÷ 8 ____
2. $\frac{2}{5}$ of 15 ____
3. 700 ÷ 10 ____
4. $\frac{7}{10} - \frac{2}{5}$ ____
5. $546.45 + $356.78
6. $560 × 7 ____
7. Increase 34 by 35. ____
8. Triple 645. ____
9. 356 + ____ = 412
10. $4782 × 7
11. 7)392
12. 9)576
13. 10)640
14. 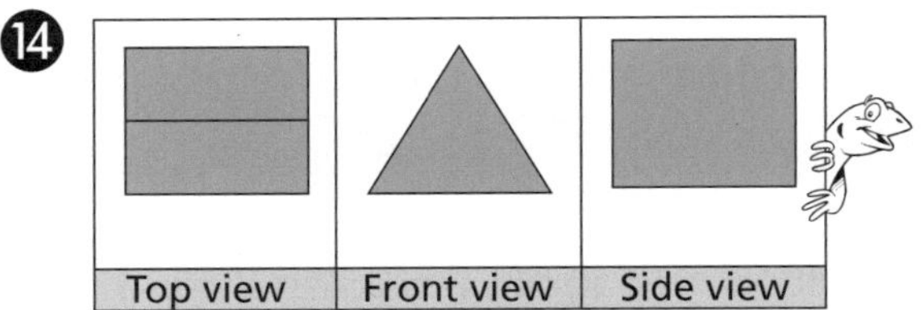

Do these views show a triangular pyramid or a triangular prism?
____
15. What is 4·65 metres less than 20 metres? ____
16. Write an estimate, to the nearest whole number, in the next algorithm then answer both questions.
   a 9·465 + 4·6 + ____
   b 7·364 + 4·7 + ____
17. I throw one standard dice. Write, as a fraction, my chance of rolling a prime number. (Note that 1 is not a prime number.) $\frac{\square}{\square}$
18. **a** Metres in 5·6 kilometres ____
   b Kilograms in 6·9 tonnes ____

Turn to ID card D on page 9.
Give the answers for these numbers.

(21) ____ (22) ____ graph
(23) ____ graph (24) ____ plot
(25) ____ graph (26) ____ graph
(27) ____ (28) ____
(29) ____ (30) ____

© PEARSON AUSTRALIA 2024 • *AUSTRALIAN SIGNPOST MATHS NSW 6 MENTALS* • ISBN 978 0 6557 0913 8

21:3 ☐ out of 12

1. Write an estimate, to the nearest whole number, in the next algorithm then answer both questions.

   a $\begin{array}{r} 3{\cdot}198 \\ +\ 3{\cdot}08 \\ \hline \end{array}$ + ______

   b $\begin{array}{r} 4{\cdot}579 \\ +\ 7{\cdot}75 \\ \hline \end{array}$ + ______

2. Arrange −2, 5 and −3 in order from smallest to largest. ______

3. In a newspaper there are 50 pages. If $\frac{1}{10}$ of the newspaper contains comics, how many pages of comics are there? ______

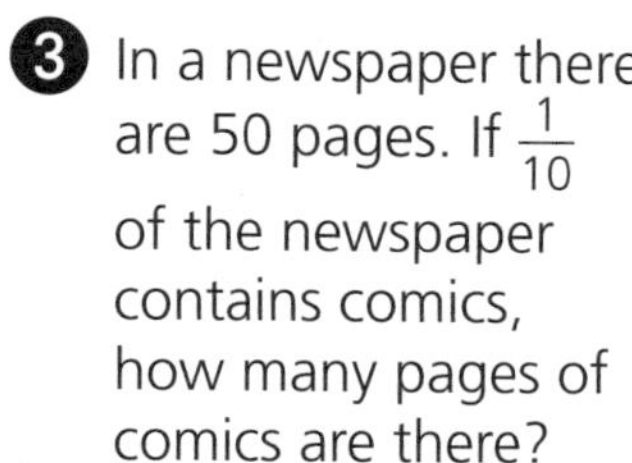

4. Arrange in ascending order: 0·06, 0·63, 0·36 ______

5. How many seeds are in a packet if a quarter of the seeds can be used to plant 3 rows of 9 seeds? ______

6. 100 − 32·8 − 0·2 ______

7. Round 298·105 to the nearest hundredth. ______

8. If you are facing north-west, what direction is to your:

   a left? ______ **b** right? ______

9. 18 − 9 + 5 − 12·15 ______

10. Round 32·6 to the nearest whole. ______

11. The temperature on Monday was −5°C. What is the temperature if it was 7 degrees colder the following Monday? ______

12. How much of the block is covered:

    a as a fraction? ______

    b as a decimal? ______

21:4 Extension ☐ out of 8

1. $\begin{array}{r} \square\cdot 7\ 0\ \square \\ +\ \ 8\cdot \square\ 5\ 9 \\ \hline 1\ 3\cdot 1\ 6\ 1 \end{array}$

2. $\begin{array}{r} 9\cdot 2\ \square\ 7 \\ +\ \ \square\cdot 9\ 6\ \square \\ \hline 1\ 2\cdot 2\ 1\ 4 \end{array}$

3. One seventh of the whole is 5. Write the value of the shaded part.

   a ______ **b** ______

4. A man born in 365 BCE died 40 years later. The year he died was ______.

5. Which one-digit number when multiplied by 7·79 gives an answer closest to 40? ______

6. The number of parallelograms of any size in this figure. ______

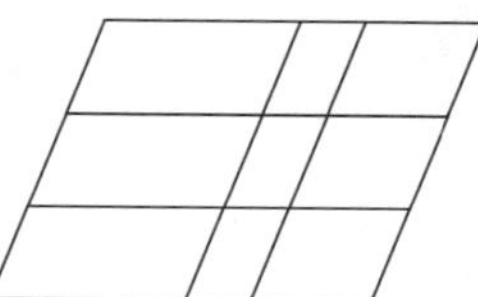

7. I ride in my car for 36·9 km every day, then ride my bike for 13·9 km. How far did I travel in:

   a a week? ______ **b** 6 weeks? ______

8. What is half of 29 plus double 12·25? ______

Challenge

Construct a number sentence to match the problem, then find the value of the missing number.

a *Five less than a number is 87.* ______

b *Twice a number, minus 2 makes 28.* ______

c *The product of a number and 6 is 90.* ______

Calculator crossnumber puzzle

Across

1 81 × 305
5 9743 − 9203
6 6^2 + 4332
8 475 ÷ 25
9 223 × 3
10 821^2

Down

1 4446 ÷ 19
2 9000 − 1631
3 275 ÷ 5
4 701 391 + 103 510
7 56^2
9 25 × 24

22:1   ☐ out of 17

1. $6{\cdot}8 + 5$ ______
2. $200 - 68$ ______
3. $30 \div 6 \times 6$ ______
4. 4 squared. ______
5. $\begin{array}{r} \$46.37 \\ +\ \$27.97 \\ \hline \end{array}$
6. 7 times 900. ______
7. $\frac{3}{5}$ of 40. ______
8. $0{\cdot}7 \times 100$ ______
9. $\frac{3}{10} + \frac{4}{10}$ ______
10. $\begin{array}{r} \$45.9 \\ \times\ \ \ 3 \\ \hline \end{array}$
11. 

How many counting numbers are:
a 2 units away from 4? ______
b less than 3 units from 4? ______
12. 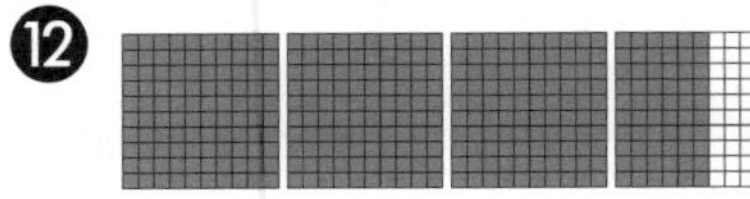 
Show this number as a:
a decimal ______
b mixed number ______
13. Rhonda drinks 600 mL of juice each day. How many litres does she drink in a week? ______
14. List all the possible outcomes if I roll 2 standard dice and add the numbers shown.
______
15. Write as an improper fraction:
a $2\frac{1}{4}$ ______ **b** $3\frac{3}{5}$ ______
16. Arrange in descending order.
75 124 911   75 241 119   75 921 977
______
17. Complete the pattern:
56·36, 58·39, 60·42, ______, ______,

22:2   ☐ out of 20

1. 99×6 ______
2. $400 \div 8$ ______
3. $5^2 + 546$ ______
4. $560 \div 8$ ______
5. $\begin{array}{r} \$26.57 \\ +\ \$74.89 \\ \hline \end{array}$
6. $6{\cdot}7$ km $\times 1000$ ______
7. $8 \div (64 - 56)$ ______
8. $\frac{8}{12} + \frac{3}{4}$ ______
9. Triple 297. ______
10. $\begin{array}{r} 35{\cdot}46 \\ \times\ \ \ \ 9 \\ \hline \end{array}$
11. $4\overline{)648}$
12. $7\overline{)936}$
13. $8\overline{)773}$
14. I used 0·8 m of ribbon to wrap each present. How many metres did I use for 8 presents? ______
15. What is the percentage probability of tossing a head when I toss a coin? ______
16. What is the difference between walking straight to school (12 072 paces) or going via the shops (16 180 paces)? ______
17. A stone is kicked 5·8 m twice, then 7·8 m, and finally 12·1 m twice. How far has it been kicked altogether? ______
18. List the factors of 18. ______
19. Write an estimate, to the nearest whole number, in the next algorithm then answer both questions.
a $\begin{array}{r} 8{\cdot}235 \\ +\ 1{\cdot}856 \\ \hline \end{array}$ + ______
b $\begin{array}{r} 7{\cdot}079 \\ +\ 3{\cdot}907 \\ \hline \end{array}$ + ______
20. I bought 600 bananas at 75c each. What was the total cost? ______

Concept

In a magic square, the sum of each row, column and diagonal is the same.

11	6	7
4	8	12
9	10	5

Here, all lines add up to 24.

Complete these magic squares.

a

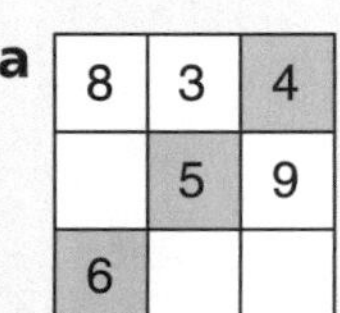

8	3	4
	5	9
6		

b

9		5
2		10
7		3

c

8		
9	7	
		6

Add any line to find the sum.

© PEARSON AUSTRALIA 2024 • *AUSTRALIAN SIGNPOST MATHS NSW 6 MENTALS* • ISBN 978 0 6557 0913 8

22:3 out of 8

1. Write an estimate to the nearest whole number in the next algorithm, then answer both questions.

   a $\begin{array}{r} 7{\cdot}108 \\ +\ 2{\cdot}897 \\ \hline \end{array}$ $\begin{array}{r} \\ + \underline{\qquad} \end{array}$ **b** $\begin{array}{r} 5{\cdot}805 \\ +\ 3{\cdot}868 \\ \hline \end{array}$ $\begin{array}{r} \\ + \underline{\qquad} \end{array}$

2. I jumped 98 cm, 98 cm, 1 m, and 1 m 11 cm. What was the sum of the jumps? ______

3. The value of the 2 in:

   a 6·32 ______ **b** 70·25 ______

4. Find the size of the reflex angle. ______

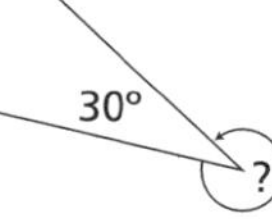

5. I poured six 0·7 L cups of water into the jug. How much did I pour into the jug? ______

6. Cara begins with $95.50. She buys:

   a What is Cara's total cost? ______

   b How much money is left? ______

   c If Cara buys this amount of milk and bread once a week, how much would she spend on this in 7 weeks? ______

7. How heavy are 8 bags of flour each weighing 4·75kg? ______

8. (28 − 14) + (89 − 67) ______

22:4 Extension out of 7

1. **a**

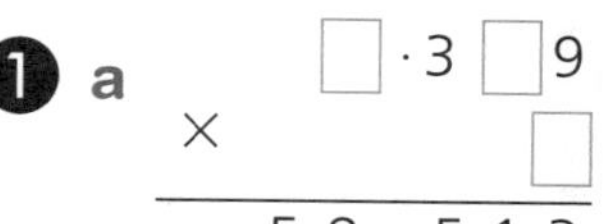

$\begin{array}{r} \square\cdot 3\ \square 9 \\ \times \qquad\ \ \square \\ \hline 58\cdot 513 \end{array}$

2. **b**

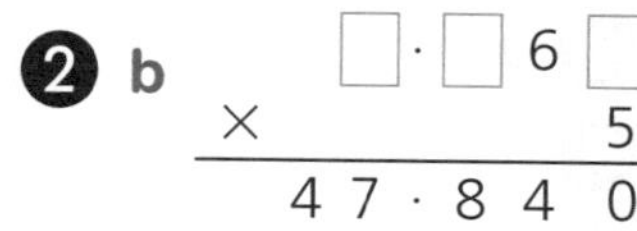

$\begin{array}{r} \square\cdot\square\ 6\ \square \\ \times \qquad\quad 5 \\ \hline 47\cdot 840 \end{array}$

3. I spent 2 hours and 15 minutes on my laptop in the morning and again in the evening, 5 days a week. On the other 2 days, I spent 3 hours and 45 minutes each day. For how long did I use my laptop over a four-week period? ______

4. A $1799 laptop was on sale for 25% off. How many could be bought with a budget of $20 000? ______

5. I have 5 shirts and 4 ties. In how many ways can I choose one of each? ______

6. 4 oranges cost $5.40 and a banana costs 40c more than an orange. David bought 5 oranges and 7 bananas. He paid and his change was $30. How much money did he start with? ______

7. Estimate the number that would be at point A on the number line. ______

   8966·5 ——— A ——— 8967·8

Challenge

Write questions, using different operations, that are equal to:

a 56 − 47 **b** 93 − 29

= ______ = ______

= ______ = ______

= ______ = ______

= ______ = ______

Calculator crossnumber puzzle

Across	Down
1 714 × 33	**1** 4148 ÷ 17
5 6463 − 5917	**2** 6000 − 807
6 975 + 3618	**3** 625 ÷ 25
8 7384 ÷ 568	**4** 328 600 + 240 945
9 $25^2 + 240$	**7** 72^2
10 675^2	**9** 6000 − 5194

1		2		3	■	4
	■		■	5		
6	7			■	■	
■	8		■	9		
■		■	■		■	
■	10					

23:1 out of 22

1. $0{\cdot}3 + 0{\cdot}7$ ______
2. $5 - 0{\cdot}5$ ______
3. $\frac{1}{4} + \frac{1}{4}$ ______
4. $63 +$ ______ $= 100$
5. $\begin{array}{r} 4{\cdot}678 \\ +\ 0{\cdot}856 \\ \hline \end{array}$
6. $756 - 136$ ______
7. $\frac{1}{4}$ of 28 ______
8. $600 - 78$ ______
9. $81 \div 9 \times 9$ ______
10. $\begin{array}{r} 8{\cdot}956\,\text{km} \\ -\ 0{\cdot}86 \\ \hline \end{array}$
11. $9\overline{)3875}$
12. $4\overline{)26606}$
13. Which is smallest, 7·77, 7·17 or 7·7? ______
14. $9 \div (45 - 42) + 34$ ______
15. Write the improper fraction for:
    a $3\frac{4}{5}$ ______ **b** $2\frac{1}{8}$ ______
16. Round 7 465 768 to the nearest million. ______
17. How many tens can be taken from:
    a 65 000 ______
    b 75 350 ______
18. True or false?
    a $576 + 765 = 765 - 576$ ______
    b $78 \times 34 = 34 \times 78$ ______
19. I gave 8 pencils to all my friends. If I gave out 72 pencils, how many friends do I have? ______
20. Change 560 mm to centimetres. ______
21. What number is 17 less than 100? ______
22. The value of 6 in 354·768. ______

23:2 out of 20

1. $\frac{16}{10} - \frac{2}{5}$ ______
2. $\frac{3}{4}$ of 24. ______
3. 67×57 ______
4. 99×34 ______
5. $\begin{array}{r} 7{\cdot}308\,\text{m} \\ \times\quad 6 \\ \hline \end{array}$
6. $0{\cdot}5 - 0{\cdot}25$ ______
7. $1345 +$ ______ $= 1600$
8. $1546 -$ ______ $= 1256$
9. 20% of \$600. ______
10. $\begin{array}{r} 4{\cdot}726\,\text{cm} \\ \times\quad 9 \\ \hline \end{array}$
11. $10\overline{)96890}$
12. $6\overline{)6966}$

13. How much would each person receive if 4 students equally shared 5 bananas? (Write your answer as a mixed number.) ______
14. $(3 +$ ______ $) \times 7 = 35$ ______
15. 3 days from now it will be Saturday. What day was it 2 days ago? ______
16. $(5 \times 10^4) + (6 \times 10^3) + (4 \times 10^2) + (9 \times 10^1) + 9 =$ ______
17. Find the size of the reflex angle. ______

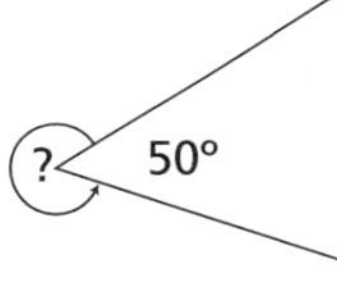

18. I printed a document 6 times. I used 9006 pieces of paper How many pages were in the document if I printed on only one side of the paper? ______

19. Change 3456 mm to centimetres. ______
20. I have \$56 867 in my bank account. How many \$10 notes could I withdraw? ______

© PEARSON AUSTRALIA 2024 • *AUSTRALIAN SIGNPOST MATHS NSW 6 MENTALS* • ISBN 978 0 6557 0913 8

23:3 out of 11

1. Write an estimate, to the nearest whole number, in the next algorithm then answer both questions.

   a 6·387 + 9·576 + ______

   b 8·99 + 4·897 + ______

2. $10\overline{)25460}$

3. $3\overline{)9036}$

4. Write as a decimal:
   a 3 and 56 hundredths ______
   b 7 and 893 thousandths ______
   c 8 point three four two ______

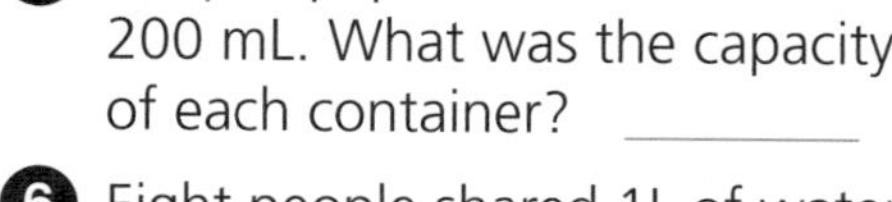

5. 8 liquid paper containers held 200 mL. What was the capacity of each container? ______

6. Eight people shared 1L of water. What is a fair share? ______

7. Change 3567 mm to centimetres. ______

8. 5400 people were placed in groups of 10 How many groups were formed? ______

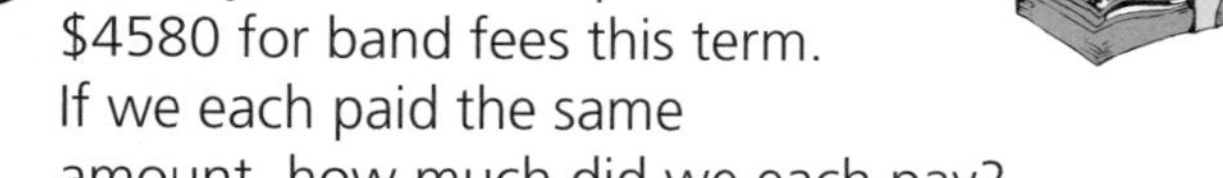

9. 9 of my friends and I paid $4580 for band fees this term. If we each paid the same amount, how much did we each pay? ______

10. a 467 km = ______ m
    b 5763 g = ______ kg
    c 7·8 t = ______ kg
    d 4657 mm = ______ m
    e 8674 mL = ______ L
    f 6 hectares = ______ m^2
    g 78·4 km = ______ m

11. What is my change from $100 after spending $56.35? ______

23:4 Extension out of 8

1. Circle the numbers that are divisible by both 4 and 5.

   610 305 1444 1600 420

2. The average of 13 numbers is 4·6. What is their sum? ______

3. It cost me $2304 to replace all the tyres on my car.
   a What was the cost of one tyre? ______
   b If the tyres were 20% off, how much would I save? ______

4. Train A is travelling at 38 km/h. Train B is travelling at 82 km/h. If they each travelled at this speed for an hour, how much further would Train B travel? ______

5. My heart beats 5040 times in an hour. How many times would it beat at this rate in 6 minutes? ______

6. 3 days from now it will be Tuesday. What day was it 30 days ago? ______

7. $65 \times 4 + 234 \div 9$ ______

8. To the total of 35, 68 and 35, add the product of 8 and 14. ______

Challenge

Toss 2 coins 25 times and colour a box for each head or tail thrown.

Heads																									
Tails																									

What was the total of:

a *heads?* ______ b *tails?* ______

What was the percentage of:

a *heads?* ______ b *tails?* ______

Complete this grid to write the distances in three ways.

8·375 km	8 km 375 m	8375 m
		2914 m
5·446 km		
	9 km 125 m	
		3546 m
9·897 km		

1000 m makes 1 km.

24:1 out of 17

1. 900 − 67 ____
2. ____ + 51 = 89
3. 81 ÷ 9 + 17 ____
4. 12 × 5 − 35 ____
5. $\begin{array}{r} 2{\cdot}613 \\ \times \quad 2 \\ \hline \end{array}$
6. $\frac{8}{10} - \frac{1}{2}$ ____
7. 3·76 × 100 ____
8. $\frac{1}{4}$ of 32. ____
9. 78 − ____ = 34
10. $\begin{array}{r} 7{\cdot}024 \\ \times \quad 3 \\ \hline \end{array}$
11. $10\overline{)7459{\cdot}0}$
12. $3\overline{)27{\cdot}09}$
13. a 456·43 ÷ 10 ____
    b 9·345 × 100 ____
    c 70·6384 ÷ 1000 ____
    d 46·5678 × 100 ____
14. How many tens in 34 567? ____
15. Measure the length of this bar.

    ____ mm or ____ cm
16. a 4·5 cm = ____ mm
    b 78 mm = ____ cm
    c 4300 m = ____ km
    d 6·8 km = ____ m
17. Which group of shapes below can be rearranged to make the flag on the right? ____

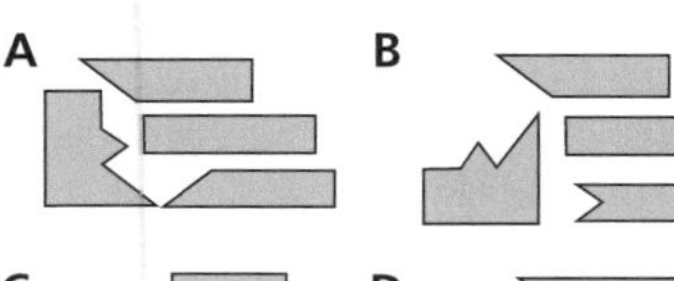

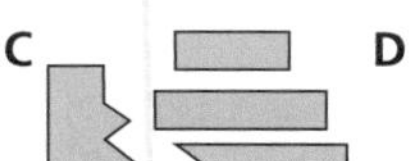

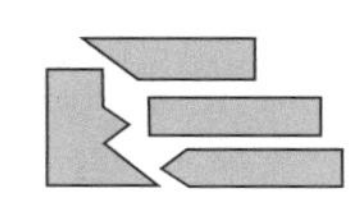

24:2 out of 18

1. $\frac{5}{6}$ of 54. ____
2. $8^2 - 48$ ____
3. $\frac{3}{4}$ of 100. ____
4. 7·896 ÷ 10 ____
5. $\begin{array}{r} 3{\cdot}496\,\text{m} \\ \times \quad 7 \\ \hline \end{array}$
6. 0·6 + 1·4 ____
7. \$15 − \$3.67 ____
8. $\frac{18}{10} - \frac{8}{5}$ ____
9. 268 + ____ = 867
10. $\begin{array}{r} 5{\cdot}989\,\text{cm} \\ \times \quad 8 \\ \hline \end{array}$
11. $10\overline{)375008}$
12. $7\overline{)89{\cdot}04}$
13. 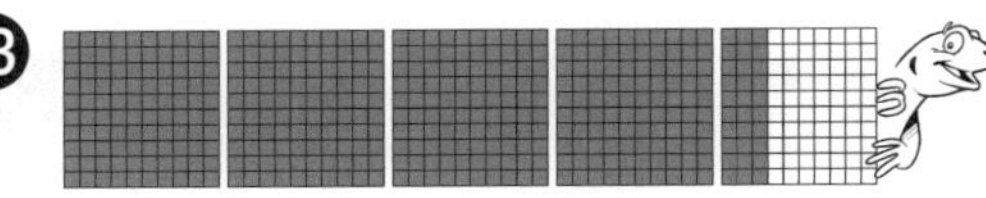

    Write this number as a:
    a mixed number ____
    b improper fraction ____
    c decimal ____
14. 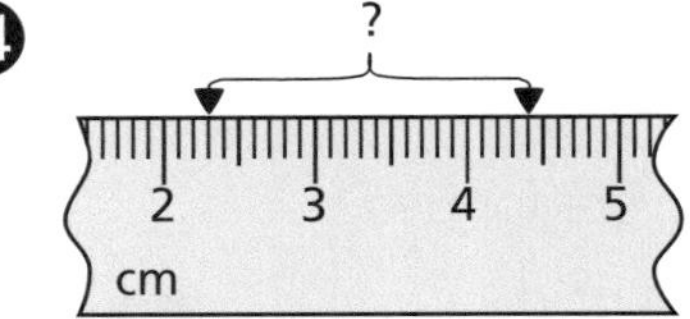

    Write the difference between the 2 marks on the ruler in:
    a centimetres ____
    b millimetres ____
15. Aimee ran an average of 4·5 km each day for 5 days. What was the total distance she ran? ____
16. a 876·45 ÷ 10 ____
    b 578·934 × 100 ____
17. a $\frac{1}{2}$ km = ____ m b $1\frac{3}{4}$ km = ____ m
18. What is my speed if I travel 178 km in 2 hours? ____

Strategy Time

Using a model

Alan, Rhonda, Rachel and Heather will sit on the four seats shown. Alan is in seat 3. Rhonda will sit between Rachel and Alan. Who will sit in seat number:

a 1? ____ b 2? ____

c 4? ____

© PEARSON AUSTRALIA 2024 • *AUSTRALIAN SIGNPOST MATHS NSW 6 MENTALS* • ISBN 978 0 6557 0913 8

24:3 — out of 11

1.
```
  5467884
   208556
     4678
+  987967
```

2.
```
  5·989 cm
×       5
```

3. $10\overline{)2658{\cdot}0}$

4. $9\overline{)26{\cdot}91}$

5. a 6247·21 ÷ 100 ______
   b 46·5678 × 1000 ______

6. What is the length of the black line in:
   a centimetres? ______
   b millimetres? ______

7. What is my speed if I travel 369 km in 3 hours? ______

8. I have walked 350 m of my 4·7 km journey. How much further have I to go? ______

9. a 9·7 km = ______ m
   b 367 mm = ______ cm
   c 8470 m = ______ km
   d 13·7 cm = ______ mm
   e $5\frac{4}{10}$ km = ______ m

10. The chance of Sophie scoring a goal at netball is about 1 in 3. About how many did she miss if she scored 7 goals? ______

11. 24 × 20 = (20 × ____) + (____ × ____)
    = ______ + ______
    = ______

24:4 — out of 6 — Extension

1. How many millimetres in 6 m? ______

2. For our excursion, 3 buses took our group 90 km to our destination. Bus A had an average speed of 60 km/h. Bus B had an average speed of 52 km/h and Bus C had an average speed of 45 km/h. How long did the passengers of Bus A have to wait at the destination until Bus C arrived? ______

3. □ − △ + ▭ = 20
   If □ − △ = 13 and □ + ▭ = 25, find the value of △. ______

4. I am walking to my Nana's house, which is 2·5 km from my place. I will stay an hour and then walk back home. If I am 467 m from my house, how much further will I have to walk to get there and then back home again? ______

5. Sue has emus and horses. These have 40 legs altogether. What is the greatest number of horses possible? ______

6. What is the largest number of squares you can make using 22 unbroken paddle pop sticks? ______

Challenge

Complete:

63·789 × 100	______	102·3 ÷ 10	______
49·028 ÷ 10	______	32·41 × 10	______
8·7034 × 1000	______	3409·8 ÷ 1000	______
9·416 × 100	______	429·37 ÷ 100	______
31·08 × 10	______	30·002 × 100	______
9002·3 ÷ 1000	______	5·1123 × 1000	______
8·325 × 100	______	9007·6 ÷ 1000	______
793·2 ÷ 10	______	2·31 × 10	______

Arkos wanted to find the thickness of a sheet of paper.
He found that the thickness of the pages in a 200-page book was 1 cm.

a How many sheets of paper make 200 pages? ______

b Complete this table.

Thickness	10 mm	1 mm	0·1 mm
Number of sheets	100		

c How thick would a book of 160 pages be? ______

25:1 ☐ out of 15

1. 80 − 59 ______
2. 800 − 59 ______
3. 0·7 + 1·3 ______
4. 7 × 8 − 30 ______
5. 365·46 − 95·48
6. $\frac{10}{12} - \frac{7}{12}$ ______
7. 36·7 × 10 km ______
8. 4°C less than 0. ______
9. 45 + ______ = 97
10. 746·24 + 36·79
11. Round the numbers in questions 5 and 10 to the nearest whole number to estimate and check your answers.
    a Round

    b Round
    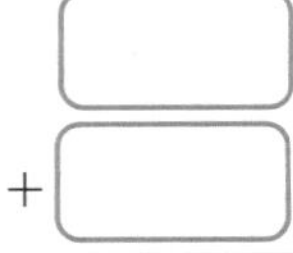
12. **a** 500 ÷ 50 (÷ 10) (÷ 10) ______ ÷ ______ = ______
    b 4·9 ÷ 0·7 (× 10) (× 10) ______ ÷ ______ = ______
13. The length of this pencil.
    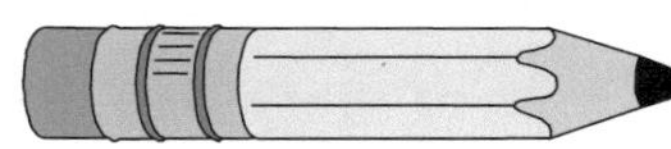
    a Estimate = ______ mm
    b Measure = ______ mm or ______ cm
14. **a** 6247·21 ÷ 10 ______
    b 46·5678 × 100 ______
15. **a** 56·9 cm = ______ mm
    b 8769 mm = ______ cm
    c 2·5 cm = ______ m
    d $8\frac{2}{10}$ km = ______ m

25:2 ☐ out of 16

1. 81 ÷ 9 × 6 ______
2. $\frac{4}{10}$ of 50 L. ______
3. 45·9 ÷ 10 ______
4. $8 - \frac{4}{5}$ ______
5. 263078 + 26478
6. $\frac{11}{12} - \frac{1}{2}$ ______
7. 62 × 74 ______
8. 54 ÷ ______ = 9
9. $7 − $3.45 ______
10. 297865 − 74986
11. Write 586 cm as metres using a decimal. ______
12. **a** 900 ÷ 30 (÷ 10) (÷ 10) ______ ÷ ______ = ______
    b 3·6 ÷ 0·6 (× 10) (× 10) ______ ÷ ______ = ______
13. Round to the nearest whole to estimate:
    a 67·5 − 28·9 ______
    b 35 ÷ 6·936 ______

14. **a** 356·6 ÷ 100 ______
    b 948·23 × 1000 ______
15. Estimate, then measure the length of this line.
    a Estimate = ______ mm
    b Measure = ______ mm or ______ cm
16. **a** 56·9 m = ______ cm
    b 87 654 m = ______ km
    c 3756 mm = ______ cm
    d 27·9 cm = ______ cm ______ mm
    e 8·846 km = ______ m

Estimation

Choose a measurement from the table as an estimate for the length of a:

a bed ______ **b** mouse ______
c bus ______ **d** paperclip ______
e shoe ______ **f** cricket bat ______
g car ______ **h** ant ______

2 cm	10 m
0·5 cm	0·5 km
2 m	50 m
2 km	4 m
100 km	8 cm
20 cm	10 km
1 mm	75 cm

© PEARSON AUSTRALIA 2024 • *AUSTRALIAN SIGNPOST MATHS NSW 6 MENTALS* • ISBN 978 0 6557 0913 8

25:3 out of 11

1.
```
   3768567
    106587
      2758
 +  357003
```

2.
```
   $3567.68
 − $ 426.03
```

3. Write 926 cm as metres using a decimal. ________

4. Each parking space in a car park is 230 cm wide. What is the width of 19 car spaces placed side by side? (Write your answer in metres.) ________

5. a 128 ÷ 16 (÷ 2) (÷ 2) ____ ÷ ____ = ____
   b 54 ÷ 18 (÷ 2) (÷ 2) ____ ÷ ____ = ____

6. Round to the nearest whole to estimate:
   a 90·3 − 73·6 ________
   b 81 ÷ 8·715 ________

7.

Write in order, from smallest to largest:
$\frac{1}{2}$, $\frac{1}{12}$, $\frac{1}{3}$, $\frac{1}{6}$, $\frac{1}{4}$ ________

8. a 892·89 ÷ 10 ________
   b 79·254 × 1000 ________

9. a 35·27 ÷ 10 ________
   b 872·1 ÷ 100 ________
   c 9138 ÷ 1000 ________

10. a 38·2 cm = ______ cm ______ mm
    b 36·67 km = ______ m

11. (3 × 70) + (9 × 400) = ________

25:4 Extension out of 4

1. (45 × 67) + (47 × 89) × 3 ________

2. Sami is 137 cm tall. How many more millimetres does he need to grow to reach 170 cm? ________

3. Jedda needs to drop off parcels at **A**, **B**, **C** and **D**.
   a Calculate the shortest route if he starts and ends at **E**. ________
   b His average speed is 60 km/h. How long will this trip take, to the nearest minute. ________

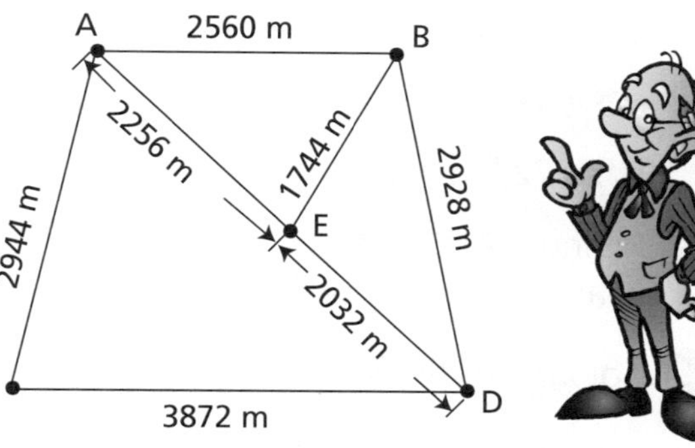

4. The shaded part has a value of 12. What is the value of the whole? ________

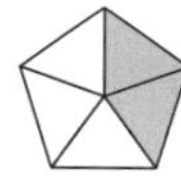

Challenge

Use a digital map (e.g. Whereis.com) to find the distance and travel time to visit landmarks from your location.

____
____
____
____

Example of factors

Draw the rectangles that have an area of 6 units^2.

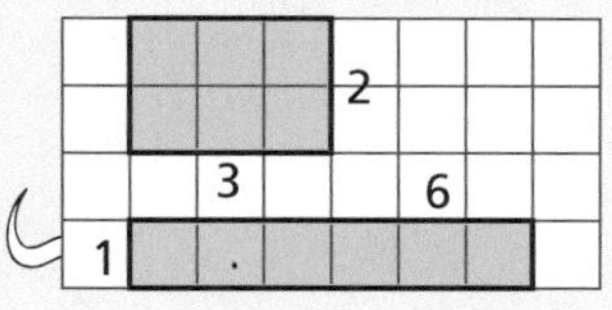

Draw rectangles of area 12 units^2.

List the factors. ________

26:1 ☐ out of 18

1. 456 + 143 ______
2. 748 − 234 ______
3. 7 × (3 + 7) ______
4. $5 - \frac{1}{2}$ ______
5. 6^2 plus 30. ______
6. $\frac{1}{2}$ of 62. ______
7. 54 + ______ = 78
8. 50% of $26. ______
9. $7\overline{)65{\cdot}94}$
10. $10\overline{)354657{\cdot}0}$
11. Estimate, then measure the length of this line.

    a Estimate = ______ mm

    b Measure = ______ mm or ______ cm
12. a 5·6 cm = ______ cm ______ mm

    b 78·72 km = ______ km ______ m
13. Round 3·876 to the nearest whole number ______
14. Colour $\frac{1}{3}$ of this shape red and $\frac{1}{4}$ of the shape blue. How much is coloured altogether? ______

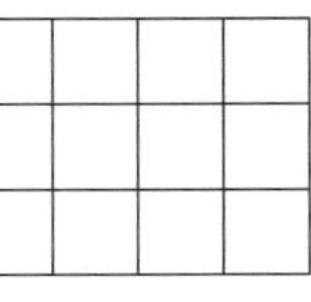

15. 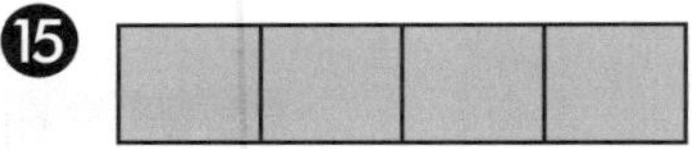

    a $\frac{1}{4} + \frac{2}{4} = \frac{\square}{\square}$ b $\frac{2}{4} + \frac{2}{4} = \frac{\square}{\square}$ = ______
16. a 546·21 ÷ 10 ______

    b 867·34 × 100 ______
17. How many tens can be taken from:

    a 573? ______   b 86 846? ______
18. (3 × 50) + (7 × 30) = ______

26:2 ☐ out of 19

1. 63 ÷ 9 × 7 ______
2. 3·7 L × 10 ______
3. $\frac{9}{12} - \frac{4}{6}$ ______
4. $50 − $12 ______
5. 78 − ______ = 27
6. 56 − 34 = ______ − 30
7. 81 + 73 = ______ + 70
8. $\frac{6}{7}$ of 49 mL. ______
9. $5\overline{)91{\cdot}55}$
10. $10\overline{)71089{\cdot}0}$
11. Write 375 cm as metres using a decimal. ______
12. My hand span is 18·4 cm long. My desk measures 4 hands spans plus 5·6 cm more. How long is my desk? ______
13. Divide 867·34 by ten. ______
14. 8·3 cm = ______ cm ______ mm
15. Estimate, then measure the length of this line.

    a Estimate = ______ mm

    b Measure = ______ mm or ______ cm
16. Naomi has 4 rulers of the same length. When placed in a line they have a length of 92 cm. How long is each ruler? ______
17. a 5·4 ÷ 0·9   (× 10) (× 10)

    ______ ÷ ______ = ______

    b 560 ÷ 70   (÷ 10) (÷ 10)

    ______ ÷ ______ = ______
18. Round to the nearest whole to estimate:

    a 4·89 × 6·214 ______

    b 56 ÷ 6·894 ______
19. $\frac{3}{8} + \frac{1}{8} + \frac{2}{8} = \frac{\square}{\square}$

Use the diagram to answer these questions.

a How many eights in one half? ______

b $1 - \frac{1}{4}$ ______   c $\frac{1}{2} + \frac{1}{8}$ ______   d $\frac{5}{8} - \frac{1}{8}$ ______

e $\frac{3}{4} - \frac{3}{8}$ ______   f $\frac{1}{2} + \frac{5}{8}$ ______   g $\frac{7}{8} - \frac{3}{4}$ ______

h $1\frac{7}{8} - \frac{1}{4}$ ______   i $2 - \frac{1}{8}$ ______   j $1\frac{1}{2} - \frac{5}{8}$ ______

© PEARSON AUSTRALIA 2024 • *AUSTRALIAN SIGNPOST MATHS NSW 6 MENTALS* • ISBN 978 0 6557 0913 8

26:3 ☐ out of 14

1. $$\begin{array}{r} 5678{\cdot}57 \\ 573{\cdot}29 \\ +\quad 36{\cdot}46 \\ \hline \end{array}$$

2. $$\begin{array}{r} 345{\cdot}67 \\ -\ 135{\cdot}79 \\ \hline \end{array}$$

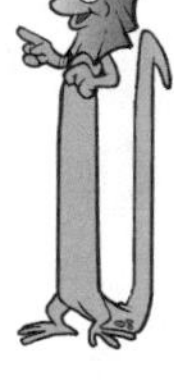

3. Emily is 65 mm taller than Sophie, and Sophie is 97 mm taller than Matthew. If Matthew is 1·450 m, how tall is Emily? ________

4. Round to the nearest whole to estimate:
   - **a** 19·839 × 3·879 ________
   - **b** 48·9 ÷ 6·85 ________

5. What is the chance as a percentage of throwing an even number using a dice made from this net? ________

	3	
5	1	5
	5	
	1	

6. (2 × 100) − (3 × 11) ________

7. Divide 367·7 by 100. ________

8. **a** $4 - \frac{1}{2}$ ________ **b** $8 - 1\frac{1}{2}$ ________

9. How many books with a spine width of 25 mm could I fit into my shelf that is 23 cm wide? ________

10. **a** 6297·3 × 10 ________
    b 834·97 × 100 ________

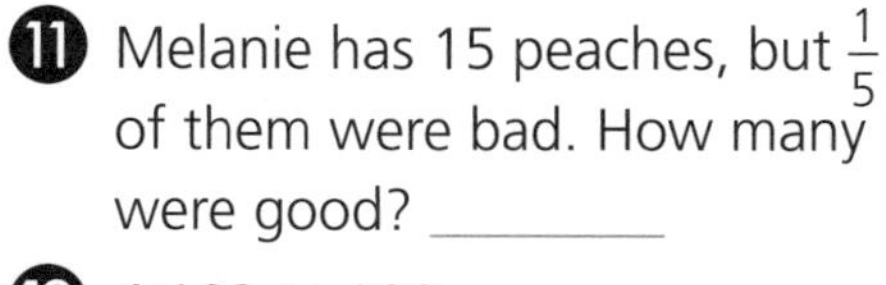

11. Melanie has 15 peaches, but $\frac{1}{5}$ of them were bad. How many were good? ________

12. 4·103 × 100 ________

13. < or >?
    a $\frac{1}{5}$ ☐ $\frac{3}{10}$ **b** $\frac{7}{10}$ ☐ $\frac{2}{5}$

14. $(7 \times 10^4) + (8 \times 10^3) + (9 \times 10^2) + (8 \times 10^1) + 4$
    = ________

26:4 ☐ out of 6

Extension

1. I used 46 cm of ribbon to wrap a large present and 36 cm to wrap a small present. How much ribbon would I need to wrap 6 large presents and 7 small presents? ________

2. A can of soup costs $3.95. Alana bought 7 cans of soup and had $67.30 cash left over. How much did she start with? ________

3. Lin has 10 times as much money as Chris and he has $567 900 less than Harry. How much does Lin have if Harry has $876 580? ________

4. Write all possible pairs of counting numbers that make this sentence true.
   31 − 17= △ × □
   ____

5. What is the sum of the first 6 consecutive even counting numbers after 156? ________

6. Colour the shortest distance from **A** to **B**.

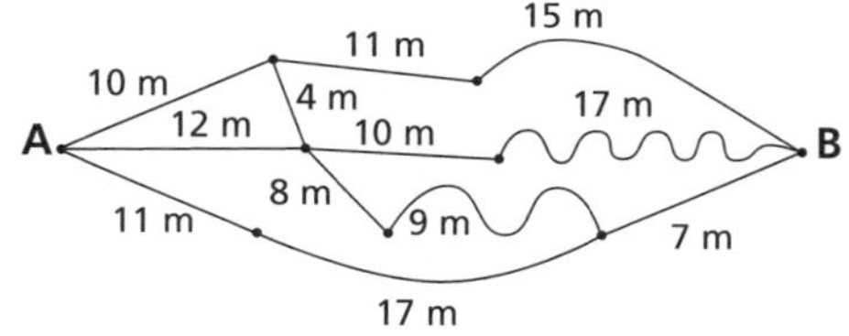

Challenge

Write facts about the number 13·452.

____
____
____
____

Concept

Use the diagram to answer these questions.

- **a** $4 - \frac{1}{2} =$ ________
- **b** $2 - \frac{1}{2} =$ ________
- **c** $3 - \frac{3}{4} =$ ________
- **d** $3 - \frac{1}{4} =$ ________
- **e** $1 - \frac{1}{4} =$ ________
- **f** $1 - \frac{3}{4} =$ ________
- **g** $4 - \frac{2}{4} =$ ________
- **h** $2 - \frac{3}{4} =$ ________

There are 16 quarters in 4 wholes.

27:1 out of 15

1. $5 \times$ ____ $= 35$
2. $\frac{1}{4}$ of 8. ____
3. 5×60 ____
4. $5{\cdot}6 \times 100$ ____
5. $(48 \div 8) + (36 \div 6)$ ____
6. $\frac{3}{4}$ of 36 m. ____
7. $56 + 24 =$ ____ $+ 20$
8. 8×900 ____
9. $9\overline{)84{\cdot}69}$
10. $10\overline{)834569{\cdot}0}$
11. a 89·3 cm = ____ mm
    b 8345 m = ____ km
    c 2978 mm = ____ cm
    d 7·2 km = ____ m
    e $3\frac{3}{4}$ km = ____ m

See page 85 for help.

12. Find the perimeter of each shape.

13.

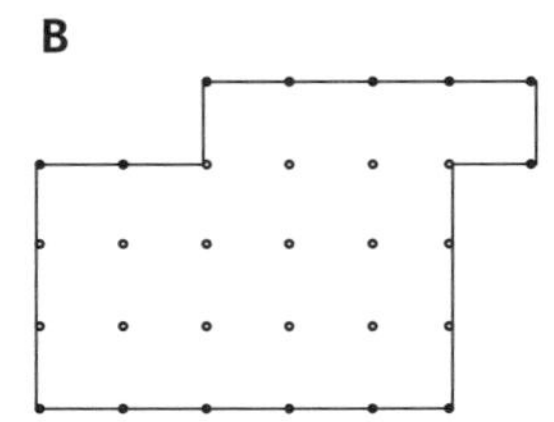

Which shape has the greater:

a area? ____ b perimeter? ____

14. a $\frac{4}{6} + \frac{1}{6}$ ____ b $\frac{10}{12} - \frac{5}{12}$ ____
15. a $15{\cdot}3 \div 10$ ____
    b $174{\cdot}762 \times 100$ ____
    c $8134{\cdot}6 \div 1000$ ____

27:2 out of 17

1. $435 + 645$ ____
2. $846 - 327$ ____
3. $6^2 - 2^2$ ____
4. $\frac{5}{6}$ of 54 L ____
5. $5 \times 6 -$ ____ $= 24$
6. $56 - 32 =$ ____ $- 30$
7. $56 + 34 =$ ____ $+ 30$
8. $8 + 20 \div 4$ ____
9. $5\overline{)85{\cdot}95}$
10. $10\overline{)290768{\cdot}0}$
11. $\frac{1}{5}$ of 20 kangaroos are male. How many are female? ____
12. $\frac{3}{4}$ of 1 litre. ____
13. a $\frac{13}{100} + \frac{4}{100}$ ____ b $\frac{18}{100} - \frac{9}{100}$ ____
    c $\frac{6}{100} + \frac{5}{100}$ ____ d $\frac{99}{100} - \frac{10}{100}$ ____
14. Find the area and perimeter of this shape.

Area = ____

Perimeter = ____

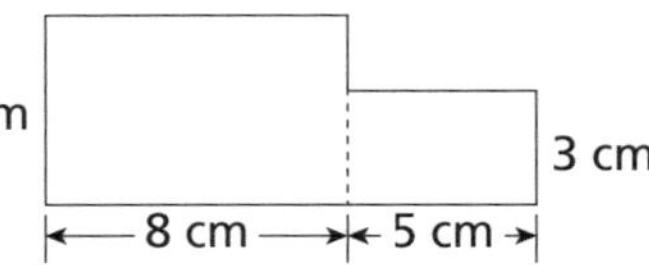

15. Write a fraction equal to:

a $\frac{6}{10}$ ☐ b $\frac{1}{4}$ ☐ c $\frac{2}{6}$ ☐

16. a $\frac{3}{4}$ of 20 ____
    b $\frac{1}{5}$ of 20 ____
    c $\frac{2}{5}$ of 20 ____
    d $\frac{4}{5}$ of 20 ____
17. 0·829 km = ____ m

Fractions to decimals using a calculator

Use a calculator to change these to decimals.

a $\frac{1}{2}$ ____ b $\frac{3}{5}$ ____ c $\frac{7}{20}$ ____

d $\frac{13}{25}$ ____ e $\frac{7}{8}$ ____ f $\frac{1}{16}$ ____

g $\frac{5}{8}$ ____ h $\frac{3}{16}$ ____ i $\frac{7}{25}$ ____

j $\frac{1}{32}$ ____ k $\frac{1}{64}$ ____ l $\frac{63}{64}$ ____

© PEARSON AUSTRALIA 2024 • *AUSTRALIAN SIGNPOST MATHS NSW 6 MENTALS* • ISBN 978 0 6557 0913 8

27:3

out of 9

❶
$$\begin{array}{r} 3546{\cdot}78 \\ 265{\cdot}78 \\ 3{\cdot}56 \\ +\ \ 939{\cdot}85 \\ \hline \end{array}$$

❷
$$\begin{array}{r} 530902 \\ -\ 253685 \\ \hline \end{array}$$

❸ Find the area and perimeter of this shape.

Area = ________

Perimeter = ________

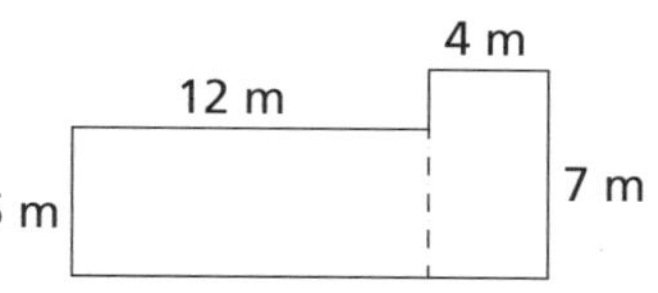

❹ a $\frac{41}{100} + \frac{22}{100}$ ________ b $\frac{50}{100} - \frac{7}{100}$ ________

c $\frac{32}{100} - \frac{11}{100}$ ________ d $\frac{6}{100} + \frac{41}{100}$ ________

❺ Round each number to the nearest whole then estimate the answer.

a $3{\cdot}4 \times 7{\cdot}2$ ________

b $9{\cdot}3 \times 6{\cdot}9$ ________

c $26{\cdot}8 - 13{\cdot}1$ ________

❻ Write all the factors of 42.

____

❼ Write a fraction equal to:

a $\frac{2}{5}$ b $\frac{4}{5}$ c $\frac{1}{5}$

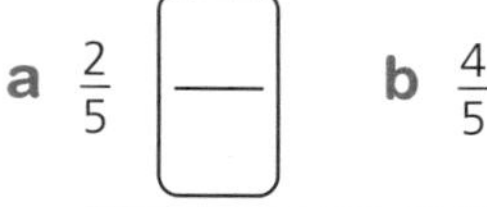

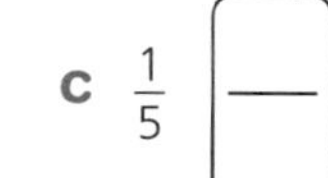

❽ $\frac{1}{4}$ of 20 oranges. ________

❾ Asha spent $100 on party decorations. Tye only spent two tenths of what Asha spent. How much did Tye spend?

____

27:4

Extension

out of 5

❶ The area of:

a the shaded part? ________

b the part not shaded? ________

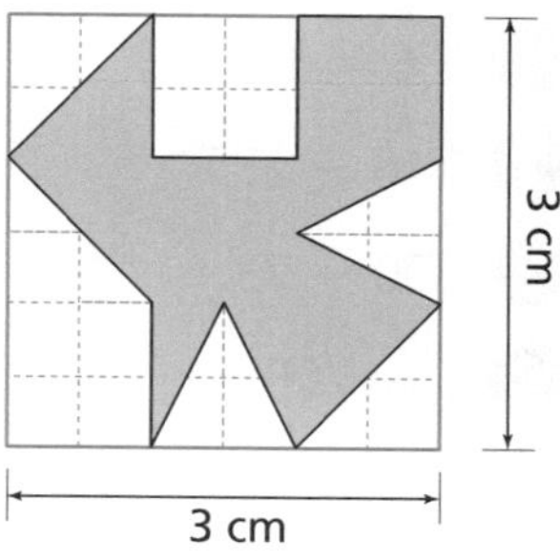

❷ A bird's head is $\frac{1}{3}$ as long as its body and $\frac{1}{4}$ as long as its tail. The bird is 48 cm long. How long is its head? ________

❸ In a test, Luis scored $\frac{3}{4}$ of the possible marks, while Peter scored $\frac{4}{5}$ of the possible marks. Which of the two boys scored the higher mark? ________

❹ Jodie ordered $\frac{1}{4}$ of a pizza for each of her 14 friends. How many pizzas did she order? ________

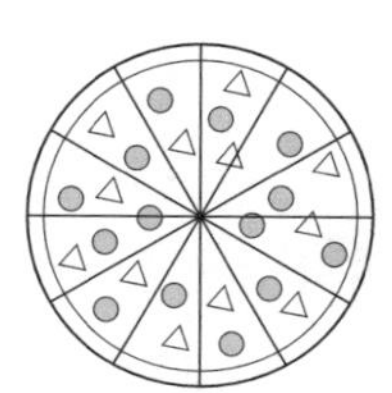

❺ a 30 squared. ________

b 300 squared. ________

Challenge

Complete this fraction wall.
Record equivalent fractions below.

$\frac{1}{2}$				$\frac{1}{2}$			
$\frac{1}{4}$							
$\frac{1}{8}$							

Note: $\frac{2}{4} = \frac{4}{8}$

28:1   ☐ out of 15

1. $5{\cdot}6 \times 10$ _____
2. $746 - 235$ _____
3. $900 - 73$ _____
4. 5×700 _____
5. $\frac{7}{12} + \frac{4}{12}$ _____
6. $45 +$ _____ $= 100$
7. 40×8 _____
8. $\frac{1}{4}$ of 24. _____
9. $8\overline{)354672}$
10. $5\overline{)73{\cdot}65}$
11. What is the perimeter of this rectangle? _____

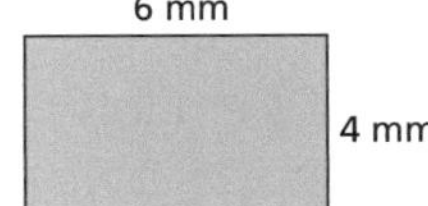

12. Write a fraction equal to:

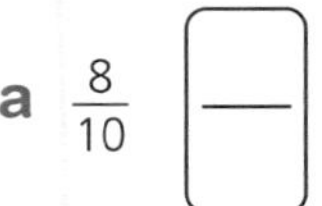

a $\frac{8}{10}$ ☐   **b** $\frac{4}{10}$ ☐   **c** $\frac{6}{10}$ ☐

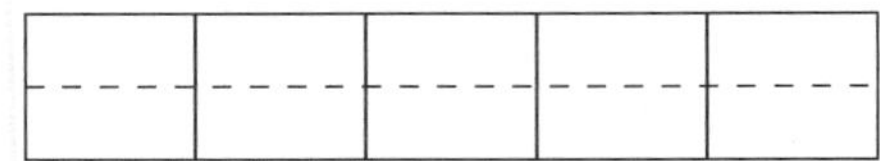

13. **a** 6·9 cm = _____ mm
    b 2947 m = _____ km
    c 5456 mm = _____ cm
    d 3·7 km = _____ m
    e $1\frac{4}{10}$ km = _____ m

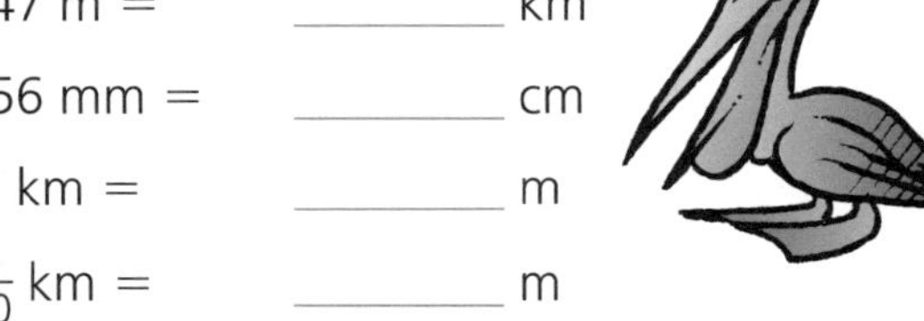

14. Find the perimeter of a square with side lengths of 89·3 m. _____
15. What is the area of this parallelogram?
    Remember the area = base × height.

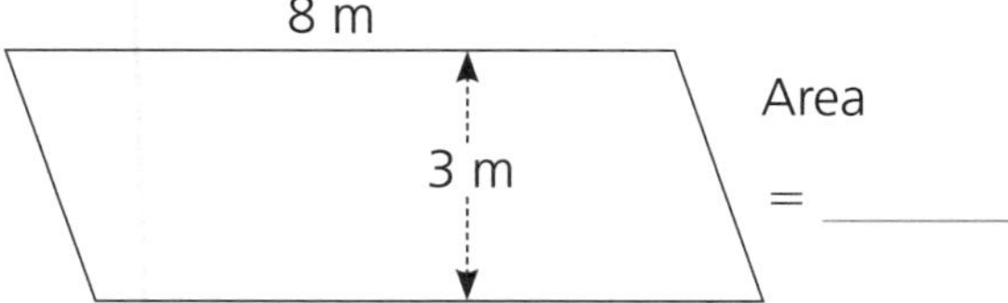

Area = _____

28:2   ☐ out of 18

1. $526 - 313$ _____
2. Triple 57. _____
3. $6 + 56 \div 7$ _____
4. $1\frac{9}{10} - \frac{7}{5}$ _____
5. $5 + 3 \times 5$ _____
6. $167 +$ _____ $= 219$
7. $6\ \text{L} \times 800$ _____
8. $\frac{4}{6}$ of 18. _____
9. $7\overline{)398062}$
10. $4\overline{)37{\cdot}76}$
11. **a**

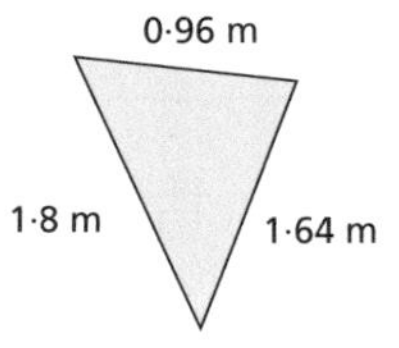

Perimeter = _____

b

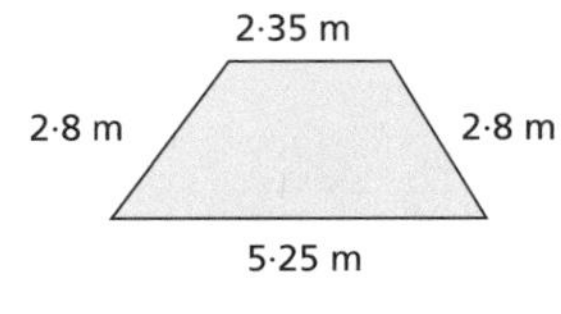

Perimeter = _____

12. **a** $\frac{1}{5} + \frac{3}{5} =$ _____   **b** $\frac{5}{8} - \frac{1}{8} =$ _____
13. **a** 4 take away $1\frac{1}{4}$. _____
14. Which fraction is bigger:
    a $\frac{3}{4}$ or $\frac{1}{3}$? _____   **b** $\frac{3}{4}$ or $\frac{2}{3}$? _____
15. **a** $\frac{4\ (\div 2)}{10\ (\div 2)}$ ☐   **b** $\frac{2\ (\times 3)}{6\ (\times 3)}$ ☐

16. Find the area of a square with side lengths of 34 m. _____
17. $\frac{2}{3} - \frac{1}{6} = \frac{☐}{☐} - \frac{☐}{☐} = \frac{☐}{☐}$

18.

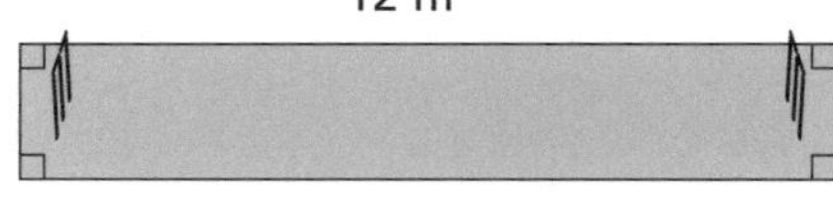

For this cricket pitch find the:
a area _____   **b** perimeter _____

Turn to ID card A on page 6.
Give the answers for these numbers.

(1) _____   (2) _____
(3) _____   (4) _____
(24) _____   (25) _____
(26) _____ : _____ _____   (27) _____ : _____
(28) _____ _____   (29) _____

The metric system is based on the number 10.

10
100
1000

© PEARSON AUSTRALIA 2024 • *AUSTRALIAN SIGNPOST MATHS NSW 6 MENTALS* • ISBN 978 0 6557 0913 8

28:3

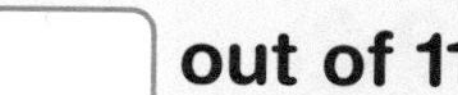

out of 11

❶
$$\begin{array}{r} 5476899 \\ 246567 \\ 97 \\ +\ \ 48670 \\ \hline \end{array}$$

❷
$$\begin{array}{r} 286908 \\ -\ 175679 \\ \hline \end{array}$$

❸ What fraction of $1 is 30c? ______

❹ Write all the factors of 32. ______

❺ The first 10 multiples of 9 are:

______

❻ **a** 5 squared ______ **b** 7 squared ______

❼ **a** $\frac{7}{8} - \frac{2}{8}$ ______ **b** $\frac{3}{6} + \frac{2}{6}$ ______

c $\frac{3}{10} + \frac{4}{10}$ ______ **d** $\frac{7}{12} - \frac{2}{12}$ ______

❽ Write a fraction equal to:

a $\frac{1}{6}$ [—] **b** $\frac{2}{8}$ [—] **c** $\frac{4}{10}$ [—]

d $\frac{5}{5}$ [—] **e** $\frac{1}{3}$ [—] **f** $\frac{4}{5}$ [—]

❾ The value of 8 in 34·798 ______

❿ What is the area (A) of these parallelograms?

a

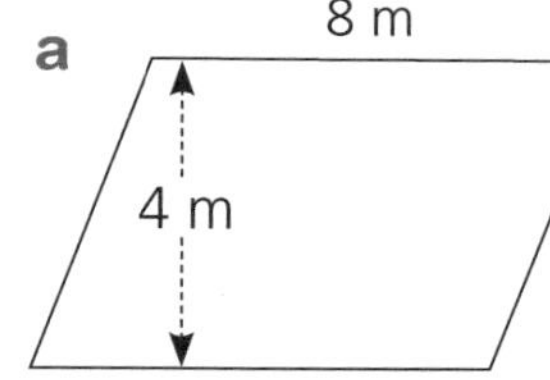

A = ______

b

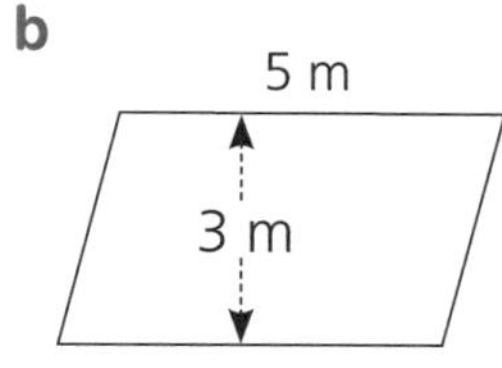
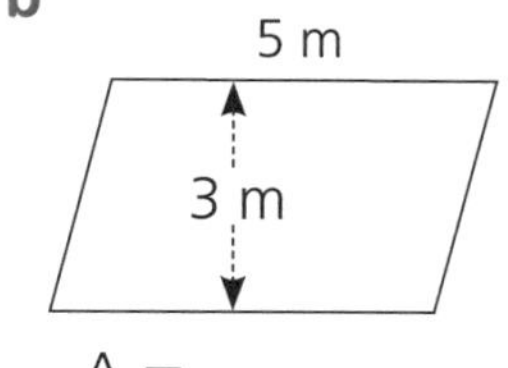

A = ______

⓫ The size of:

a angle **A** ______

b angle **B** ______

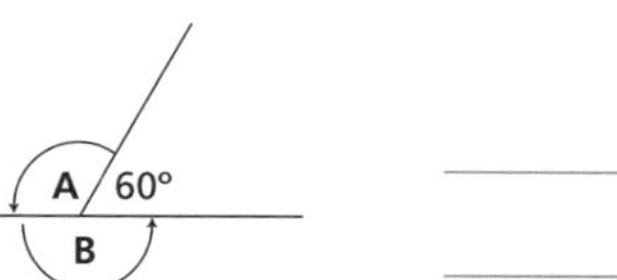

28:4

Extension

out of 6

❶ In 1984, my age was half my father's age. 23 years later, my age was 21 years younger than my father. If my father was 65 at this time, in which year was:

a I born? ______

b my father born? ______

❷ Find the area and perimeter of this shape.

Area = ______

Perimeter = ______

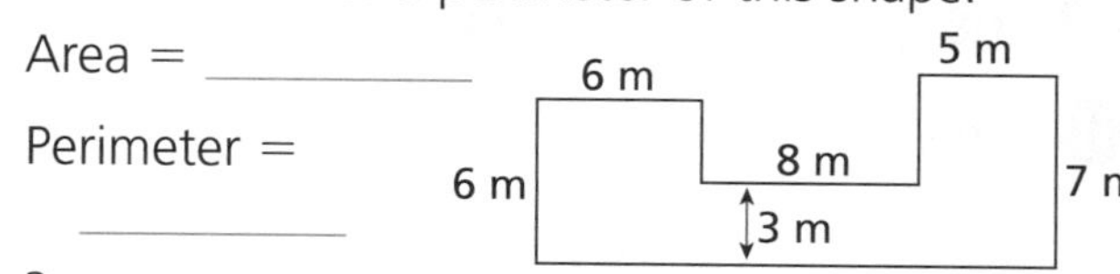

❸ $\frac{3}{4}$ of 8 L ______

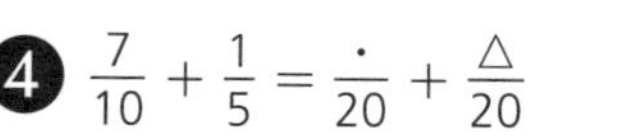

❹ $\frac{7}{10} + \frac{1}{5} = \frac{\cdot}{20} + \frac{\triangle}{20}$ $\cdot$ = ______, $\triangle$ = ______

❺ For this shape find the:

a perimeter

______

b area

______

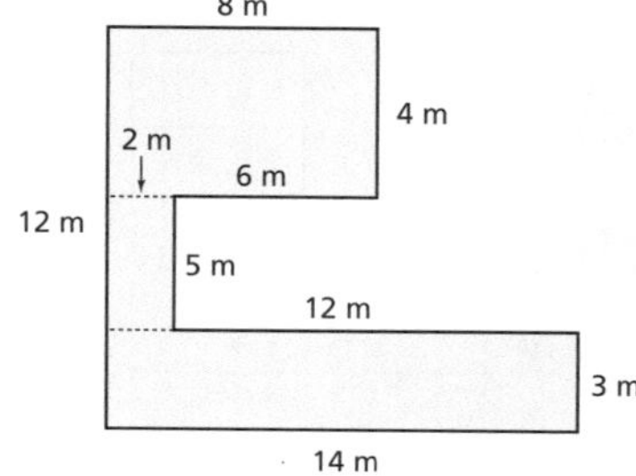

❻ **a** (265 − 49) + 63 = ______

b (176 − 128) ÷ 4 = ______

Challenge

Draw and describe the features of a parallelogram.

______

______

______

______

a To get to camp, Year 6 used 8-seater vans and 5-seater cars. There were 10 vehicles used. If there were 59 seats, how many vans were used? ______

b In the paddock, kangaroos and cows grazed together. The 31 animals had 100 legs altogether. How many of each type of animal were in the paddock?

kangaroos: ______ cows: ______

© PEARSON AUSTRALIA 2024 ISBN 978 0 6557 0913 8

29:1 ☐ out of 17

1. 100 − 37 ____
2. 7 × 80 ____
3. 4·5 × 10 ____
4. 5 × 3 + 7 ____
5. Factors of 17. ____
6. $\frac{1}{4}$ of 16. ____
7. 35 + ____ = 80
8. $\frac{5}{8} - \frac{1}{2}$ ____
9. $3\overline{)857032}$
10. $7\overline{)85\cdot75}$
11. Write a fraction equal to:
    a $\frac{2}{5}$ ☐ b $\frac{1}{2}$ ☐ c $\frac{3}{4}$ ☐
12. 15 birds are in a flock. One third fly away. How many are left? ____

13. $\frac{3}{4}$ plus $\frac{3}{4}$. ☐

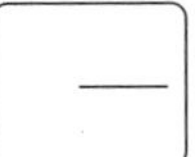

14. What is the area (A) of these shapes?

a 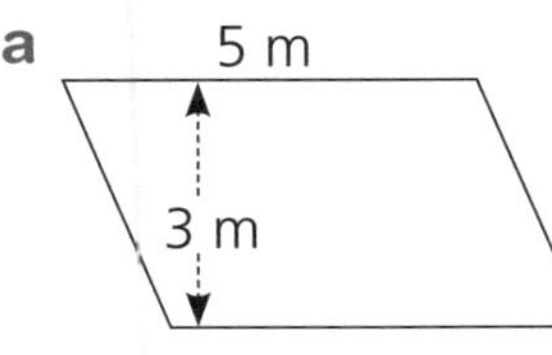

A = ____

b 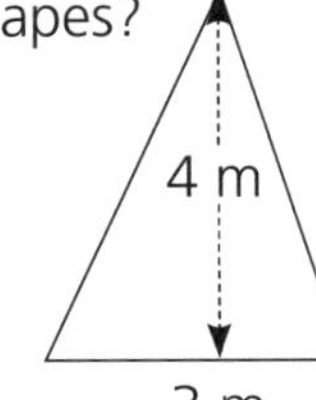

A = ____

15. a $\frac{1}{4}$ plus $\frac{1}{4}$ ____
    b $\frac{1}{4}$ plus $\frac{1}{2}$ ____

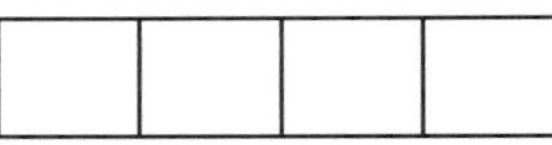

16. What is the area of a rectangular dance floor that has a length of 9 m and a width of 6 m? ____

17. What is 20% of 60? ____

29:2 ☐ out of 21

1. 56 × 3 ____
2. $\frac{3}{4}$ of 36 L. ____
3. 64 ÷ 8 + 9 ____
4. 85 − 43 − 8 ____
5. $\frac{4}{12} + \frac{3}{6}$ ____
6. 256 − 34 = ____ − 30
7. 7 × 700 ____
8. 25% of $24. ____
9. $7\overline{)285678}$
10. $8\overline{)25\cdot52}$
11. < or >?
    a $\frac{1}{2}$ ☐ $\frac{4}{6}$ b $\frac{3}{4}$ ☐ $\frac{3}{8}$
12. What is 30% of $50? ____
13. How many weeks in half a year? ____
14. What is the area (A) of these triangles?

a 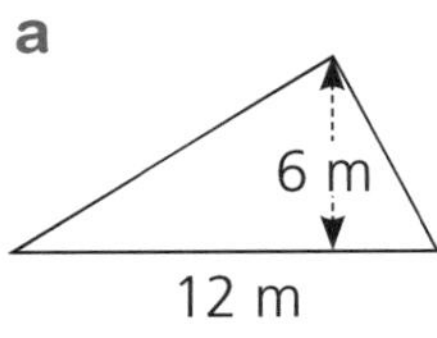

A = ____

b 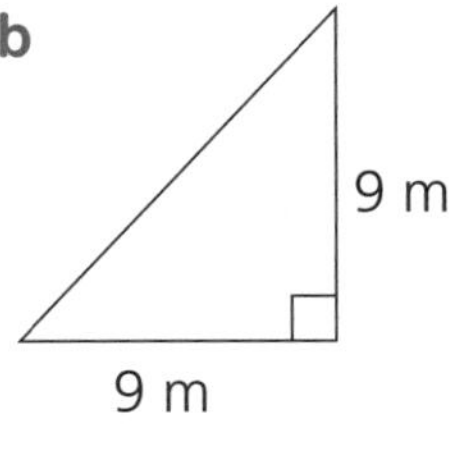

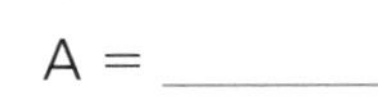

A = ____

15. $\frac{3}{10} + \frac{1}{2} = \frac{\square}{\square} + \frac{\square}{\square} = \frac{\square}{\square}$

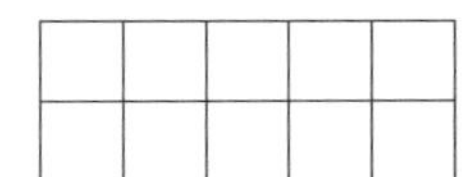

16. What fraction is equal to 25%? ____
17. a Write 8 and 7 tenths as a decimal. ____
    b Write 897 thousandths as a decimal. ____
18. Find the perimeter of a square with side lengths of 56·4 cm. ____
19. How many hours in 2 days? ____
20. Find the area of a square with side lengths of 9 m. ____
21. (56 + 35) − 5 × 5 ____

Average speed = distance travelled for each unit of time

Find the average speed if:

a 200 metres is covered in 10 seconds. ____ per second

b 144 kilometres is covered in 3 hours. ____ per hour

c 980 kilometres is covered in 4 days. ____ per day

d 60 millimetres is covered in 5 seconds. ____ per second

© PEARSON AUSTRALIA 2024 • *AUSTRALIAN SIGNPOST MATHS NSW 6 MENTALS* • ISBN 978 0 6557 0913 8

29:3 ☐ out of 11

1
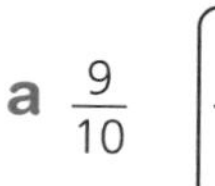

$$\begin{array}{r} 9456499 \\ 189567 \\ 2989 \\ +\ 234000 \\ \hline \end{array}$$

2
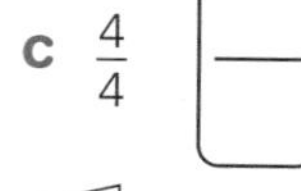

$$\begin{array}{r} 703000 \\ -\ 296849 \\ \hline \end{array}$$

3 Write a fraction equal to:

a $\frac{9}{10}$ ☐ **b** $\frac{1}{3}$ ☐ **c** $\frac{4}{4}$ ☐

4 Find the area of this triangle. ______

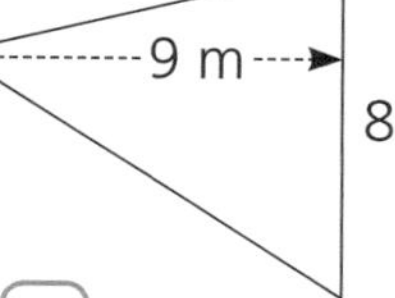

5 $\frac{3}{6} + \frac{1}{3} = \frac{\square}{\square} + \frac{\square}{\square} = \frac{\square}{\square}$

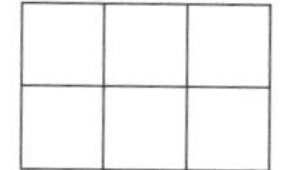

6 **a** 6·546 kg = ______ g
b 4795 m = ______ km
c 88 millimetres = ______ cm

7 What is the value of the bold digits?
a 7**4**1 865 ______
b 989 3**5**0 ______
c 354·56**8** ______

8 **a** Name this shape. ______
b Is this shape a quadrilateral? ______

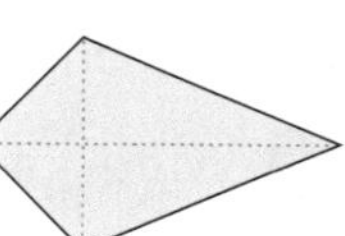

9 What is 40% of $70? ______

10
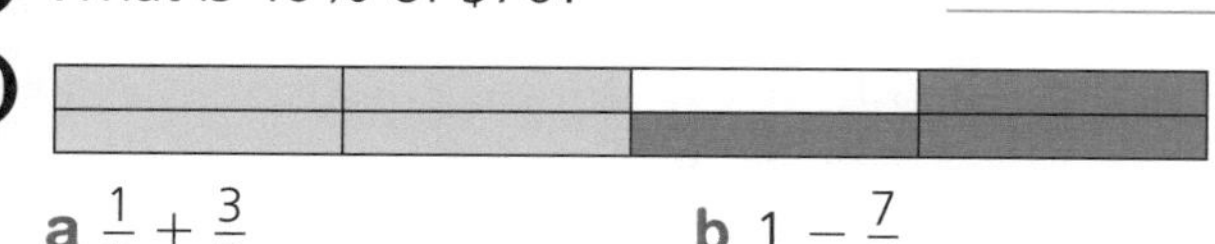

a $\frac{1}{2} + \frac{3}{8}$ ______ **b** $1 - \frac{7}{8}$ ______

11 Calculate the:
a area ______
b perimeter ______

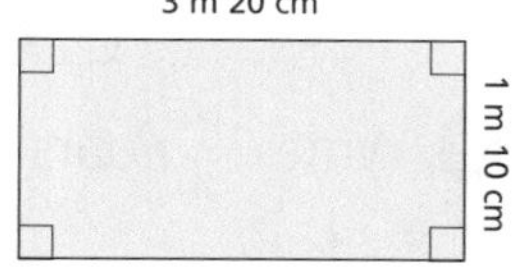

29:4 Extension ☐ out of 4

1 One fifth of a whole is 9.
Write the value of the shaded part.

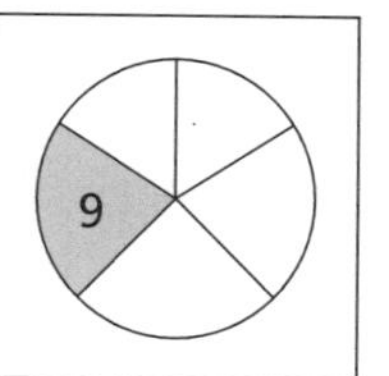

a

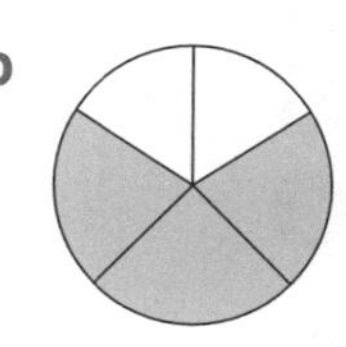

b

______ ______ ______

2 30% of the townspeople were men, 27% were women and 51% were male
If there were 4000 townspeople, how many people were:

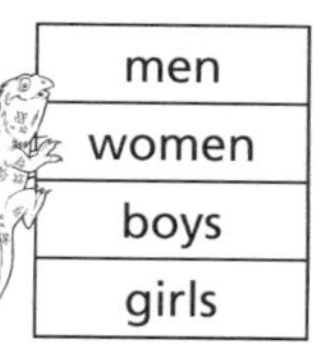

a male? ______ **b** boys? ______
c women? ______ **d** girls? ______

3 Compare these two shapes. What is the difference between the:

a perimeter of each? ______
b area of each? ______

4 These are finishing times for a race. Who came 2nd? ______

Ty	21:54·69
Kim	21:53·45
Ron	22:01·56
Sue	21:54·71

Challenge

Write facts about the number 356 467 453.

______

______

______

Strategy Time

Use the clues to fill in the tables.

Put a tick for YES ☑
Put a cross for NO ☒

	Drama	Gym	Tennis	Monday	Tuesday	Friday
Heather						
Naomi						
Luke						

Heather, Naomi and Luke are in different clubs. One of the girls goes to gym on Monday. Naomi goes to her club on Tuesday. Luke does not do drama. His club meets on Friday.

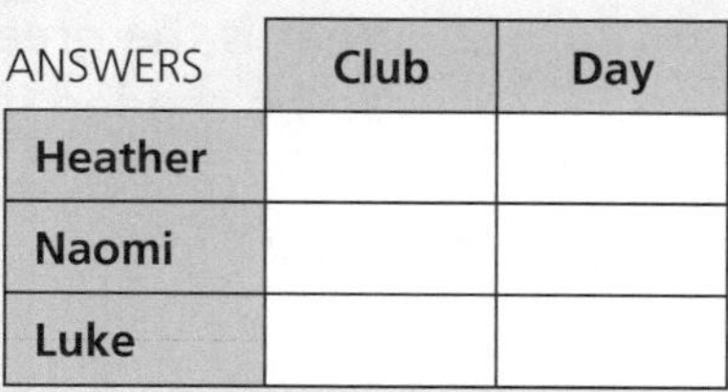

ANSWERS	Club	Day
Heather		
Naomi		
Luke		

30:1

☐ out of 15

1. 534 + 253 ____
2. 867 − 253 ____
3. Triple 25. ____
4. $\frac{5}{6} - \frac{5}{12}$ ____
5. 20% of 100. ____
6. $\frac{3}{10} + \frac{4}{10}$ ____
7. 56 ÷ 7 + 13 ____
8. 100 × 6·5 cm ____
9. **a** $\frac{5}{7} = \frac{\square}{28}$, $\square$ = ____
   b $\frac{2}{7} = \frac{\square}{28}$, $\square$ = ____
   c $\frac{1}{4} = \frac{\square}{28}$, $\square$ = ____
   d $\frac{3}{4} = \frac{\square}{28}$, $\square$ = ____

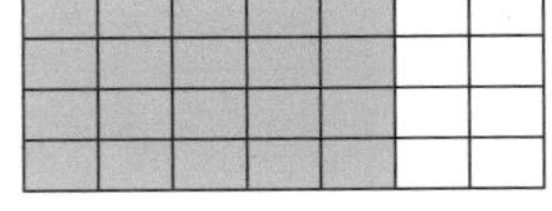

10. The size of each missing angle.
    a

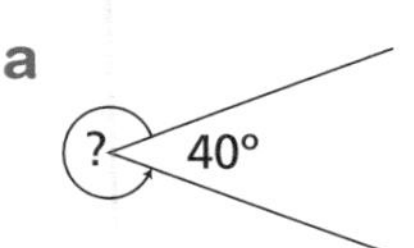

____

    b

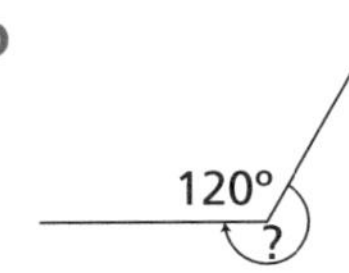

____

11. A rectangle measures 7 cm by 8 cm.
    What is its:
    a perimeter? ____
    b area? ____

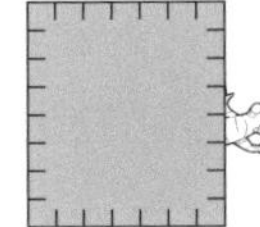

12. What is the area (A) of these triangles?
    a

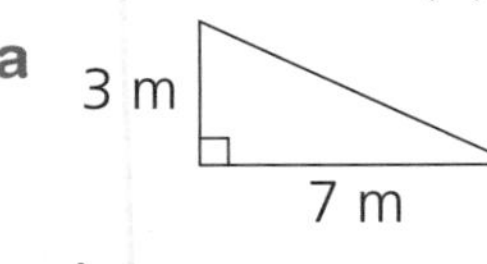

A = ____

    b

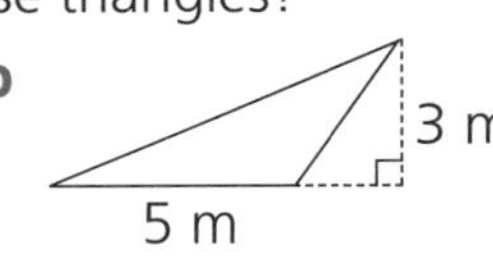

A = ____

13. What is 40% of $70? ____
14. (16 − 7) × (5 + 3) ____
15. **a** 29·6 cm = ____ mm
    b 2980 m = ____ km

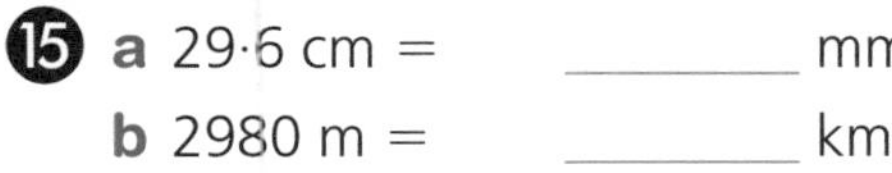

30:2

☐ out of 18

1. 81 ÷ 9 + 8 ____
2. 351 − 247 ____
3. 6 × 90 L ____
4. $\frac{2}{6} + \frac{1}{2}$ ____
5. 456783 + 96783
6. 25% of 50. ____
7. 72 ÷ 9 × 5 ____
8. 18 − 12 ÷ 4 ____
9. 76 + ____ = 116
10. 935734 − 94759
11. What is the area of a parallelogram with a base of 6 cm and a height of 4 cm? ____
12. $\frac{4}{5} - \frac{2}{10} = \frac{\square}{\square} - \frac{\square}{\square} = \frac{\square}{\square}$

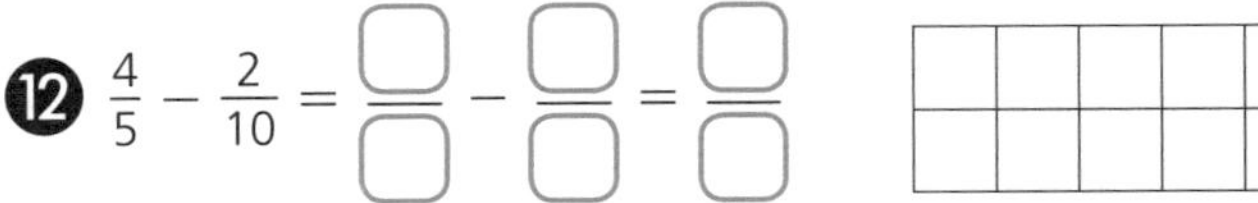

13. Our school has 10 soccer balls.
    6 of them were used today.
    What percentage were not used? ____
14. Calculate the:
    a perimeter ____
    b area ____

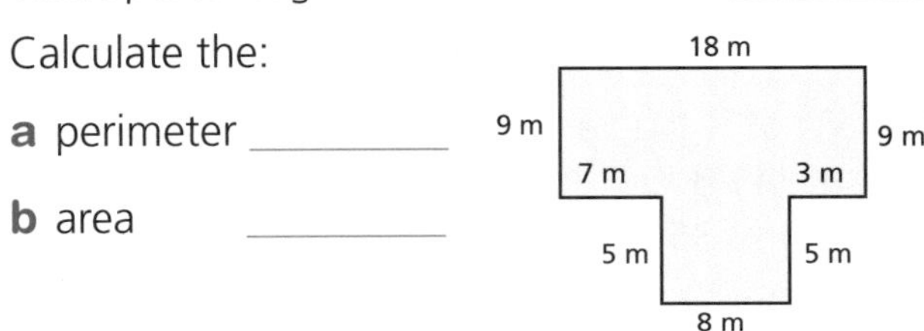

15. What is the area of a triangle with a base of 5 m and a height of 7 m? ____
16. Write $\frac{1}{4}$ as a percentage. ____
17. Find the lowest common denominator, then find:
    a $\frac{1}{2} + \frac{1}{3} = \frac{\square}{\square} + \frac{\square}{\square} = \frac{\square}{\square}$
    b $\frac{3}{4} + \frac{1}{5} = \frac{\square}{\square} + \frac{\square}{\square} = \frac{\square}{\square}$

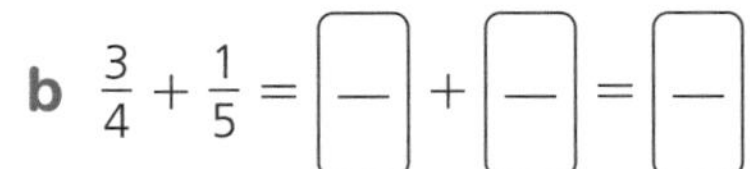

18. Write $7\frac{1}{4}$ hours as a decimal. ____

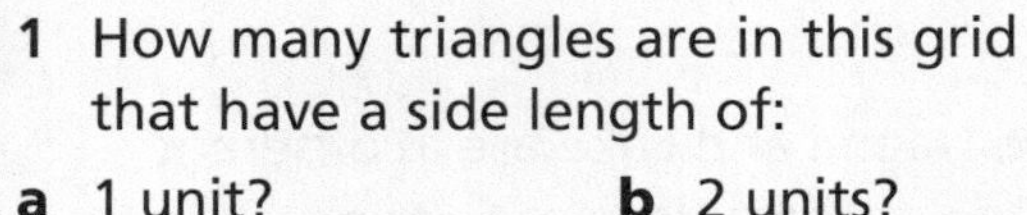

1 How many triangles are in this grid that have a side length of:
a 1 unit? ____ **b** 2 units? ____ **c** 4 units? ____

2 What is the greatest number of small triangles that can be shaded if no two shaded triangles share:
a a side? ____ **b** a corner? ____

Some triangles will point down.

© PEARSON AUSTRALIA 2024 • *AUSTRALIAN SIGNPOST MATHS NSW 6 MENTALS* • ISBN 978 0 6557 0913 8

30:3 ☐ out of 11

1
$$\begin{array}{r} 4657809 \\ 300800 \\ 6859 \\ +\ 269895 \\ \hline \end{array}$$

2
$$\begin{array}{r} 306003 \\ -\ 230035 \\ \hline \end{array}$$

3 What is 5% of $20? ______

4 < or >?

a $\frac{1}{10}$ ☐ $\frac{4}{5}$ **b** $\frac{5}{6}$ ☐ $\frac{2}{3}$

5 What is the area (A) of these triangles?

a

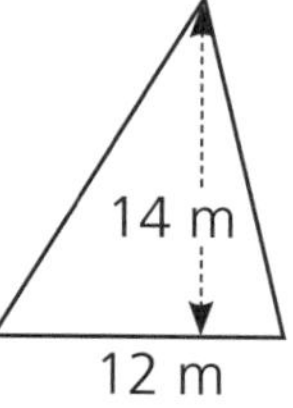

b

9 m
6 m

A = ______ A = ______

6 50 + 20 ÷ (8 ÷ 2) − 24 ______

7 Find the lowest common denominator, then find:

a $\frac{3}{5} - \frac{1}{2} = \frac{\square}{\square} - \frac{\square}{\square} = \frac{\square}{\square}$

b $\frac{3}{4} - \frac{1}{3} = \frac{\square}{\square} - \frac{\square}{\square} = \frac{\square}{\square}$

8

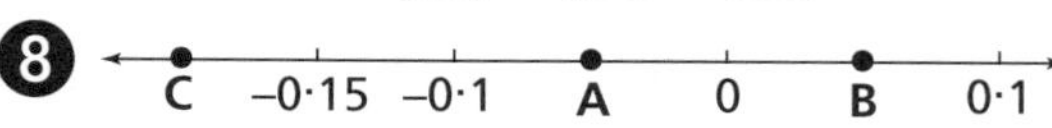

What number would be at:

a A? ____ **b** B? ____ **c** C? ____

9 Write $\frac{2}{10}$ as a percentage. ______

10 Write 25% as a fraction. ______

11
a 3·4 cm = ______ mm
b 8937 m = ______ km
c 845 mm = ______ cm
d 2·8 km = ______ m

30:4 Extension ☐ out of 6

1 Ethan ate $\frac{1}{3}$ of the orange and Lucas ate $\frac{1}{4}$. What fraction of the orange was left? ______

2 Sam raised $1657 more than Harry, and Riley raised half as much as Harry. What did they raise in total if Harry raised $658? ______

3 Oliver had green, blue, white and red balls. $\frac{3}{12}$ were green, $\frac{1}{4}$ were blue, $\frac{1}{3}$ were white, and 4 were red.
How many were green or blue? ______

4 10% reduction was given on the price of a TV marked at $890. How much was paid? ______

5 76 less than a third of my number is divided by 5 to get 34. My number is ______.

6 Linda weighs 57·45 kg. She was holding $8\frac{1}{2}$ kg of groceries when she stepped onto the scales.

a What was the total weight? ______

b How much less than 100 kg is the total weight? ______

Challenge

Make up questions like Question 5 above, to challenge your friends. Write the answers somewhere else in your book. Guess my number:

______

______

______

______

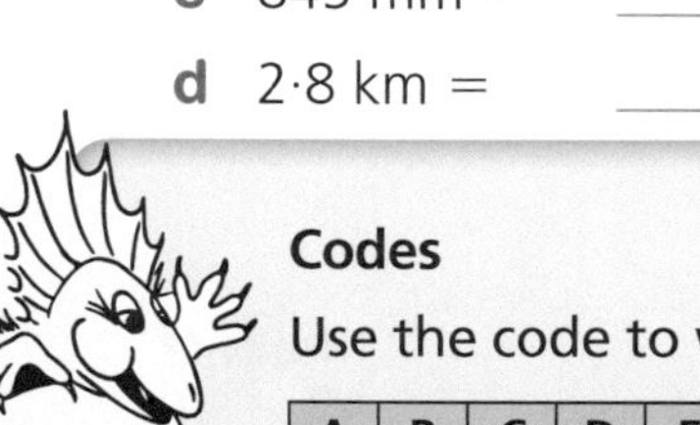

Codes

Use the code to write 'true' or 'false' for each code statement.

A	B	C	D	E	F	G	H	I	J	K	L	M	N	O	P	R	S	T	U	V	W	Y
1	*	9	&	4	?	0	/	2	(	+	7	<	5	#	)	3	$	=	8	@	>	6

=384 is the code for true.

a 1 7#50 (#83546 $=13=$ >2=/ (8$= #54 $=4). ______

b $8994$$ &4)45&$ 7130476 #5 /13& >#3+. ______

c <156 34942@4 1&@294, =/4 >2$4)3#?2= ?3#< 2=. ______

31:1

out of 16

1. 6 × ____ = 36
2. 50% of 24. ____
3. 7 × 4 − 25 ____
4. 3 × 8 + 6 ____
5.
```
  4675·2
+  364·7
```
6. $\frac{1}{4} + \frac{3}{8}$ ____
7. 159 − 59 ____
8. $\frac{1}{4}$ of 32. ____
9. 34 + 39 = ____ + 40
10.
```
  365·18
−  33·24
```
11. What is the cost of 13 balls if they are $8 each? ____
12. I walked at 5 km/h for 6 hours. How far did I walk? ____
13. Which of these is the net of an open cube? ____

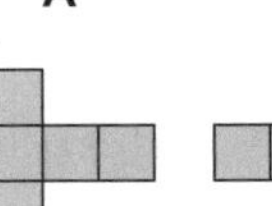

14. Find the area of:

a 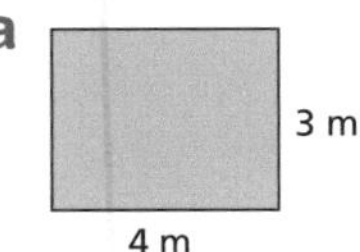

b 

15. Find the lowest common denominator, then find:

a $\frac{1}{5} + \frac{4}{10} = \square + \square = \square$

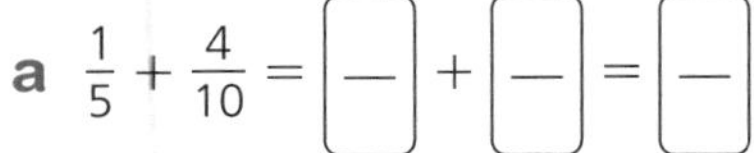

b $\frac{3}{6} + \frac{2}{12} = \square + \square = \square$

16. Find the equal measures: (See page 85.)

a 3 L = ____ mL

b 9 L 261 mL = ____ mL

c 2·734 L = ____ mL

31:2

out of 16

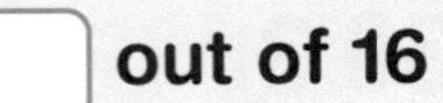

1. 20% of 50. ____
2. $\frac{1}{3}$ of 12 ____
3. 35 × 20 ____
4. 0·6 × 10 ____
5. 5 × 50 ____
6. 42 ÷ 2 − 8 ____
7. 58 + 147 = ____ + 150
8. 271 − 38 = ____ − 40
9. $5\overline{)356455}$
10. $6\overline{)73·38}$
11. What is the greatest number of shape A that could be cut out from shape B? ____

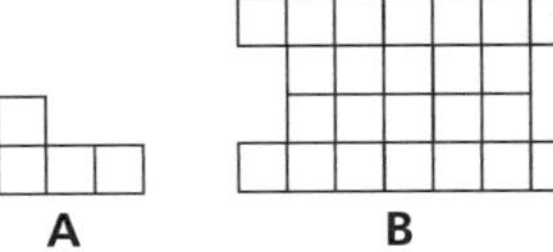

12. 2 × 25 − 30 − 5 = ____
13. Find the lowest common denominator, then find:

a $\frac{8}{10} - \frac{1}{2} = \square - \square = \square$

b $\frac{5}{7} + \frac{2}{10} = \square + \square = \square$

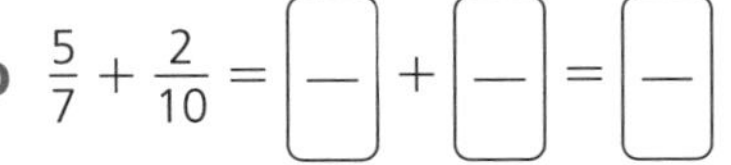

14. What is 25% of $40? ____
15. If the time is 8:39 pm on December 31st, how long will it be until the new year? ____
16.

red	yellow	green	blue
20	11	10	59

This table shows the results from a survey of 100 children in my school. Students were asked what their preferred colour was. If you asked 10 students their preferred colour, predict how many would say:

a red? ____ b green? ____

Concept: Order of operations

Order
1 ( )
2 × and ÷
3 + and − (going from left to right)

a 40 − 6 − 9 ____

b 39 − 36 + 11 ____

c 9 + 4 × 6 ____

d 16 − 4 × 4 ____

e 28 ÷ 7 × 6 ____

f 30 − (4 + 16) ____

g 16 − (2 × 2) ____

h 50 − 6 × 4 ____

i 5 × (39 − 36) ____

j 18 ÷ (56 − 50) ____

k 35 + 3 × 5 − (49 − 9) ÷ (50 − 46) ____

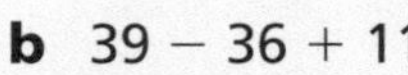

© PEARSON AUSTRALIA 2024 • *AUSTRALIAN SIGNPOST MATHS NSW 6 MENTALS* • ISBN 978 0 6557 0913 8

31:3 ☐ out of 10

1. $4\overline{)84656}$
2. $7\overline{)30.24}$
3. My painting time totalled 525 minutes over 3 days. On average, for how long did I paint each day? ______
4. The Olympic Games are held every 4 years . They were held in Sydney in 2000. Will they be held in 2065, 2066, 2067 or 2068? ______

5. Stickers were stuck on a dice so that the faces showed three 3s, two 5s and one 6. The dice was rolled 120 times.

   a Which number would you expect to see most often? ______

   b About how many times would you expect to see an even number? ______
6. Use decimals to write these as litres.

   a 8000 mL = ______ L

   b 9465 mL = ______ L

   c 7 L 234 mL = ______ L
7. Find the estimate by rounding each number to the nearest 10.

   a 19 × 56 = ______

   b 28 × 123 = ______

   c 498 × 31 = ______

See page 85 for help.

8. Find the equal measures:

   a 8 L = ______ mL

   b 4839 mL = ______ L
9. 5 + (56 − 48) ÷ 2 ______
10. 13 children hold hands in a line. How many hands are being held? ______

31:4 Extension ☐ out of 4

1. This shape has already been folded along either a vertical or horizontal axis of symmetry. Draw all four possible original shapes.

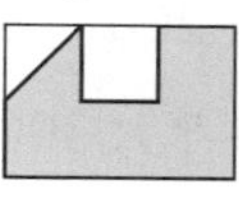

a

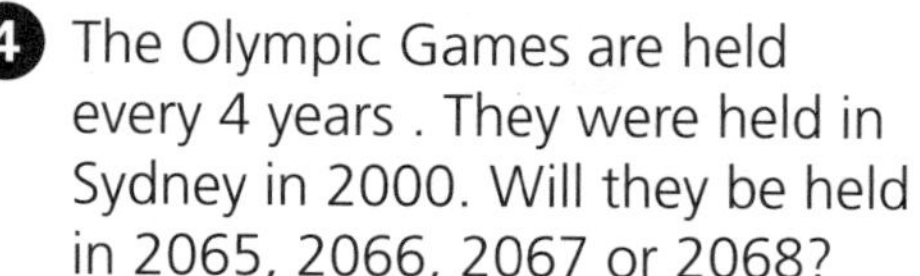

b

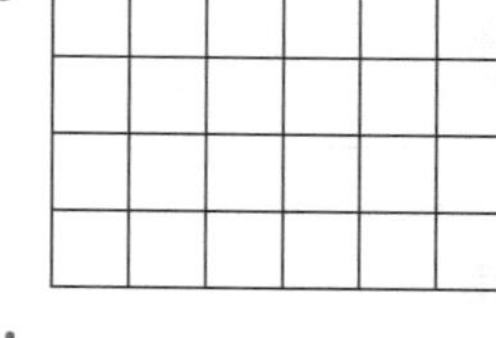

c

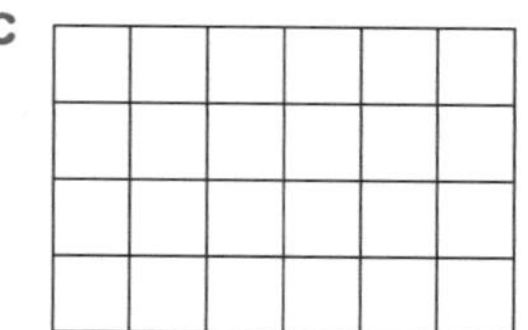

d

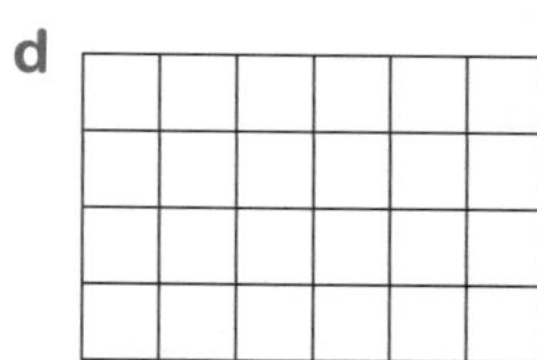

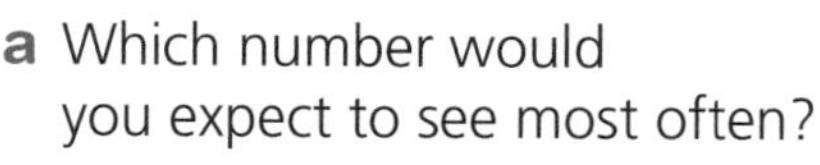

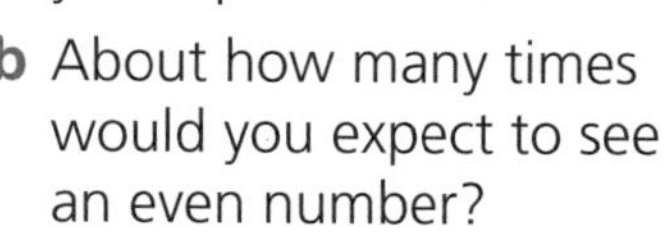

2. I read 45 minutes a night for 28 days. For how long did I read? ______
3. How many days are there until Christmas this year? ______
4. I take 7 steps forward, then 2 back, and then repeat this pattern. If I take one step every second, how many seconds will it take for me to go 14 steps forward from my starting position? ______

Challenge

Survey 20 people. Ask them how many siblings (brothers and sisters) they have. Tally the results in the table.

Siblings		Total
0		
1		
2		
3		
other		

Which vowel is used the most?

a Which vowel do you think is used the most? ______

b Use this tally to record the vowels in this activity box.

	a	e	i	o	u
Tally					

c Which vowel was used the most? ______

© PEARSON AUSTRALIA 2024 • *AUSTRALIAN SIGNPOST MATHS NSW 6 MENTALS* • ISBN 978 0 6557 0913 8

32:1 out of 17

1. $5 \times 6 + 7$ ______
2. $200 - 36$ ______
3. 8×300 ______
4. $9 \times 4 + 3$ ______
5. $\begin{array}{r} 9567{\cdot}3 \\ +\ \ 746{\cdot}4 \\ \hline \end{array}$
6. $\frac{4}{10} - \frac{3}{10}$ ______
7. $672 - 150$ ______
8. $\frac{1}{4}$ of 12. ______
9. $46 + 53 =$ ____ $+ 50$
10. $\begin{array}{r} 735{\cdot}07 \\ -\ \ 47{\cdot}93 \\ \hline \end{array}$

11. 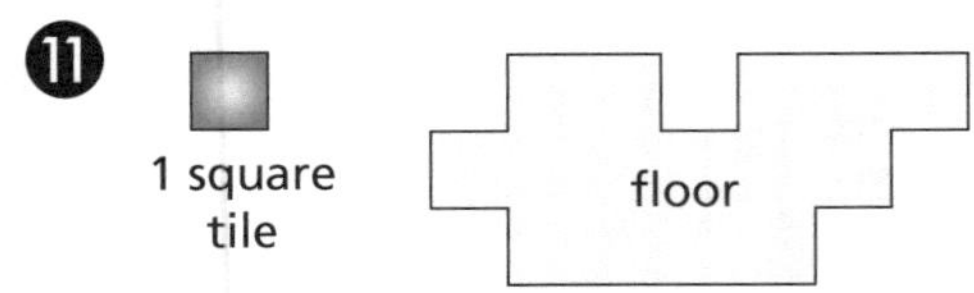

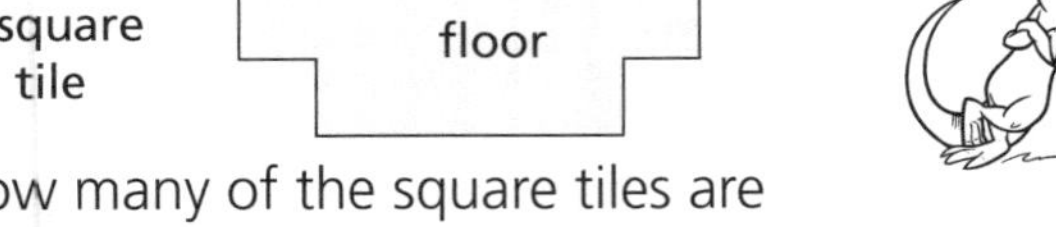
How many of the square tiles are needed to cover the floor? ______

12. 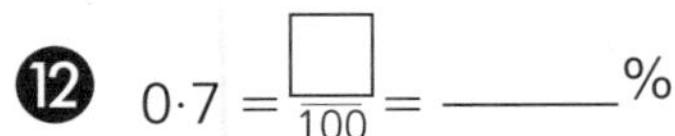
$0{\cdot}7 = \frac{\square}{100} =$ ______%

13. How many squares will there be if each side of the rectangle is made twice as long? ______
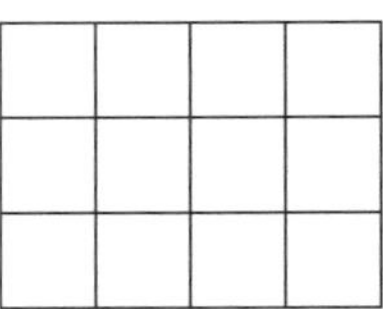

14. Find the lowest common denominator, then find:
   a $\frac{2}{10} + \frac{3}{4} = \frac{\square}{\square} + \frac{\square}{\square} = \frac{\square}{\square}$
   b $\frac{3}{4} + \frac{1}{3} = \frac{\square}{\square} + \frac{\square}{\square} = \frac{\square}{\square}$

15. Find the equal measures: (See page 85.)
   a $6{\cdot}846$ L = ______ mL
   b 7 L 278 mL = ______ mL

16. 98% as a fraction is ______.

17. a 7×70 ______
   b 7×7000 ______
   c 50×7000 ______

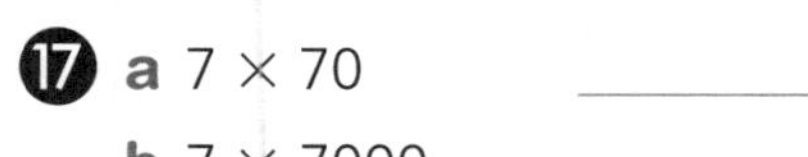

32:2 out of 15

1. 5×60 L ______
2. $\frac{1}{3}$ of 21. ______
3. 49×20 ______
4. 50% of 18. ______
5. 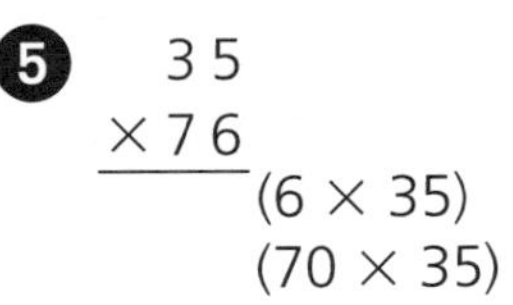
$\begin{array}{r} 35 \\ \times 76 \\ \hline \end{array}$
______ (6×35)
______ (70×35)
6. 20% of \$20. ______
7. 58×300 ______
8. $47 + 239 =$ ____ $+ 240$
9. $364 - 49 =$ ____ $- 50$
10. 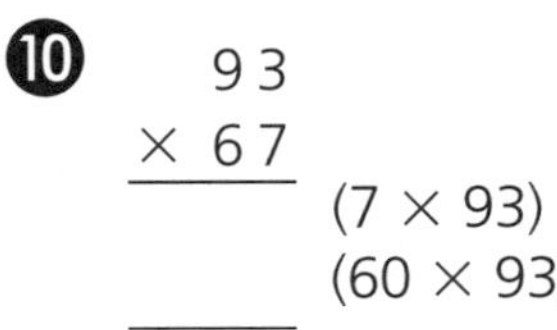
$\begin{array}{r} 93 \\ \times\ 67 \\ \hline \end{array}$
______ (7×93)
______ (60×93)

11. If the sides of this rectangle are made 4 times as long, how many times as big will its area be? ______
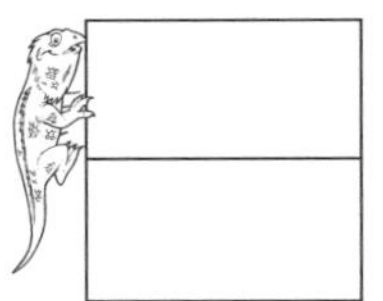

12. $100 \times 50 - 50 - 15 =$ ______

13. Find the lowest common denominator, then find:
   a $\frac{6}{7} - \frac{3}{10} = \frac{\square}{\square} - \frac{\square}{\square} = \frac{\square}{\square}$
   b $\frac{3}{10} + \frac{1}{3} = \frac{\square}{\square} + \frac{\square}{\square} = \frac{\square}{\square}$

14. Find the area of this shape.
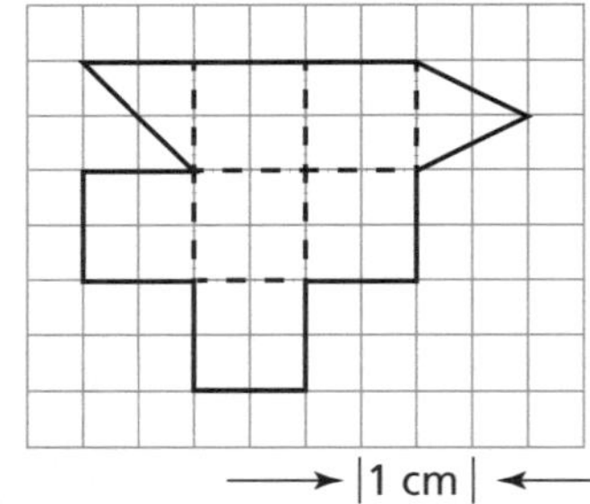

______

15. Use decimals to write these as litres.
   a 846 mL = ______ L
   b 58 mL = ______ L

× Tables

× 6	× 7	× 8
10, 50, 80, 100, 40, 90, 60, 30, 70, 20	40, 50, 60, 100, 10, 90, 80, 30, 70, 20	50, 20, 40, 100, 80, 70, 30, 10, 60, 90

© PEARSON AUSTRALIA 2024 • *AUSTRALIAN SIGNPOST MATHS NSW 6 MENTALS* • ISBN 978 0 6557 0913 8

32:3 ☐ out of 10

1. $6\overline{)38094}$

2. $3\overline{)23 \cdot 61}$

3.
```
   2 3
 × 4 5
 ─────  (5 × 23)
 ─────  (40 × 23)
```

4.
```
   8 6
 × 6 7
 ─────  (7 × 86)
 ─────  (60 × 86)
```

5. Find the lowest common denominator, then find:

   a $\frac{8}{12} - \frac{1}{4} = \frac{\square}{\square} - \frac{\square}{\square} = \frac{\square}{\square}$

   b $\frac{3}{4} + \frac{1}{10} = \frac{\square}{\square} + \frac{\square}{\square} = \frac{\square}{\square}$

6. Use decimals to write these as litres.

   a 298 mL = ________ L

   b 46 mL = ________ L

   c 7 mL = ________ L

7. Daniel was paid $20 an hour for 78 hours of work. How much was he paid altogether? ________

8. Find the estimate by rounding each number to the nearest 10.

   a $21 \times 99 =$ ________

   b $48 \times 121 =$ ________

   c $504 \times 21 =$ ________

See page 85 for help.

9. Find the equal measures:

   a 15 L = ________ mL

   b $4\frac{1}{4}$ L = ________ mL

   c 76·3 kg = ________ g

   d $3\frac{1}{2}$ kg = ________ g

   e $57\frac{3}{4}$ km = ________ m

10. $(76 - 35) + 8 \times 4 =$ ________

32:4 Extension ☐ out of 5

1. a How many small squares are in this rectangle? ________

   b How many are in an area 4 times as long and 3 times as wide? ________

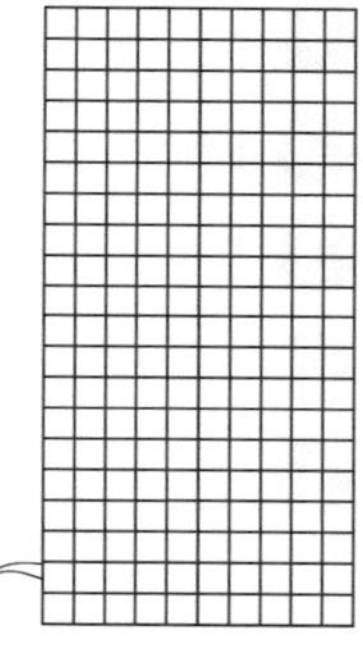

2. I spent $\frac{1}{4}$ of my money on a t-shirt, $\frac{1}{3}$ of my money on pants and $\frac{1}{6}$ of my money on lunch. I had $18 left. How much money did I start with? ________

3. Rachel swims 26 laps and Marika swims 33 laps of the 50 m pool every Thursday. How much further does Marika swim on:

   a one visit? ________

   b 8 visits? ________

4. Jody started with a number, doubled it, divided by 3, then subtracted 52. She finished with 8. What did she start with? ________

5. To the total of 14, 18 and 38, add the product of 45 and 167. ________

Challenge

Find containers that hold millilitres. List each name and capacity below, e.g. tomato sauce 500 mL.

____

____

____

____

____

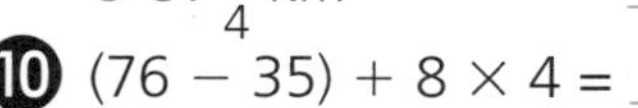

To divide numbers by 4, halve the number, then halve it again.

a 72 students were put into 4 equal teams. How many were put in each team? ________

b How many rows of 4 can be made with 96 mugs? ________

c Naomi, Alana, Luke and Heather shared 128 grapes. How many did each receive? ________

33:1 out of 16

1. $8 \times 9 + 14$ ______
2. $600 - 39$ ______
3. 5×600 ______
4. $7 \times 6 \div 7$ ______
5. $\begin{array}{r} 67 \\ \times \quad 8 \\ \hline \end{array}$
6. $\frac{5}{10} - \frac{4}{10}$ ______
7. 20% of \$40. ______
8. 6·434 m × 1000 ______
9. 3 × 800 L ______
10. $\begin{array}{r} 42 \\ \times \quad 9 \\ \hline \end{array}$

11. **a** 5·926 L = ______________ mL

    b 2 L 978 mL = ______________ mL

    c $6\frac{3}{4}$ L = ______________ mL

12. How much further must this car travel before the odometer shows 1000 km?

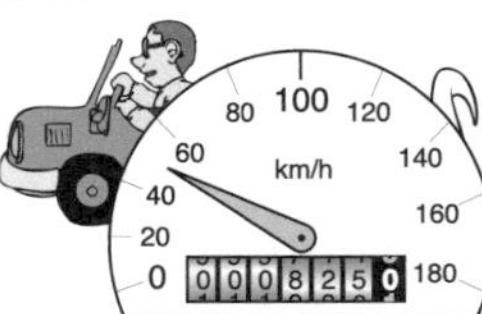

____

13. Underline the units that have been correctly written.

KG	G	gm	g.	Kg
g	kg.	kg	G.	kG

14. **a** The abbreviation for millimetres is ______.

    b The abbreviation for millilitres is ______.

    c The abbreviation for tonnes is ______.

15. Find the equal measures: (See page 85.)

    a 6 t = __________ kg

    b 3000 kg = __________ t

16. **a** Is $\frac{2}{10}$ the same as $\frac{1}{5}$? ______

    b Is $\frac{5}{10}$ the same as $\frac{1}{2}$? ______

    c $\frac{2}{10} + \frac{5}{10}$ ______

    d $\frac{1}{5} + \frac{1}{2}$ ______

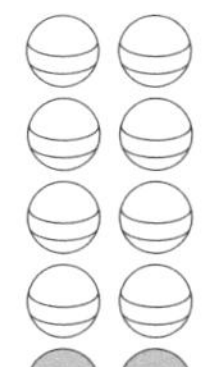

33:2 out of 15

1. $473 + 387$ ______
2. $894 - 354$ ______
3. $69 - 56 \div 8$ ______
4. $\frac{1}{3}$ of \$27. ______
5. $\begin{array}{r} 59 \\ \times 46 \\ \hline \end{array}$ (6 × 59) (40 × 59) ______
6. $\frac{7}{10} + \frac{1}{5}$ ______
7. \$20 − \$6.73 ______
8. 376 − 89 = ______ − 90
9. 437 + 38 = ______ + 40
10. $\begin{array}{r} 71 \\ \times 53 \\ \hline \end{array}$ (3 × 71) (50 × 71) ______

11. $(7 \times 10^4) + (8 \times 10^3) + (2 \times 10^2) + (9 \times 10^1) + 1$

    = ______________

12. Lachlan's Nanna gave \$5 for every goal scored in the soccer season.

    a If he scored 58 goals, how much money did he receive?

    ____

    b If his sister Felicity scored 36, how much did she receive? ______________

13. Use decimals to write these as litres.

    a 298 mL = ______________ L

    b 84 mL = ______________ L

    c 19 mL = ______________ L

14. **a** 7·4 t = ______________ kg

    b 90 000 kg = ______________ t

15. 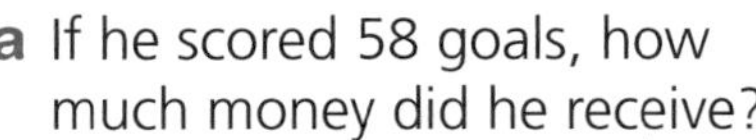

    Each dog has a mass of about 15 kg. Calculate the approximate mass of:

    a 5 dogs ____________ **b** 14 dogs ____________

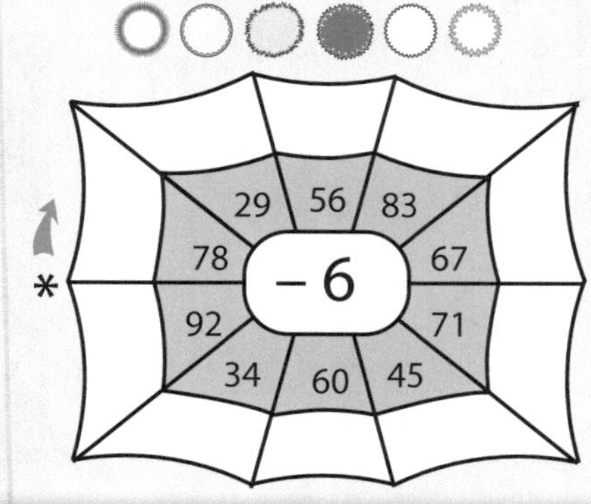

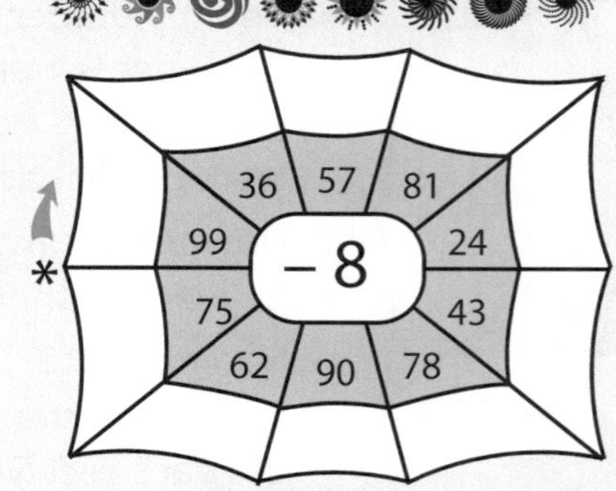

© PEARSON AUSTRALIA 2024 • *AUSTRALIAN SIGNPOST MATHS NSW 6 MENTALS* • ISBN 978 0 6557 0913 8

33:3 ☐ out of 9

1
$$\begin{array}{r} 83 \\ \times 76 \\ \hline \end{array}$$
(6 × 83)
(70 × 83)

2
$$\begin{array}{r} 926 \\ \times \quad 78 \\ \hline \end{array}$$
(8 × 926)
(70 × 926)

3 **a** A whale weighs 140 000 kg. How many tonnes is this? ______

b A car had a mass of 1·8 t. How many kg is this? ______

4 **a** 2·97 t = ______ kg

b 30 000 kg = ______ t

5 **a** Write this as 24-hour time. ______

b What will be the 24-hour time in 18 minutes? ______

6 Round each number to the nearest whole, then estimate the answer.

a 10·2 × 5·9 ______

b 12·5 + 29·8 ______

c 52·6 − 30·5 ______

d 42 × 3·4 ______

7 Use decimals to write these as litres.

a 289 mL = ______ L

b 37 mL = ______ L

c 106 mL = ______ L

See page 85 for help.

8 **a** 3·6 L = ______ mL

b $9\frac{1}{4}$ L = ______ mL

c 627 mL = ______ L

d 92 mL = ______ L

9 **a** Write 65% as a decimal. ______

b Write $\frac{14}{100}$ as a percentage. ______

33:4 ☐ out of 4

Extension

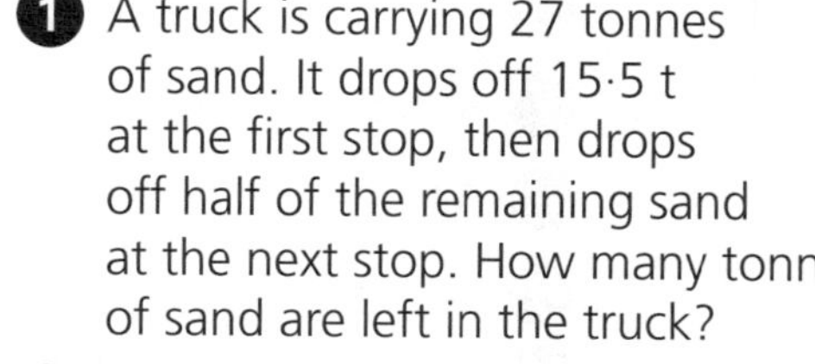

1 A truck is carrying 27 tonnes of sand. It drops off 15·5 t at the first stop, then drops off half of the remaining sand at the next stop. How many tonnes of sand are left in the truck? ______

2 Draw the missing part of this pattern.

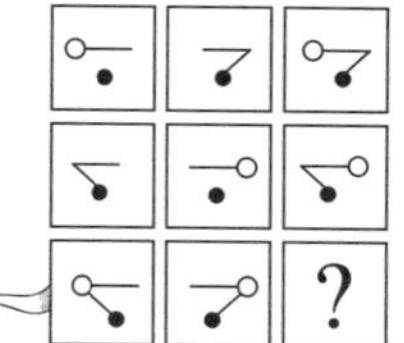

3 Tanya and Karyn took 60 cakes each to the cake stall. Tanya sold $\frac{9}{12}$ of her cakes and Karyn sold $\frac{11}{12}$ of her cakes.

a How many cakes did they sell altogether? ______

b How many did they have left? ______

4 If you double the length, width and height of this shape, how many times as big will its volume be?

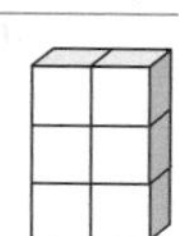

______

Challenge

Research objects that are measured in tonnes. List each below with an approximate mass if appropriate, e.g. Semitrailer ______.

______

______

______

______

______

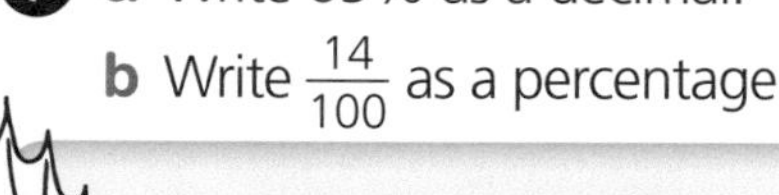

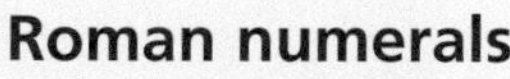

Roman numerals

Concept

1	I	one finger	
5	V	one hand	
10	X	two Vs	
50	L	half of a C	
100	C	centum = 100	
500	D	half of an ⓘ	
1000	M	mille = 1000	

IX = 10 − 1 = 9 | XC = 100 − 10 | CD = 500 − 100

1 Write our numeral for:

a XCVI ______ **b** CLX ______

c DCX ______ **d** CCIV ______

e LXVI ______ **f** XXXVI ______

2 Write the Roman numeral for:

a 75 ______ **b** 830 ______

c 378 ______ **d** 2567 ______

e 635 ______ **f** 3999 ______

34:1

☐ out of 17

1. ____ + 8 = 10
2. 18 + ____ = 30
3. $\frac{3}{8} + \frac{2}{8}$ ____
4. 7 × 6 − 12 ____
5.
$$\begin{array}{r} 87 \\ \times \quad 6 \\ \hline \end{array}$$
6. 40% of $80. ____
7. 8·475 m × 1000 ____
8. 634 − 213 ____
9. $6 − $2.50 ____
10.
$$\begin{array}{r} 21 \\ \times \ 32 \\ \hline \\ \hline \end{array}$$

11. Find the equal measures: (See page 85.)

Tonnes	Kilograms
7t	
	70 000 kg
7·546 t	

Litres	Millilitres
9L	
	2000 mL
8·3 L	

12. Write this as 24-hour time. ____

13. 192 − ☐ = 65,  ☐ = ____
14. Write 678 thousandths as a decimal. ____
15. Use am or pm to write the time 1 hour after:
    - **a** 15:35 ____
    - **b** 03:09 ____
16. What is the best unit to measure the mass of a:
    - **a** full suitcase? ____
    - **b** semitrailer? ____
    - **c** shoe? ____
17. Name this solid. ____

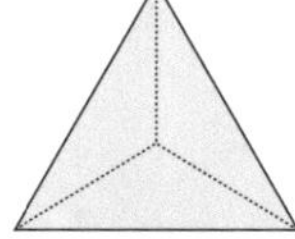

34:2

☐ out of 17

1. ____ + 47 = 100
2. $\frac{4}{7}$ of 63 ____
3. 56 ÷ ____ = 8
4. $\frac{1}{2} + \frac{5}{12}$ ____
5.
$$\begin{array}{r} 42 \\ \times \ 89 \\ \hline \\ \hline \end{array}$$
6. $27 − $5.60 ____
7. Triple 325. ____
8. 6 × 5 = 57 − ____
9. ____ − 142 = 4 × 8
10.
$$\begin{array}{r} 836 \\ \times \ \ 57 \\ \hline \\ \hline \end{array}$$

11.
$$\begin{array}{r} 2\cdot5 \\ \times 4\ \ 6 \\ \hline \\ \hline \end{array}$$
12.
$$\begin{array}{r} 3\cdot9 \\ \times 5\ \ 7 \\ \hline \\ \hline \end{array}$$
13.
$$\begin{array}{r} 3\cdot4 \\ \times 7\ \ 4 \\ \hline \\ \hline \end{array}$$

14. Kim's bus came at 7:50 am. She arrived at the station at 8:20 am. How long did the journey take? ____

15. Write the equal masses.

Tonnes & kilograms	Tonnes
7 t 300 kg	
	9·546 t
5 t 476 kg	

16. 17 − ☐ = 47 − 39, 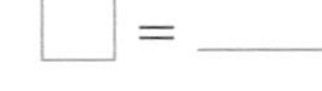 ☐ = ____
17.
    - **a** 4768 g = ____ kg 
    - **b** $4\frac{3}{4}$ kg = ____ g
    - **c** 67 t = ____ kg 
    - **d** 46·8 kg = ____ g
    - **e** $10\frac{1}{4}$ kg = ____ g

Concept

Scale: 1 cm represents 50 cm

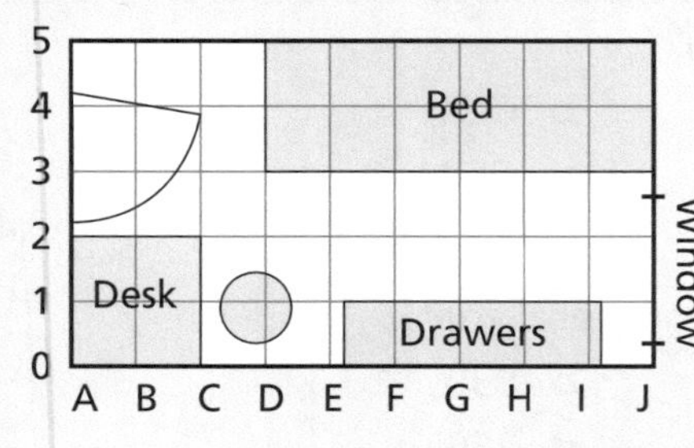

Scale drawing

- **a** The scale of this drawing ____ : ____

What is the actual length of:

- **b** the bed? ____
- **c** the drawers? ____

What is at the coordinate position:

- **d** G4? ____ 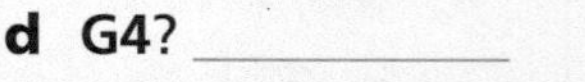 **e** B1? ____
- **f** Which coordinates could be used for the window? ____

© PEARSON AUSTRALIA 2024 • *AUSTRALIAN SIGNPOST MATHS NSW 6 MENTALS* • ISBN 978 0 6557 0913 8

34:3 out of 14

1. $\begin{array}{r} 35 \\ \times\ 68 \\ \hline \end{array}$

2. $\begin{array}{r} 73 \\ \times\ 18 \\ \hline \end{array}$

3. $\begin{array}{r} 384 \\ \times\ 46 \\ \hline \end{array}$

4. $\begin{array}{r} 5 \cdot 9 \\ \times\ 1\ \ 3 \\ \hline \end{array}$

5. $\begin{array}{r} 8 \cdot 4 \\ \times\ 2\ \ 5 \\ \hline \end{array}$

6. $\begin{array}{r} 9 \cdot 8 \\ \times\ 5\ \ 5 \\ \hline \end{array}$

7. The mass of 3 trucks is 9·1 t.
What is the mass of:
a 6 trucks? ______
b 30 trucks? ______

8. Complete: $\frac{1}{2} = \frac{2}{4} = \frac{\square}{8} = \frac{5}{\square}$

9. **a** 9·1 t = ______ kg
b 40 000 kg = ______ t

10. 1000 − 37 − 37 − 37 − 37 ______

11. What is the total mass, in kilograms, of a bag of 9 potatoes, each with an average mass of 326 g? ______

12. If a train leaves at 11:38 am and arrives at 12:12 pm, how long does the journey take? ______

13. 600 children were each given $20. How much money was given altogether? ______

14. Use am or pm to write the time 1 hour after:
a 18:27 ______
b 03:09 ______

34:4 Extension out of 6

1. A boat weighs the same as 46 people. How many people would weigh the same as 12 boats? ______

2. Write all possible pairs of counting numbers that make this number sentence true.
2707 − 2635 = △ × □ ______

3. My trolley contained three 1700 g bags of potatoes and a pumpkin weighing 3·56 kg.
a What is the total mass of my groceries? ______
b How much short of 10 kg is the mass of my groceries? ______

4. 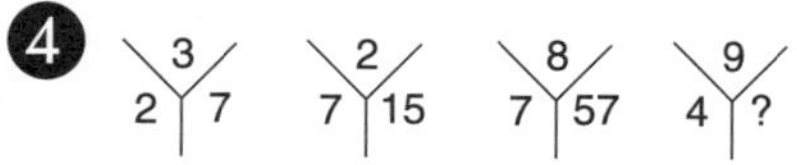

What is the missing number? ______

5. 1000 milligrams (mg) = 1 gram
If an ant's mass is 3·75 mg, how much could it carry if it can carry 35 times its weight? ______

6. 10 000 − 256 − 256 − 256 − 256 ______

Challenge

Complete:

a △ + 7 = 16 so △ = ______
b ▱ − 62 = 23 so ▱ = ______
c 2 × △ = 98 so △ = ______
d ▱ ÷ 9 = 7 so ▱ = ______
e △ + 84 = 106 − 9 so △ = ______
f 8 × ▱ = 45 + 19 so ▱ = ______

Coordinates

(1R, 3U) is the point 1 right and 3 up from zero. Join the coordinates in order, to complete the picture.

(1R, 3U), (3R, 5U), (8R, 5U), (10R, 4U), (12R, 6U), (12R, 1U), (10R, 3U), (8R, 2U), (3R, 2U), (1R, 3U)

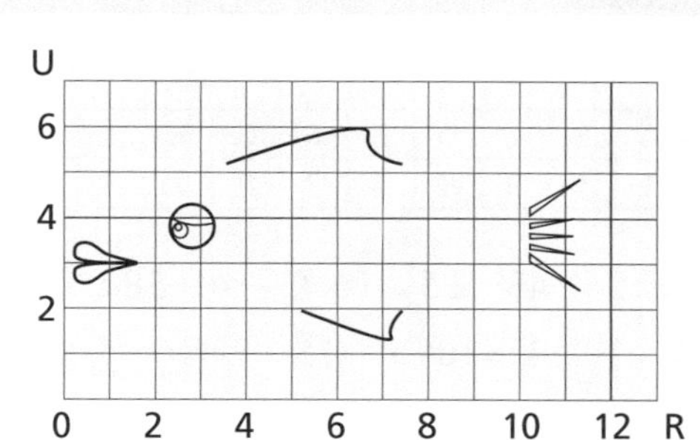

35:1 out of 17

1. 100 − 24 ____
2. 10% of 60. ____
3. 7 × ____ = 56
4. $\frac{3}{4} - \frac{1}{4}$ ____
5. $\begin{array}{r} 87 \\ \times \quad 6 \\ \hline \end{array}$
6. 78 + 39 = ____ + 40
7. 35 − ____ = 5 × 6
8. 5·498 L × 1000 ____
9. $5 × 80 ____
10. $\begin{array}{r} 28 \\ \times 11 \\ \hline \\ \hline \end{array}$
11. 128 ÷ ☐ = 32 ☐ = ____
12. a 7 t = ____ kg
    b 8000 kg = ____ t
    c 0·276 kg = ____ g
    d 7 kg 925 g = ____ g
13. Which of +, −, × and ÷ will make 3 □ 3 △ 3 = 4 true? □ = ____, △ = ____
14. Complete this pattern:

Decagons	1	2	3	4	5
Sides	10	20			

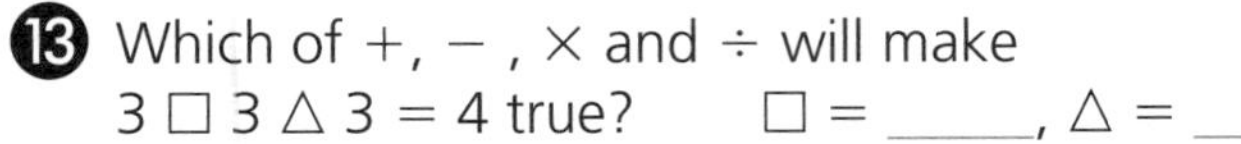

15. a $\frac{8}{10}\frac{(\div 2)}{(\div 2)} = \frac{\square}{\square}$ b $\frac{1}{4}\frac{(\times 3)}{(\times 3)} = \frac{\square}{\square}$
16. a A prime number has ____ factors, 1 and ____.
    b A composite number has more than ____ factors.
17. Show the digital and analog time for 19 minutes after 07:53.
    a 
    b 

35:2 out of 16

1. 453 + 646 ____
2. 684 − 298 ____
3. $\frac{2}{5} + \frac{4}{10}$ ____
4. $10 - 8\frac{2}{5}$ ____
5. $\frac{2}{3}$ of 27. ____
6. 25% of 50. ____
7. 7 × (67 − 62) ____
8. $\frac{4}{6} - \frac{2}{3}$ ____
9. $\begin{array}{r} 2 \cdot 8 \\ \times 1\ 5 \\ \hline \\ \hline \end{array}$
10. $\begin{array}{r} 7 \cdot 6 \\ \times 6\ 7 \\ \hline \\ \hline \end{array}$
11. $\begin{array}{r} 7 \cdot 5 \\ \times 8\ 8 \\ \hline \\ \hline \end{array}$
12. a 7·76 t = ____ kg
    b 20 000 kg = ____ t
    c 0·456 kg = ____ g
    d 2 kg 487 g = ____ g
    e $9\frac{3}{4}$ kg = ____ g
13. A bag of carrots weighs 0·427 kg. If there are 7 carrots in the bag, what is the average mass of each carrot? ____
14. Circle the prime numbers.
    17 21 29 46 83 67 49
15. (3 + △) × 7 = 35, △ = ____
16.

Bus timetable	
May St	08:54
Joy Ave	09:12
Red St	09:37
Fig St	09:48
Rae St	10:04

How long does it take to travel from:
a May St to Joy Ave? ____
b Red St to Rae St? ____
c May St to Rae St? ____

Codes

Concept

Use the code to write 'true' or 'false' for each code statement.

A	B	C	D	E	F	G	H	I	J	K	L	M	N	O	P	R	S	T	U	V	W	Y
1	*	9	&	4	?	0	/	2	(	+	7	<	5	#	)	3	$	=	8	@	>	6

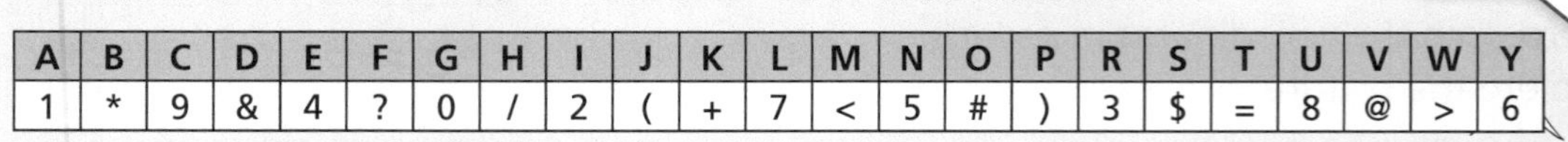

a $4@45 2$ 1)32<4 58<*43 ____
b 1)45=10#5 /1$?2@4 $2&4$ ____
c 420/= 2$ #54 ?19=#3 #? =>45=6 ?#83 ____

© PEARSON AUSTRALIA 2024 • *AUSTRALIAN SIGNPOST MATHS NSW 6 MENTALS* • ISBN 978 0 6557 0913 8

35:3 ☐ out of 12

1. $\begin{array}{r} 73 \\ \times\ 29 \\ \hline \end{array}$

2. $\begin{array}{r} 5\cdot 7 \\ \times\ 3\cdot 6 \\ \hline \end{array}$

3. $\begin{array}{r} 381 \\ \times\ 23 \\ \hline \end{array}$

4. $\frac{3}{4} + \frac{1}{8} = \frac{\square}{\square} + \frac{\square}{\square} = \frac{\square}{\square}$

5. a 4·34 t = ________ kg
   b 50 000 kg = ________ t
   c 0·907 kg = ________ g
   d 5 kg 264 g = ________ g

6. a ☐ + 56 = 93, ☐ = ____
   b ☐ − 13 = 47, ☐ = ____
   c ☐ × 8 = 992, ☐ = ____

7. The mass of a horse is 0·7 tonnes.
   Find the mass of:
   a 18 horses ________
   b 38 horses ________

8. The mass of 10 men is 0·8 t.
   What is the mass of
   a 30 men? ________ b 50 men? ________

9. Aaron mowed the lawn from 3:39 pm till 5:06 pm. How long did he take?
   ____

10. Use 24-hour time to write 5:26 pm. ________

11. Use am or pm to write the time 3 hours after:
    a 23:24 ________ b 09:56 ________

12. a How many minutes in $5\frac{1}{4}$ hours? ________
    b How many minutes in $7\frac{3}{4}$ hours? ________

35:4 Extension ☐ out of 5

1. Felicity was born on 23rd June 2016 at 05:20. How many hours (to the nearest hour) has she been alive, if it is now 14:27 on 27th June 2016? ________

2. If a snail travelled 4·8 metres per hour, how long would it take to travel:
   a 15 cm (to the nearest minute)? ________
   b 50 cm (to the nearest minute)? ________
   c 2 m (to the nearest minute)? ________

3. What number is missing? ________

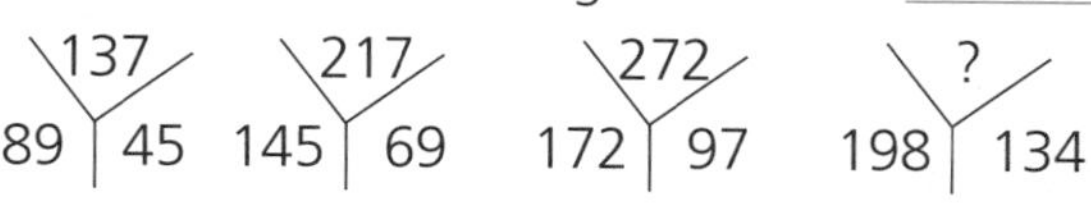

4. a $\begin{array}{r} 6\cdot\square\square 7 \\ +\ \square\cdot 0\,4\,\square \\ \hline 14\cdot 976 \end{array}$
   b $\begin{array}{r} 8\cdot\square 5\square \\ +\ \square\cdot 8\square 8 \\ \hline 16\cdot 630 \end{array}$

5. 1000 milligrams (mg) = 1 gram (g)
   A male fly weighs about 11·5 mg and a female fly weighs about 17·5 mg. What is the difference between the mass of 6 male flies and 6 female flies? ________

Challenge

Research objects that are measured in milligrams. List each below with an approximate mass, e.g. A grain of rice weighs ________.

____
____
____
____
____

Concept

Example of factors

Draw the rectangles that have an area of 8 units².

The numbers used are factors of 8.

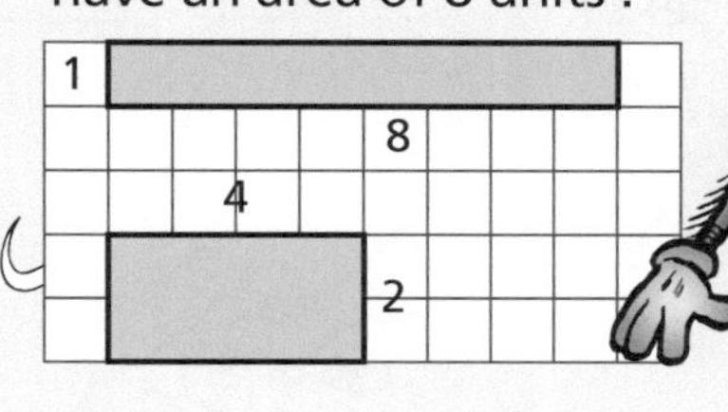

Draw rectangles of area 15 units².

List the factors. ________

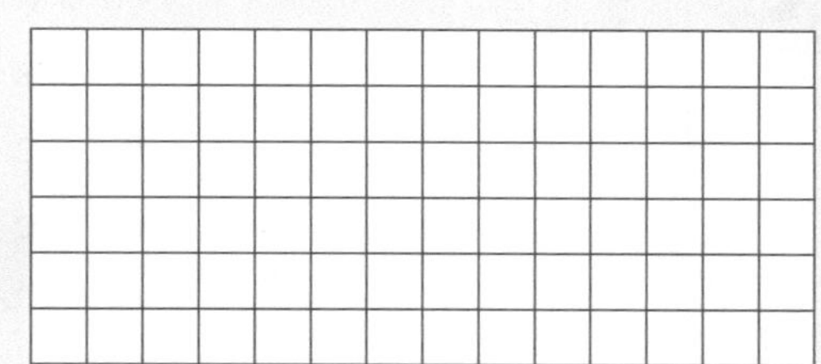

36:1 ☐ out of 15

1. 409 + 356 ____
2. 600 − 57 ____
3. \$9 × 400 ____
4. 20% of 40. ____
5.
$$\begin{array}{r} 375{\cdot}89 \\ +\ 857{\cdot}46 \\ \hline \end{array}$$
6. 7 × ____ = 47 − 40
7. 75 − 35 = ____ − 40
8. 8 + 4 ÷ 2 ____
9. $\frac{9}{10} - \frac{3}{10}$ ____
10.
$$\begin{array}{r} \$9786.37 \\ -\ \$\ \ 978.36 \\ \hline \end{array}$$
11. Circle the composite numbers.

    5 9 12 17 11 6 15

12. What is the volume of this solid? ________ blocks

13. List the factors for each number. Put a tick next to the prime numbers.

1			
2			
3			
4			

5				
6				
7				
8				

14. Show the digital and analog time for 3 hours and 12 minutes after 16:19.

a  

b 

15.     

A B C D E

Which have a top view that is:

a a circle? ________

b a rectangle? ________

36:2 ☐ out of 19

1. 60 ÷ 2 + 54 ____
2. $8^2 + 2^2$ ____
3. $\frac{3}{5}$ of 40. ____
4. $\frac{8}{10} - \frac{2}{5}$ ____
5.
$$\begin{array}{r} 50{\cdot}9006 \\ -\ \ 7{\cdot}5673 \\ \hline \end{array}$$
6. 6 × 7 = ____ − 58
7. 90 + 3 × 15 − 8 ____
8. $6 - \frac{5}{6}$ ____
9. 5·624 m × 1000 ____
10.
$$\begin{array}{r} 900{\cdot}004 \\ -\ \ 46{\cdot}896 \\ \hline \end{array}$$
11. 7 + △ × 2 = 10 + 5, △ = ____

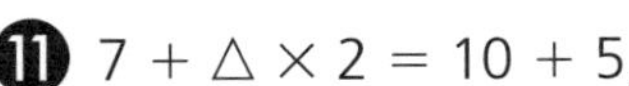
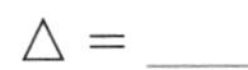

12. A B C

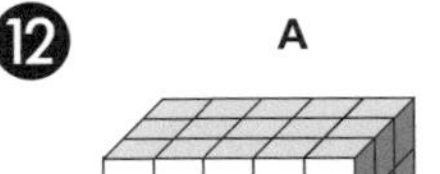
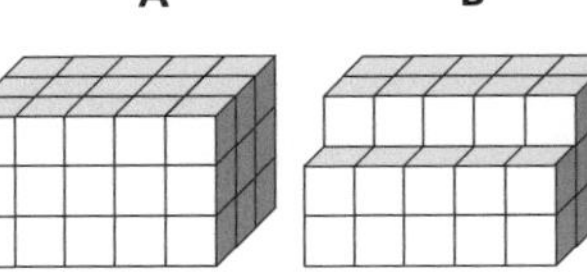
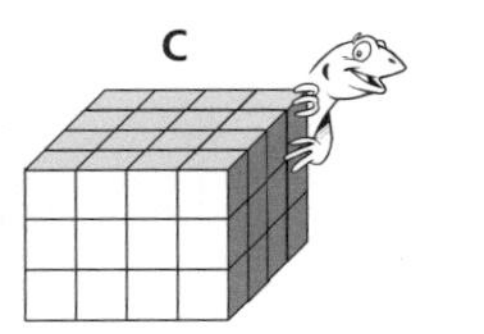

Which uses the most cubes? ________

13. Circle the numbers that are divisible by 5. (The last digit must be 5 or 0.)

    852 790 555 231 685 917 080

14. Hours from 10 am to:

    a 3 pm ________ **b** midnight ________

    c 1 am ________ **d** 7:00 pm ________

15. Circle the prime numbers.

    19 45 31 69 47 51 62

16. List all the factors of 42.

    ____

17. Write 4:28 pm in 24-hour time. ________

18. What time has elapsed between 5 pm Tuesday and 2 am the following day? ________

19. **a** Minutes in $1\frac{1}{2}$ hours? ________

    b Minutes in $3\frac{1}{4}$ hours? ________

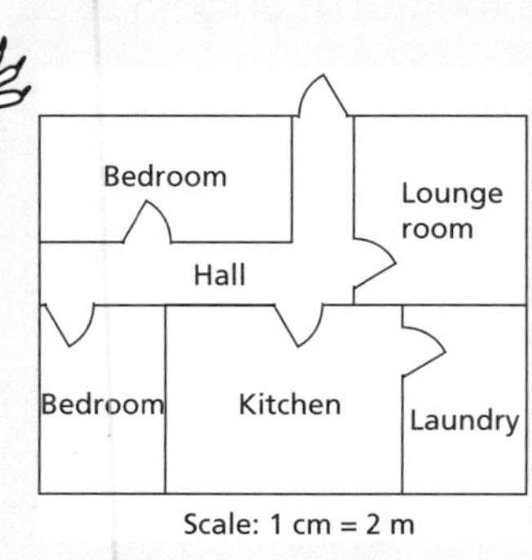

Scale drawing

Find the real length (the longest side) of:

a the laundry ________

b the lounge room ________

c the kitchen ________

d What is the real perimeter of the kitchen? ________

© PEARSON AUSTRALIA 2024 • *AUSTRALIAN SIGNPOST MATHS NSW 6 MENTALS* • ISBN 978 0 6557 0913 8

36:3 ☐ out of 11

❶
$$\begin{array}{r} 4572{\cdot}94 \\ 835{\cdot}08 \\ 2{\cdot}45 \\ +\ 845{\cdot}37 \\ \hline \end{array}$$

❷
$$\begin{array}{r} \$9678.25 \\ -\ \$3656.93 \\ \hline \end{array}$$

❸ **a** I took one hour to do my homework. Alana took half as long. Heather took one third as long as Alana. How long did Heather take? ______

b In part a, how much time was spent on homework altogether? ______

❹ 100 − 7 − 7 − 7 − 7 − 7 ______

❺ ☐ × 4 = 200, ☐ = ______

❻ The bath's water level was 21·3 cm before Archimedes got in and 25·7 cm after. What was the difference in water level? ______

❼ List all the prime numbers less than 30.

______

❽ Use am or pm to write the time $4\frac{1}{4}$ hours after:

a 18:30 ______ **c** 21:45 ______

b 02:09 ______ **d** 09:08 ______

❾ List the factors for each number.
Put a tick next to the prime numbers.

9						
10						
11						
12						

13					
14					
15					
16					

❿ Circle the numbers that are divisible by 10.

2307 800010 410043 8310 7850

⓫ List all the factors of 100.

______

36:4 ☐ out of 6

Extension

❶ Write the missing numbers in the algorithms.

a
$$\begin{array}{r} \square 5 \square \\ \times\ \ \square 8 \\ \hline 6\,0\,7\,2 \\ 2\,2\,7\,7\,0 \\ \hline \square \end{array}$$

b
$$\begin{array}{r} \square \\ \times\ \ 54 \\ \hline 1696 \\ 21200 \\ \hline \square \end{array}$$

c
$$\begin{array}{r} \square \\ \times\ \ 39 \\ \hline 2664 \\ 8880 \\ \hline \square \end{array}$$

❷ 30 000 − 89 − 89 − 89 − 89 ______

❸ Draw the missing part of this pattern.

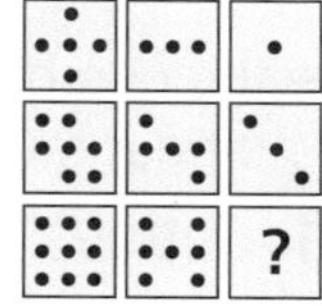

❹ Colour the models that represent one cubic metre.

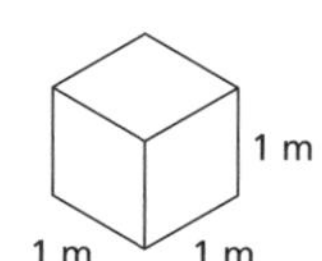

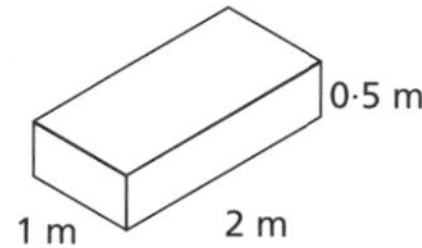

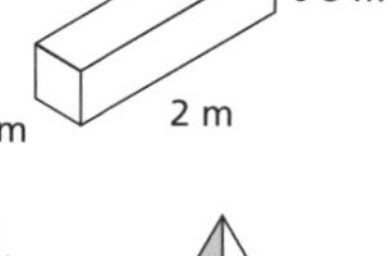

❺ The shaded part has a value of 48.

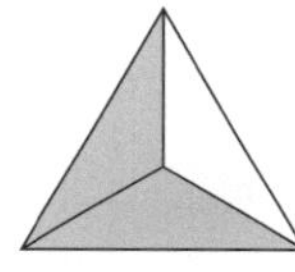

a What is the value of the whole? ______

b What is the value of $7\frac{1}{3}$ whole triangles like this? ______

❻ $1^2 + 2^2 + 3^2 + 4^2 + 5^2 + 6^2 + 7^2$ ______

Challenge

Record a time line for your life.
Fit in as many events and dates as you can.

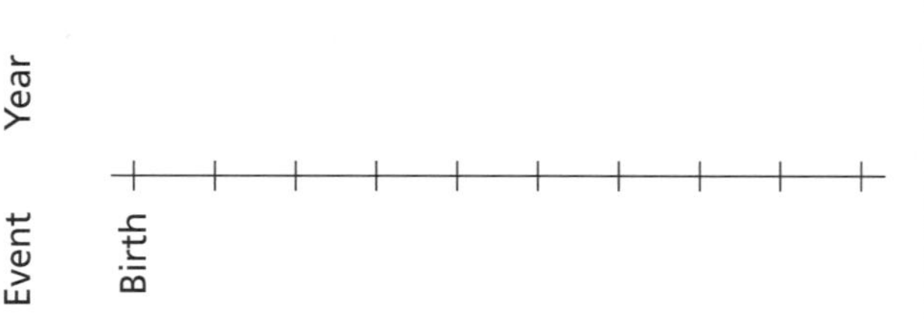

Testing divisibility rules using a calculator

a Choose any 10 large numbers ending in 0 or 5. Is each one divisible by 5? ______

b Choose any 10 large numbers whose last two digits are divisible by 4 (like 810 912). Is each one divisible by 4? ______

c Choose any 10 large numbers whose sum of digits is divisible by 3 (like 411 441). Is each one divisible by 3? ______

One number is divisible by another if the answer is a whole number when you divide.

© PEARSON AUSTRALIA 2024 • *AUSTRALIAN SIGNPOST MATHS NSW 6 MENTALS* • ISBN 978 0 6557 0913 8

37:1 out of 15

1. $0{\cdot}2 + 0{\cdot}6$ ____
2. 20% of 80. ____
3. $5 + 14 \div 2$ ____
4. $\frac{6}{8} + \frac{1}{8}$ ____
5. $364700 - 48678$
6. $7 − $2.80 ____
7. $0{\cdot}4 - 0{\cdot}3$ ____
8. $8\,345 \times 1000$ ____
9. $57 + \_\_\_\_ = 100$
10. $490080 - 37567$

11. Circle the numbers that are divisible by 2. (The number must be even.)

6578 29053 6475 2080 35245

12. **a** What ingredient is used most in making a quiche? ____

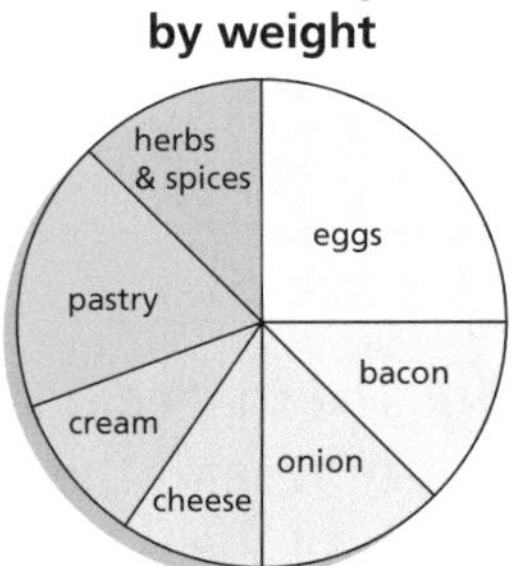

b What fraction of the final quiche is made from eggs? ____

c If the quiche weighs 400 g, how many 50 g eggs were used in the recipe? ____

Which does the recipe use more of: ____

d bacon or cheese? ____

e pastry or onion? ____

13. If the rule is F + 5 what will the answer be if F is:

a 7? ____ **b** 16? ____

14. My car can travel 12 km on one litre of petrol. How far can I go with four litres? ____

15. The value of the 3 in $78{\cdot}943$. ____

37:2 out of 14

1. $2{\cdot}8 + 0{\cdot}5$ ____
2. $1{\cdot}5 \times 10$ ____
3. $45 - 4 \times 7$ ____
4. $8\frac{7}{8} - \frac{1}{2}$ ____
5. $500.00 + $692.49
6. $\frac{3}{8}$ of 64. ____
7. $893 - 536$ ____
8. $100 - \_\_\_\_ = 6 \times 7$
9. $\frac{7}{10} + \frac{8}{5}$ ____
10. $7500.00 − $ 936.93

11. Matilda's ring box is 4 cm long, 5 cm wide and 3 cm high. What is the volume? ____

12.

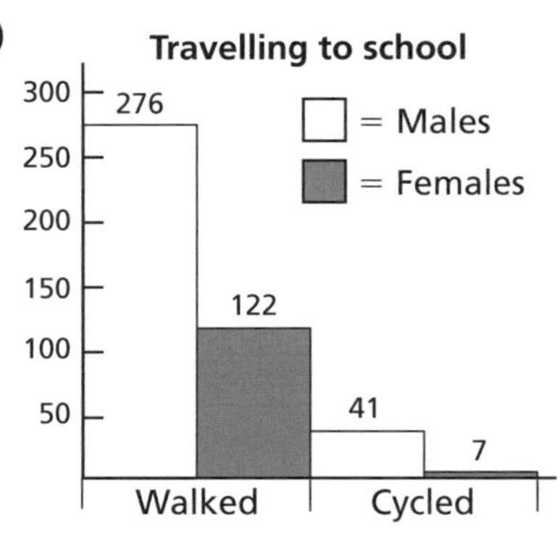

a How many people who walked were females? ____

b Is it more likely that the next person to arrive at school by walking will be male or female? ____

c How many people walked altogether? ____

13. Circle the numbers that are divisible by 4. (The number made by the last 2 digits must be divisible by 4.)

36 100 812 561 4000

14. Find the volume in cm^3 of a block 2 cm high, 8 cm wide and 10 cm long. ____

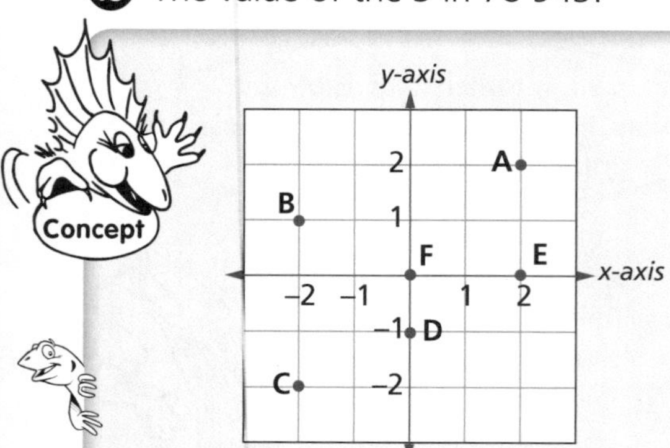

The 4 quadrants

Write the coordinates for:

(a) **A** ____ (b) **B** ____

(c) **C** ____ (d) **D** ____

(e) **E** ____ (f) **F** ____

Write the name and coordinates for a 2D shape.

____

© PEARSON AUSTRALIA 2024 • *AUSTRALIAN SIGNPOST MATHS NSW 6 MENTALS* • ISBN 978 0 6557 0913 8

37:3 ☐ out of 10

1. 456×8

2. $800000 - 7946$

3. $(5 \times 10^4) + (6 \times 10^3) + (4 \times 10^2) + (0 \times 10^1) + 4 =$ ______

4. Complete the table.

Number of horses	1	2	3	4	5
Number of legs	4				

   a Write a rule to describe the pattern.

   ______

   b How many legs are on 592 horses? ______

5. What is the volume of a container 4 m long, 3 m wide, and 6 m high? ______

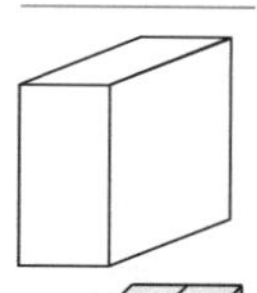

6. a What is the surface area of this model? ______

   b What is the volume of this model? ______

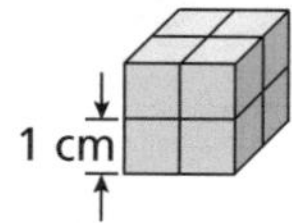

7. $9 \times 2 + \square = 25$, $\square =$ ______

8. **Number of siblings**

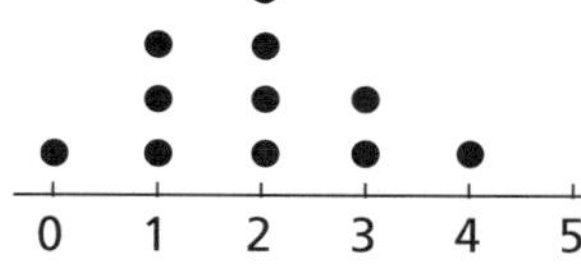

Key: ● = 10 people
(Data is rounded to the nearest 10.)

   a How many people had 4 siblings? ______

   b Which number of siblings was the most common? ______

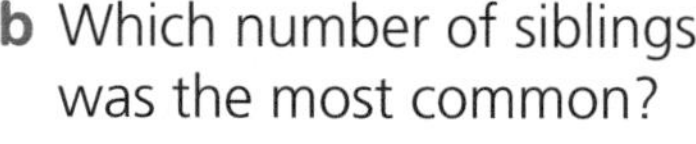

9. Circle the numbers that are divisible by 3.
(The sum of the digits must be divisible by 3.)

   2307 800010 410043 8310 7850

10. 16, 20, 24 and 28 are all divisible by ______.

37:4 Extension ☐ out of 4

1. a $7\overline{)\square}$ = 75 b $4\overline{)\square}$ = 216 r 5 c $7\overline{)\square\cdot\square}$ = 11·28

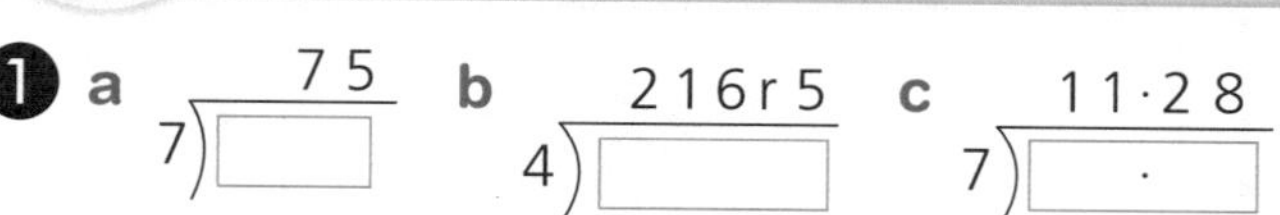

2. If → means 'is taller than', who is the tallest?

   ______

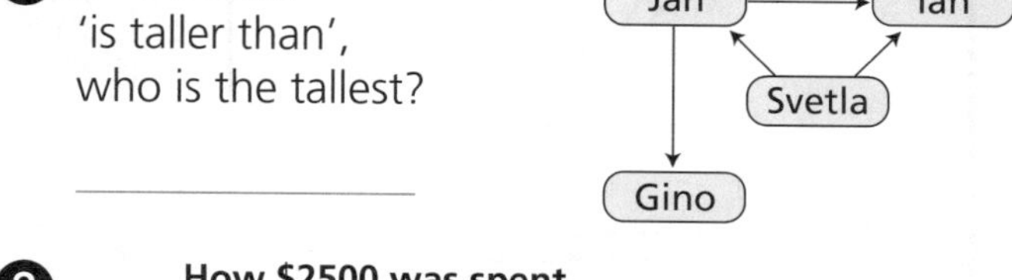

3. **How $2500 was spent**

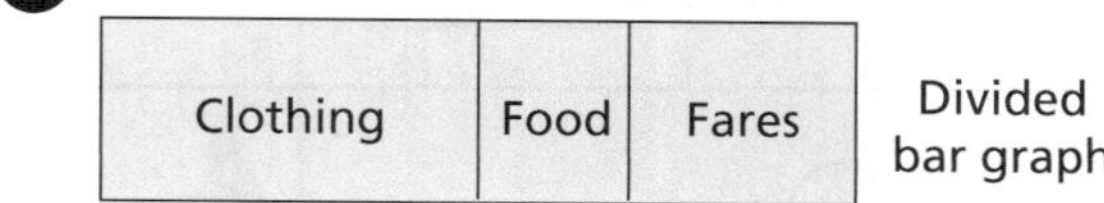

   a What % was spent on fares? ______

   b What % was spent on food? ______

4. Calculate how many bird seed packets can fit in the box. ______

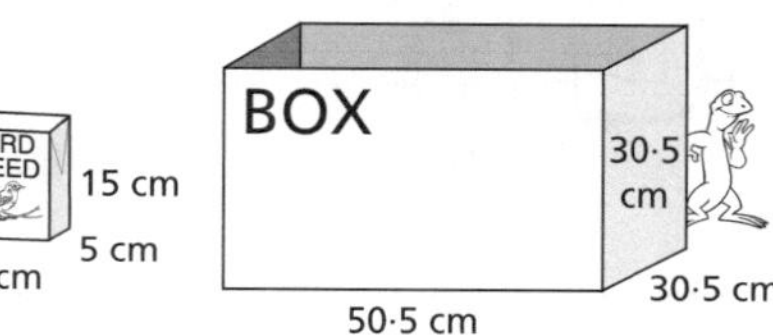

Challenge

Survey 20 people. Ask them what country they would most like to visit out of Canada, Fiji, South Africa and China. Tally the results in the table.

		Total
Canada		
Fiji		
South Africa		
China		

Discuss the results with your family.

Fill in this table for the person measured in Unit 1.

Name: ______ **Date:** ______

Age: ______	Mass: ______ kg	Shoe size: ______
Height: ______ cm	Waist: ______ cm	Neck size: ______ cm

How have these measurements changed since Unit 1? ______

______

Examples of measurements

1

2

3

4

5

6

1
- The width of a finger is about 1 cm.
- The length of a place-value tens block is 10 cm.

2
- The height of the girl is a little more than 1 m.

3
- The container of milk holds 2 L.
- The can of softdrink holds 375 mL.
- The teaspoon holds 5 mL.

4
- The boy has a mass of 40 kg.
- The margarine has a mass of 500 g.

5
- A double page of the newspaper has an area of half of 1 m^2.
- The top of a place-value ones block has an area of 1 cm^2.

6
- 30°C is a hot day.
- 3°C is a very cold day.

Use the pictures above to estimate the answers to these questions.

1 a How high is the glass?
b How wide is the table?

2 a How wide is the clothes line?
b How tall is the woman?

3 a How much will the bucket hold?
b How much will the cup hold?

4 a What is the mass of the dog?
b What is the mass of 2 L of milk?

5 a What is the area of the window?
b What is the area of the top of a matchbox?

6 a What is the temperature on a very hot day?
b What is the temperature on a cool day?

© PEARSON AUSTRALIA 2024 • *AUSTRALIAN SIGNPOST MATHS NSW 6 MENTALS* • ISBN 978 0 6557 0913 8

Tables of number and measurement

Length

1 centimetre	=	10 millimetres
1 metre	=	100 centimeters
1 metre	=	1000 millimetres
1 kilometre	=	1000 metres

Area

1 hectare (ha)	=	10 000 m^2
1 square metre	=	10 000 cm^2
1 square kilometre	=	10 00 000 m^2
1 square kilometre	=	100 ha

Mass

1 kilogram	=	1000 grams
1 tonne	=	1000 kilograms
1 gram	=	1000 milligrams (mg)

Capacity and volume

1000 millilitres	=	1 litre
1000 litres	=	1 kilolitre
1 millilitre	=	1 cm^3
1 litre	=	1000 cm^3

1 litre of water has a mass of 1 kg.

1 kilolitre	=	1000 litres
1 megalitre (ML)	=	1000 kilolitres (kL)

A teaspoon holds about 5 mL.

5 mL

A carton of milk holds 1 L.

Time

1 minute	=	60 seconds
1 hour	=	60 minutes
1 day	=	24 hours
1 week	=	7 days
1 fortnight	=	2 weeks
1 year	=	52 weeks
1 year	=	365 days
1 leap year	=	366 days
1 decade	=	10 years
1 century	=	100 years

am stands for **ante meridiem**.
am means **before midday**.

pm stands for **post meridiem**.
pm means **after midday**.

It is important to learn your tables!

The **freezing point** of water is **0°C**.
The **boiling point** of water is **100°C**.

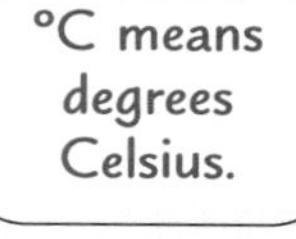

A temperature of **5°C** is a **cold** day.
A temperature of **35°C** is a **hot** day.

Roman numerals

1	= I		**6**	= VI		**20**	= XX		**90**	= XC
2	= II		**7**	= VII		**30**	= XXX		**100**	= C
3	= III		**8**	= VIII		**40**	= XL		**200**	= CC
4	= IV		**9**	= IX		**50**	= L		**500**	= D
5	= V		**10**	= X		**60**	= LX		**1000**	= M

Months of the year

Thirty days has September, April, June and November. All the rest have thirty-one, except February alone, which has twenty-eight days clear and twenty-nine days each leap year.

You can use the knuckles of your hands to find the number of days in each month.

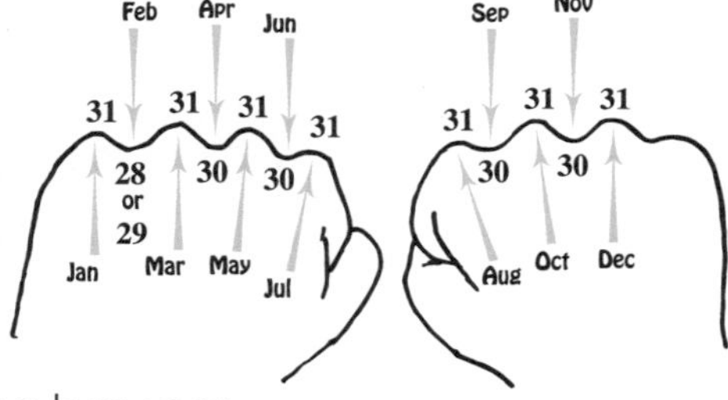

Every 4th year is a leap year.

24-hour time

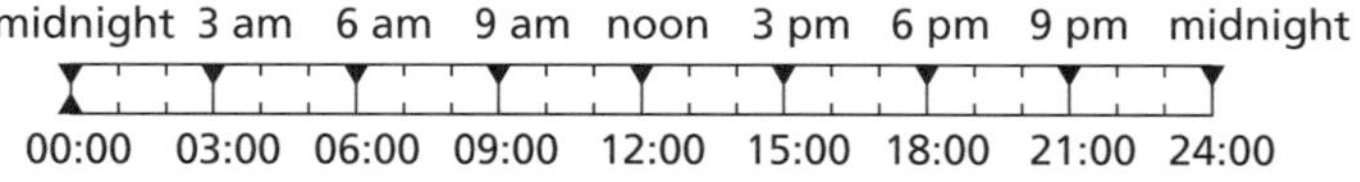

Seasons

Summer: December, January, February
Autumn: March, April, May
Winter: June, July, August
Spring: September, October, November

Multiplication tables

1 × 2 = 2	1 × 3 = 3	1 × 4 = 4	1 × 5 = 5	1 × 6 = 6	1 × 7 = 7	1 × 8 = 8	1 × 9 = 9	1 × 10 = 10
2 × 2 = 4	2 × 3 = 6	2 × 4 = 8	2 × 5 = 10	2 × 6 = 12	2 × 7 = 14	2 × 8 = 16	2 × 9 = 18	2 × 10 = 20
3 × 2 = 6	3 × 3 = 9	3 × 4 = 12	3 × 5 = 15	3 × 6 = 18	3 × 7 = 21	3 × 8 = 24	3 × 9 = 27	3 × 10 = 30
4 × 2 = 8	4 × 3 = 12	4 × 4 = 16	4 × 5 = 20	4 × 6 = 24	4 × 7 = 28	4 × 8 = 32	4 × 9 = 36	4 × 10 = 40
5 × 2 = 10	5 × 3 = 15	5 × 4 = 20	5 × 5 = 25	5 × 6 = 30	5 × 7 = 35	5 × 8 = 40	5 × 9 = 45	5 × 10 = 50
6 × 2 = 12	6 × 3 = 18	6 × 4 = 24	6 × 5 = 30	6 × 6 = 36	6 × 7 = 42	6 × 8 = 48	6 × 9 = 54	6 × 10 = 60
7 × 2 = 14	7 × 3 = 21	7 × 4 = 28	7 × 5 = 35	7 × 6 = 42	7 × 7 = 49	7 × 8 = 56	7 × 9 = 63	7 × 10 = 70
8 × 2 = 16	8 × 3 = 24	8 × 4 = 32	8 × 5 = 40	8 × 6 = 48	8 × 7 = 56	8 × 8 = 64	8 × 9 = 72	8 × 10 = 80
9 × 2 = 18	9 × 3 = 27	9 × 4 = 36	9 × 5 = 45	9 × 6 = 54	9 × 7 = 63	9 × 8 = 72	9 × 9 = 81	9 × 10 = 90
10 × 2 = 20	10 × 3 = 30	10 × 4 = 40	10 × 5 = 50	10 × 6 = 60	10 × 7 = 70	10 × 8 = 80	10 × 9 = 90	10 × 10 = 100